CITIES AND DISASTER

AMERICAN SOCIETY FOR INDUSTRIAL SECURITY
1625 PRINCE STREET
ALEXANDRIA, VA 22314
(703) 519–6200

CITIES AND DISASTER
North American Studies in Emergency Management

RICHARD T. SYLVES, PH.D.
Department of Political Science
University of Delaware

WILLIAM L. WAUGH, JR., PH.D.
Institute of Public Administration
and Department of Urban Studies
Georgia State University

CHARLES C THOMAS • PUBLISHER
Springfield • Illinois • U.S.A.

Published and Distributed Throughout the World by

CHARLES C THOMAS • PUBLISHER
2600 South First Street
Springfield, Illinois 62794-9265

© *1990 by* CHARLES C THOMAS • PUBLISHER

ISBN 0-398-05635-8

Library of Congress Catalog Card Number: 89-37355

Printed in the United States of America
SC-R-3

Library of Congress Cataloging-in-Publication Data

Cities and disaster : North American studies in emergency management /
[edited by] Richard T. Sylves, William L. Waugh, Jr.
    p. cm.
   Includes bibliographical references.
   ISBN 0-398-05635-8
   1. Disaster relief—United States—Planning. 2. Local government—
United States. 3. Central—local government relations—United
States. I. Sylves, Richard Terry. II. Waugh, William L.
HV555.U6C58 1989
336.3'456'0973—dc20
                                                     89-37355
                                                        CIP

CONTRIBUTORS

Virginia Bott; professor of political science at California State University, Fullerton, has done extensive research on city governments. She has investigated ethnic politics, intergovernmental relations, and the impact of California's Proposition 13. She received her Ph.D. from Johns Hopkins University.

Raymond J. Burby; professor of city and regional planning at the University of North Carolina at Chapel Hill and former coeditor of the *Journal of the American Planning Association.* He has written extensively on the application of land use planning procedures to mitigate environmental hazards. He is coeditor of *Floodplain Land Use Management: A National Assessment, Hazardous Materials in North Carolina: A Guide for Decision Makers in Local Government,* and *Drinking Water Supplies: Protection Through Watershed Management.* He has authored numerous articles and his latest book, *Cities Under Water,* was published in 1988.

Beverly A. Cigler; professor of public administration and policy at Pennsylvania State University, Harrisburg. She has published widely on such topics as small governments, fiscal stress, flood hazard management, and energy management. She serves on the editorial boards of several journals and chairs the American Society for Public Administration's (ASPA) Section on Public Administration Education.

Jack D. Kartez; associate professor of environmental science and regional planning at Washington State University. He has advised emergency training and planning staff at the Tennessee Emergency Management Agency, the Washington State Division of Emergency Management, and the National Emergency Training Center of the U.S. Federal Emergency Management Agency (FEMA). His research has been supported by the National Science Foundation and FEMA. During a recent leave he collaborated in research of government financial strategies for damages to public facilities from natural hazards at University of North Carolina's Center for Urban Studies.

Michael K. Lindell; associate professor of industrial/organizational psychology at Michigan State University. His principal research area is the response of individuals and organizations to the threat of disaster. His previous research projects have investigated factors influencing individuals' responses to warnings of imminent dangers and how individuals adjust to a variety of natural and technological hazards. He has developed planning guides for emergency organizations.

Thomas J. Pavlak; recently appointed professor of public administration and director of the Institute of Public Administration at Fairleigh Dickinson University. He received his Ph.D. in political science from the University of Illinois at Urbana-Champaign in 1971. He has taught at the University of Missouri-St. Louis, the University of Illinois-Chicago and the University of Pittsburgh. His current research concerns issues in administrative justice, organization effectiveness and performance appraisal.

Joseph Scanlon; professor of journalism and director of the Emergency Communications Research Unit at Carleton University in Ottawa, Canada. He has written more than 100 articles, monographs, and book chapters on emergency management and emergency communications, including *The Peel Regional Police Force and the Mississauga Evacuation* and *May Day at St. Joseph's: Fire and Evacuation at a Major City Hospital.*

Charles B. Schepart; policy analyst with the Los Angeles Unified School District. He earned a doctorate in public administration from University of Southern California. He lived in Windsor Locks, Connecticut when it was struck by a tornado and was at the time a city official in nearby West Hartford. His research of Windsor and Windsor Locks in the aftermath of the disaster became the basis for his dissertation.

Allen K. Settle; professor in the School of Communicative Arts and Humanities at the California State University, San Luis Obispo. He is vice-mayor of San Luis Obispo and is author of *Emergency Management in Public Administration Education, Legal Issues in Emergency Management: The Coalinga Earthquake,* and coauthor of *American Public Administration: Concepts and Cases.* He is a member of the Senior Executive Policy Center at FEMA's National Emergency Training Center.

Robert A. Stallings; associate professor of public administration and sociology at the University of Southern California, Los Angeles. He has written about the public sector in natural disasters for a period of twenty years. He recently published *Post-Impact Field Studies of Disasters and Sociological Theory Construction.* His "Conflict in Natural Disasters: A Codification of Consensus and Conflict Theories" appears in the September 1988 issue of *Social Science Quarterly.*

Sandra Sutphen; professor of political science at University of California, Fullerton and coordinator of the MPA program there. She also teaches in Women's Studies. She entered the field of disaster research with a major study of a flood disaster in Lake Elsinore, California, a community near her home.

Richard T. Sylves; professor of political science at the University of Delaware and editor/publisher of *Emergency Management Dispatch,* the quarterly newsletter of the ASPA Section on Emergency Management. He earned his Ph.D. at University of Illinois at Urbana-Champaign and authored *The Nuclear Oracles: A Political History of the General Advisory Committee of the U.S. Atomic Energy Commission, 1947–77* published in 1987. In 1986–87, he won a University Public Service Fellowship and worked as a producer/researcher at WHYY TV-12 Philadelphia/Wilmington public television. He has published numerous book chapters and journal articles.

M. Elliot Vittes; associate professor of political science at University of Central Florida. He received his Ph.D. in political science at the University of Massachusetts, Amherst. He has published in *The Journal of State Government, Policy Studies Review,* and elsewhere. His specialties include environmental politics and policy making, and federalism.

William L. Waugh, Jr.; associate professor of public administration and political science and associate director of the Institute of Public Administration and Department of Urban Studies at Georgia State University. He wrote *International Terrorism: How Nations Respond to Terrorists, Terrorism and Emergency Management,* coedited *Handbook of Emergency Management Policies and Programs* and *Antiterrorism Policies: An International Comparison,* and has published numerous journal articles, book chapters, and reports.

Frances E. Winslow; emergency services coordinator, City of Irvine, and adjunct faculty of National University in Orange County, California. She graduated from Drew University and earned a doctorate in Planning from New York University. She has written many articles about emergency preparedness, emergency planning, and law enforcement.

To my wife Claire Sylves
and our sons Nathan and Eric

To my wife Deb Waugh

FOREWORD

Emergency managers today find themselves involved in systems controlled by increasingly complex forces that simultaneously stimulate and constrain their actions, thus directly affecting the successful integration and implementation of any comprehensive emergency program. These forces include technical concerns, such as attempts to quantify factors we know little about; sociopolitical pressures; conflicting and interdependent programs; and management strategies that have not been verified or proven because of insufficient field testing.

The emergency manager must be the organizational leader who manages conflicts that inevitably arise from differing philosophies and territorial imperatives, and facilitates the integration and implementation of emergency management policies, plans, and programs. Furthermore, traditional managers must engage in serious personal development activities and support organization development programs if the challenges of comprehensive emergency management are to be met. This must be done to overcome the problems created by the traditional functionally-oriented organizations that tend to impose significant limits on meeting complex system demands.

This book builds upon the new body of literature in emergency management and provides an analysis of broad-based data derived from several local government comparative analyses. It is a logical complement to the recently published case book, *Crisis Management*, edited by Michael T. Charles and John Choon Kim.

The contribution made by this book is its emphasis on the need for states and local governments to increase their capacity to plan for and respond to emergencies. The authors stress the need for improved planning and internal coordination. They also note the urgent need for professionalization of emergency management at the individual and organizational levels, and along social and technical dimensions.

Emergency management is increasing in importance within local government. This book will aid in developing a better and more comprehensive understanding of this complex area of local government. It is the next in a series of emergency management books produced by the participants of the May–June 1984 workshop on emergency management sponsored by the Federal Emergency Management Agency for faculty from university programs in public administration.

As a participant in that workshop, I had the personal pleasure and professional benefit of having worked with both Dr. Richard Sylves and Dr. William Waugh. I am honored to have been asked to write the foreword to this book. I congratulate them on their effort and their continuing contribution to the body of knowledge necessary to professionalize the field of emergency management. This book is an important addition to the field of public administration and emergency management. I commend it to your study.

WILLIAM J. PETAK
Professor and Executive Director
Institute of Safety & Systems Management
University of Southern California

INTRODUCTION

A plane crash near Gander, Newfoundland, a gasoline pipeline rupture in Irvine, California, a building collapse in New York City, a tornado in Windsor Falls, Connecticut, a flood in Princeton, British Columbia—at first glance each incident appears to be wholly unrelated to the others. Disasters and emergencies can stem from many different causes. Consequently, disaster or emergency incidents may vary dramatically both in their causes and effects, but how local officials are prepared to respond to them should not. Assembled here is a collection of original work that analyzes and surveys American and Canadian *local emergency management*.

The heart of this compilation is local government. Each contributor examines a different aspect of the general question, "is City Hall, and local government in general, prepared for disaster?" Answers to such a question must, of course, involve degrees of preparedness rather than an absolute "yes" or "no" answer. Why be concerned with local government if, as the common mythology implies, state and national governments can be counted on to rescue (or bail out as the case may be) local governments that suffer emergencies and disasters? Former U.S. House Speaker Tip O'Neill was fond of saying that "all politics is local politics." Add to this Disaster Sociology expert Henry Quarantelli's repeated claim that most disasters are really "local disasters." We should pay heed to the wisdom of O'Neill and Quarantelli because it is usually local government that first responds to disasters and emergency incidents. Local governments are not always overwhelmed by the disasters they confront. Actually, local governments are completely incapacitated by disaster very rarely. Many local governments cope quite well with the calamities they encounter, and many have leaders quite adept at securing outside help and resources from other local governments, their state or province, and their national government.

We are concerned here with local governments in Canada and in the United States. Admittedly, Canada and the United States have different colonial histories and different governmental institutions. Yet each has a federal system of government that decentralizes much public policy making and perhaps even more public policy implementation. One very decentralized public policy is disaster policy. The study does inspect various elements of U.S. and Canadian national authority in disaster policy and emergency management, but this is not the focal point of the study. Addressed are U.S. state and Canadian provincial roles in disaster policy and emergency management, but again our chief concern is at the municipal level.

PART 1

Part 1 examines how and why local officials often fail to plan effectively for community response to disaster, plus how and why the U.S. Federal Emergency Management Agency (FEMA) failed in its effort to set forth a coherent criteria for the issuance of presidential disaster declarations, one that replaces the present arbitrary, politically subjective method.

In Chapter I, Jack D. Kartez and Michael K. Lindell tell us that 80 percent of U.S. local governments have formal disaster plans, but most of their leaders continue to be surprised when, in disaster conditions, those plans often prove to be useless or irrelevant. Furthermore, local governments often fail to improve their plans after they have experienced a disaster. Kartez and Lindell seek to discover why this happens through analysis of a 450-city survey and through a conceptual model of disaster response preparedness. Among their many findings, lack of experience with disaster is an obstacle to adaptive planning for community disaster response, but not as great an obstacle as one might expect. Failure to apply what was learned from disaster experience often occurs when the municipality has no planning process upon which to imprint that knowledge within the organization's model of disaster needs. They conclude that cities with broad planning activities that encourage extensive participation of people from local agencies and that employ a face-to-face learning process in planning, are most likely to prepare disaster response strategies adapted to the city's disaster environment.

In Chapter II, Allen K. Settle informs us that over time about 41 percent of all U.S. states and localities that have requested a Presidential disaster declaration have had their request denied. It remains unclear to most state and local officials what factors or information is decisive in obtaining federal disaster aid. Settle explains that the U.S. Federal Emergency Management Agency itself has been blocked from reforming its disaster and emergency declaration criteria. His study examines criteria that may serve as guidelines in determining which states or communities are entitled to a Presidential disaster declaration and a commensurate amount of federal financial help. Settle's analysis runs simultaneously on two levels. He provides a discussion and description of existing federal rules and procedures that apply in securing Presidential declarations, and he reviews what happens once a declaration has been made. On another level, Settle shows why local governments are often unable to prove their deservedness for federal disaster assistance and why they often fail to secure from state and federal government all the aid they are entitled to receive. His "autopsy" of FEMA's failed reform effort is followed by an overview of the Stafford Act of 1988, a new U.S. law that clarifies federal disaster policy and programs, simplifies FEMA administration, promotes predisaster hazard mitigation, and furnishes additional fund eligibility in some categories of relief. What Stafford fails to do is replace FEMA's existing, awkward, and politically subjective case-by-case method of declaration request review.

PART 2

Part 2 concerns disaster types and effectiveness of emergency response. It provides important lessons about the willingness of communities to address hazards, the impact of organizational stress on a community's willingness to prepare for disaster, the problems inherent in multijurisdictional (particularly multinational) response to hazards, and the impact of community size and demography in disaster response.

In Chapter III, Beverly A. Cigler and Raymond J. Burby examine the "intergovernmental paradox," that is, while local governments and their leaders are most likely to have to respond to flood disasters, local governments are often run by people least likely to view emergency management as a priority. They assess U.S. local flood mitigation programs through a national survey of officials in "flood prone" communities. They find that flood hazard management is not a major priority of government in those communities. Cigler and Burby posit that the greatest impetus for local government action is the National Flood Insurance Program with its elaborate regulations and requirements. They also conclude that flood hazard mitigation in most communities tends to concentrate on new development leaving older existing structures less protected and more vulnerable. They do not find many local governments using innovative approaches toward flood mitigation even though many promising and effective approaches are available.

In Chapter IV, Robert A. Stallings and Charles B. Schepart compare the disaster responses of two Connecticut communities to a major tornado that struck both. Based on work originally published in the November 1987 issue of the *International Journal of Mass Emergencies and Disasters*, the study shows how in one community the response was directed entirely by the city manager, but in the other emergency activities were personally directed by the state's governor without any pretext of local control. They contrast how the two towns handled the emergency by examining the formal structure of the two local governments; Windsor had a council-manager structure and Windsor Locks a council-mayor form. Also significant is the history of each town's intergovernmental relations. Windsor, a city that had formulated its own disaster plan before the tornado, took on much more authority and responsibility in pursuing its own disaster recovery. Windsor Locks quickly abdicated response and recovery authority to the state and to an anxious governor. Stallings and Schepart reveal the advantages and disadvantages of each town's approach to disaster recovery. For example, Windsor's independence encouraged it to later enact worthwhile emergency management-related city ordinances, but its assertiveness may have cost it a sizable sum of state and federal disaster recovery money. Windsor Locks benefited by not having to spend nearly as much of its local revenue in disaster recovery as its neighbor, but it had to tolerate considerable state agency mismanagement and error as well as the interference of a well-meaning but meddlesome governor.

In Chapter V, M. Elliot Vittes analyzes the phenomenon of "extra-federalism." It is emerging to address the chronic man-made problem of acid rain deposition. Because acid rain's origins and effects are not yet completely understood in scientific terms, and because its impact is gradual, insidious, and geographically widespread, it is controversial. Some may question whether acid rain is really an agent of disaster. It must be understood that acid rain is an agent of environmental disaster that carries with it innumerable political, economic, and social consequences. Vittes shows how Reagan administration acid rain policy was so inactive, skeptical, and obstructionist that it unintentionally impelled a cross-section of American states and Canadian provinces to form sub-national policy networks and extra-federal relationships. Certain U.S. state and local governments have combined with certain Canadian provincial and local governments, to abate acid rain. Vittes informs us, however, that their lack of jurisdiction over sub-national governments that tolerate acid rain-causing pollution emissions seriously impedes their ability to attack the problem at its source. He demonstrates that the trans-border environmental problem of acid rain has opened new avenues of interaction for sub-national officials that may work to the benefit of North American disaster management.

In Chapter VI, Joseph Scanlon and Richard T. Sylves provide a comparative study of aviation disaster response. The mid-air collision of a PSA jetliner and a light plane over San Diego, California in 1978 created a localized disaster on the ground. In 1985, a military charter jetliner failed to gain altitude shortly after take-off and crashed into an isolated wooded area not far from Gander, Newfoundland. Each crash killed all passengers and crew members almost immediately. Nonetheless, Scanlon and Sylves contend that a well-managed postcrash local emergency response expedites thorough search for, and rescue of, possible survivors; protects people and property on the ground from further harm; deploys only needed responders and resources; facilitates investigation of the cause of the crash; ensures site security; manages media access and briefing; and, accelerates the long-term recovery of areas affected by the crash, among other things. They show from detailed investigation and interviewing that Gander responders did a much better job than their San Diego counterparts. This is not merely attributable to the demographic differences of each site. It is explained by comparing and contrasting how well prepared authorities were for aviation disaster before each crash, how officials from different (often conflictive) agencies interacted, how media and public access to the crash zone was controlled, how each went about identifying and collecting bodies, aircraft parts, and debris, how decision making and the chain of command worked, and how the common problem of post disaster convergence of emergency responders was addressed. Scanlon and Sylves make it apparent that the local handling of aviation disaster can be managed professionally or it can be bungled such that the tragedy is compounded.

PART 3

In Part 3, the mayors and managers of cities become the focal point. What do city officials think about emergency management? Do demographic and attitudinal variables explain why some city officials place priority on emergency management while others discount it? When a disaster incident befalls a city, how do city officials mobilize their staffs to address the many short- and long-term effects of the incident? Some city leaders formulate and implement sound emergency management in advance of disaster. Leaders of other cities do not. Do cities that have leaders attuned and responsive to emergency management before disaster strikes, do a better job responding to disaster than cities led by officials who were indifferent to emergency management before the disaster?

In Chapter VII, Sandra Sutphen and Virginia Bott analyze results of their two-staged survey of 400 California city managers. Their survey instrument contains a great many questions about local government in general and a few about emergency management specifically. Their most significant finding is not encouraging for emergency managers. They discovered that very few city managers place a high priority on emergency management. This is surprising and alarming given California's frequency and variety of disaster experience. They found that female city managers, as well as nonwhite city managers, are more likely to emphasize emergency management than are men and whites respectively. Managers with fewer years of experience are more likely to stress emergency management than managers with more years of experience. Less surprising are these findings. City managers whose municipalities have requested and received FEMA disaster aid in the past are more likely to consider emergency management essential than are managers whose cities have not asked for or received FEMA aid. Also, city managers who think that their localities will confront serious hazardous materials problems in the future are also those who are likely to think that emergency management deserves more local attention. They end maintaining that most California city managers will not be compelled to undertake emergency management until disaster has hit their city.

In Chapter VIII, Frances E. Winslow takes us inside Irvine (California) city government recounting what she did as an emergency services coordinator assisting the city manager in the aftermath of a gasoline pipeline rupture. This is a detailed case study of an emergency incident provided by an insider practitioner. Winslow lets us get very close to the wheels of municipal administration during the response and recovery phases of the emergency. Moreover, her personal chronology conveys a strong sense of how her duties shifted and transformed over the course of the incident. Her work involved legal protection of Irvine, coordination with other levels of government, information dissemination to the city manager and to elected officials, information source for concerned parties (usually corporation executives), and developer and archivist of visual documentation. Winslow shows us how she learned emergency management experientially, something that thousands of other city officials probably have done and/or will do.

In Chapter IX, Joseph Scanlon introduces us to emergency management in Canada. As head of an Emergency Communications Research Unit—supported in part by Emergency Preparedness Canada (comparable to the U.S. FEMA)—Scanlon and his staff have years of experience researching Canada's emergencies and disasters, often in the field shortly after incidents occur. Scanlon tells us that emergency management orthodoxy holds that a key to effective local emergency management is the active support of the mayor or city chief executive officer. Yet, he claims, this proposition is seldom tested empirically. His study seeks to validate this proposition. Nineteen emergency or disaster incidents are examined. For each it was determined whether the mayor or local chief executive was actively involved in, or measurably in support of, emergency response and preparedness activity *before the incident occurred in the locality.* From this, categories of "active" and "inactive" mayor cities are established. Then Scanlon reviews how cities in each group actually responded to emergency or disaster. He proves from his research that "active" mayor communities carried out more effective emergency response than did "inactive" mayor communities. His analysis is not based on impressionistic observations. It rests on evidence that cities used, or did not use, common emergency management techniques and practices. Scanlon adds that an intervening force affecting pre-incident mayoral interest in emergency management was provincial pressure. Communities in provinces that had promoted local emergency preparedness through laws and public agencies dedicated to emergency management, were more likely to have "active" mayors and the requisite elements of local emergency response.

PART 4

Part 4 brings us to a case study of how North America's most populous city conducts emergency management. In addition, it provides an introspective essay concerning state and local government capacity to undertake emergency management.

In Chapter X, Richard T. Sylves and Thomas J. Paviak describe how New York City plans for, and attempts to manage, major emergencies and disasters. They show that the essence of emergency management in New York is interdepartmental and intradepartmental coordination of preparedness, response, and recovery. They examine a variety of emergencies and disaster threats that the city has experienced, has planned for, or has classified as too remote to be concerned about. Sylves and Pavlak review city organization, the official city definition of emergency, plus emergency planning, budgets, mobilization, and communications, most particularly city 911 operations. They show that municipal labor strikes can create civil emergencies for New York and that city officials are acutely aware that this is part of emergency management. They also reveal that jurisdiction over emergency management can be a source of interdepartmental friction, as it has been between the police and fire departments of New York. They close with the proviso that "domain consensus" and "unit diversity" will be a continuing challenge for the small but highly professional New York City Office of Emergency Management.

In Chapter XI, William L. Waugh, Jr., examines the current status and future prospects of state and local emergency management. His essay paints emergency management and disaster policy on a broad canvas of public policy problems and local governmental conditions. He reviews the progress of comprehensive emergency management's diffusion among U.S. sub-national governments, inspects the capacity of local government in light of Reagan administration "New Federalism" and its perpetuation under President Bush, arrays obstacles to effective emergency management, discusses national budgetary effects on emergency management programs, and reminds us that FEMA has been encouraged to enhance its military-related programs at the expense of its other disaster and emergency management programs. Waugh's assessment is not totally bleak. He sees hope in the further professionalization of emergency management, the proliferation of more emergency management academic and professional associations, the admission by many local officials that lack of emergency preparedness and mitigation can open the municipality to lawsuits and political criticism, and the realization that many states and localities have the political, economic, and administrative wherewithal to design, implement, and maintain effective emergency management programs.

We, the editors of this volume, hope that it will find its way into graduate and undergraduate courses that address disaster policy and emergency management. We also hope that the good people who work in all realms of emergency management will read with high interest this and related works. We earnestly hope that it contributes to a deep and sophisticated appreciation of the field and profession of emergency management.

R. Sylves and W. Waugh

ACKNOWLEDGMENTS

The editors of the project would like to thank our respective employers and their staffs for having provided the labor and resources that made this study possible. The University of Delaware's Department of Political Science and Georgia State University's Institute of Public Administration provided computer facilities, wordprocessing resources, and typing services essential in this work. Professor Sylves would like to single out for special thanks the students of his Politics and Disaster course of 1989. They read, discussed, and critiqued many of the chapters of this book and, by so doing, helped make this a more suitable text for course use.

We would also like to thank the Federal Emergency Management Agency (FEMA) and the National Association of Schools of Public Affairs and Administration for having brought the editors, as well as many chapter contributors of this volume, together at FEMA's Senior Executive Policy Center in Emmitsburg, Maryland, in mid-1984. The occasion was a Public Administration Faculty Workshop on Emergency Management. This intensive two-week exercise created friendships, associations, and a cadre of dedicated emergency management scholars.

CONTENTS

                                                               Page

Foreword xi

Introduction xiii

PART I

    I. Adaptive Planning for Community Disaster Response 5
        Jack D. Kartez and Michael K. Lindell

   II. Disaster Assistance:
       Securing Presidential Declarations 33
        Allen K. Settle

PART II

  III. Local Flood Hazard Management:
       Lessons From National Research 59
        Beverly A. Cigler and Raymond J. Burby

  IV. Contrasting Local Government Responses
       to a Tornado Disaster in Two Communities 75
        Robert A. Stallings and Charles B. Schepart

   V. Acid Rain as Disaster Agent 91
        M. Elliot Vittes

  VI. Conflict and Coordination in Responding to Aviation Disaster:
       The San Diego and Gander Experiences Compared 109
        Joseph Scanlon and Richard T. Sylves

PART 3

  VII. Issue Salience and Preparedness
       as Perceived by City Managers 133
        Sandra Sutphen and Virginia Bott

VIII. The Role of Emergency Services Coordinator:
       It Starts When the Emergency Ends 155
        Frances E. Winslow

IX. Political Leadership and Canadian Emergency Planning:
     The Role of the Mayor.................................. 165
     Joseph Scanlon

PART 4

X.   The Big Apple and Disaster Planning:
     How New York City Manages Major Emergencies............ 185
     Richard T. Sylves and Thomas J. Pavlak

XI. Emergency Management and
     State and Local Government Capacity.................... 221
     William L. Waugh, Jr.

Bibliography... 239
Index... 247

CITIES AND DISASTER

PART 1

Chapter I

ADAPTIVE PLANNING FOR COMMUNITY DISASTER RESPONSE

Jack D. Kartez and Michael K. Lindell

INTRODUCTION

Formal disaster plans have been adopted by over 80 percent of U.S. localities, yet a recent assessment by the International City Management Association concluded that "local governments continue to be surprised when the standard procedures in their lengthy plans prove irrelevant in the real disaster."[1] Local governments often fail to improve their plans even after a major disaster has been experienced.[2] What factors influence how lessons from experience come to be used or ignored by local government emergency agencies? One conceptual model of disaster response preparedness is developed here and tested in a sample of 400 municipalities.

This model is based on a review of much discussed failures of local government to effectively plan for the demands of a communitywide disaster response. Different critics have attributed these failures to different factors, including: (1) a lack of relevant experience with disaster response; (2) a failure to learn from experience; (3) a lack of commitment to carrying out a disaster planning program, and; (4) doing the wrong kind of planning. The model developed here draws on recent views about managerial cognition, which concern how managers and organizations learn to recognize and interpret the demands of professional problems, especially unfamiliar or hard to predict ones like a disaster.

The following section discusses examples of disaster demands that local governments are frequently accused of ignoring in their emergency preparations. The barriers to effective preparedness are reviewed and a conceptual model of disaster planning is proposed and empirically tested in a nationwide sample. Finally, some of the management implications for federal, state, and local government are explored.

PROBLEMS IN LOCAL DISASTER PLANNING

Social scientists studying community disasters argue that authorities can improve coping performance by paying more attention to recurring patterns of community and organizational behavior in response plans.[3] Dangers are heightened when the well-documented dynamics of behavior in disaster are ignored, as in the case of a 1982 Louisiana air crash that killed 154 people and demolished a neighborhood. A nearby freeway allowed hordes of spectators and would-be helpers to converge on the scene. Inaccurate and hasty radio publicity that blood was needed at the scene doubled crowds. In the absence of predetermined action cues, fire departments from over ninety miles away acted precipitously in flooding the area with unneeded equipment.[4] These actions frustrated the response of local officials, and are examples of individual and organizational convergence—a phenomenon that was documented more than 25 years ago by disaster researchers. Such response by individuals is typically:

> ... motivated by anxiety over missing kin and friends, sympathy for the stricken population and the desire to help it, and interest in an unusual or unfamiliar event. For these needs to be satisfied, the disaster management must provide adequate information, positive direction, and guidance, rather than indiscriminate restraint.[5]

One specific strategy for achieving this aim is to make prior arrangements for disseminating emergency-related information from response agencies to the public via emergency media information centers.[6] Another strategy would be to develop crisis phone centers to meet the inevitable overload of agency phone systems caused by citizens seeking information on how to react. The frequently observed influx of unofficial helpers in disasters can be better coped with if the organization has anticipated the phenomenon and expanded its procedures to incorporate volunteers rather than ignore them.[7]

Emergency managers also must recognize the problems that emerge in dealing with other response organizations. Under disaster conditions, some organizations attempt to protect their autonomy by acting unilaterally. However, a coordinated response by the community as a whole may require that each emergency organization voluntarily surrender a significant degree of the autonomy that it exercises over the functions that it performs. When disaster impacts are severe and the time pressure to respond is intense, situational demands may necessitate a degree of coordination typically achieved only by means of a centralized authority system. In the presence of such conflicting tendencies towards the simultaneous assertion of, and resistance to, centralized control, plans need to identify strategies suitable to disaster conditions for managing the loosely coupled systems that Thomas Drabek refers to as "emergent multi-organizational networks."[8]

A prime example of a strategy for managing the organizational response is the development of a mutual aid plan that specifies the types of aid available from each organization and the appropriate mechanism for initiating a request for support. Just as there are good practices for managing citizen response, the suggested strategies for organizational response focus not on "agent-generated" demands (such as how to clear debris) but on "response-generated" demands, such as how to organize the agencies or individual volunteers to clear the debris.[9]

Barriers To Adaptive Disaster Planning

Disaster research has attributed failures in anticipating response-generated demands both to individuals and to their organizations. It would be an oversimplification to attribute the problem solely to a lack of direct experience with disaster demands. Even when the organization does have disaster experience, as Henry Quarantelli has suggested, failures to learn from experience occur when individual managers reject information which conflicts with their prior but erroneous perceptions.[10] For example, plans (and actual responses, as well) emphasize crime control and view citizens as problems, rather than provide adaptive strategies to work with citizens as partners. Even when a manager's own experience in disaster fails to confirm his or her expectations of panic, looting and other myths of disaster response, this is not accepted as evidence that plans should be changed. Observed instances of citizens functioning as valuable resources in disasters are viewed as unique "exceptions to the rule."

One early study by Jack Weller of the Disaster Research Center compared the major changes in law enforcement after experience with civil disorders to the minimal change in disaster plans after major calamities. He concluded that changes in disaster plans fail to occur because of a lack of normative and resource support within organizations and professions.[11] Others pursuing this line of investigations have suggested that the internal constituency for disaster planning among the organi-

zation's specialized agencies is often quite limited.[12] The individual
charged with maintaining disaster plans is typically a coordinator whose
status is modest, at best. Yet this person is faced with a vague charter to
promote collaboration among units with such different domains and
disciplinary backgrounds as fire, police, and public works departments.

The ambiguous goals and limited power given to the coordinator
often result in minimal participation by the units with command over
key resources. When those units must coordinate operations during a
disaster, their conflicting perceptions of task priorities and methods and
their competition for scarce resources can create new problems that
hinder performance. Confusion is even greater because each unit "responds
to its own private emergency.[13] Finally, disaster preparedness lacks the
external support of a vocal constituency among the public. In consequence,
public executives give minimal attention to disaster planning and allocate resources to matters having more immediate public preference.[14]

In 1978 the National Research Council argued that an effective disaster planning process must have a "social as well as technical dimension"
wherein learning takes place through the "sharing of experience and
knowledge among participants."[15] Emergency exercises are mandated in
funding requirements for local planning, because they provide opportunities for multiunit interaction. But exercises are often conducted in
such a manner as to satisfy the minimum requirements of funders, and
attempts to share experience and knowledge often result in standardized
plans which fail to recognize the decentralized forms of organization that
are available to cope with the demands of a disaster.

Blame for standardized, rather than novel, thinking is often attributed
to the written disaster plans emphasized by state and national government funding requirements. By convention these plans are lengthy
procedural documents descended from hierarchical military command
models. Such plans often attempt to assert a centralized system of control
rather than facilitate the adaptation of the organization to changing
circumstances. They may be developed in isolation by a technical specialist,
with minimal involvement from the very managers whose actions the
plans are intended to guide. Thus a planning process which lacks frequent participation from units in the organization and which emphasizes
noninteractive methods, results in failures to properly prepare for the
recurrent demands of major urban emergencies.

A CONCEPTUAL MODEL FOR DISASTER PLANNING

Ineffective disaster preparations can be blamed on both individuals and their organizations. But what are the conditions that facilitate the adoption of effective disaster response strategies? Information about possible disaster environments must be processed by individuals before it can be used by the organization. This includes information from direct experience with events and experience gained vicariously from planning activities such as exercises that involve response to simulated emergencies.

Disagreements about disaster demands may exist in the organization as a result of individual differences in *access to* disaster relevant information. Differences in the *interpretation of* direct and vicarious experiences of disasters are also highly likely. Individual differences in beliefs about what to plan for must therefore be reconciled by the organization through activities that involve identification and evaluation of key aspects of "disaster schemas." These organizational activities are the elements of the planning process.

Planning activities can give meaning to experience (including vicarious experience) by creating a *shared schema* for disaster among personnel who must devise response strategies for future crises. In this context, schemas are organized sets of beliefs that individuals use to guide their appraisals of situations, expectations of future events and assessments of alternative coping responses.[16]

Because disasters are infrequent and seemingly unique events, however, development of valid schemas is difficult. Disaster researchers frequently complain that public officials fail to recognize the underlying commonalities of disaster events. Instead, by focusing on the superficial dissimilarities, officials tend to conclude that "all disasters are different."[17] Research has demonstrated that common attributes do indeed exist, and much of this information has been disseminated by training programs and professional associations. But this information may simply not "add up" over time for managers lacking an accurate disaster schema. New information cannot be easily fitted by an individual to a contradictory personal model such as "all disasters are different;" that individual may well consider each event to be unique. Unfortunately, this view can be quite maladaptive, because similarities do exist and, hence, can be adapted to in advance if recognized.

Individuals have also been found to adjust their explanations of observed events to fit their own expectations, rather than use new observations to revise that mode.[18] Spurious explanations may be assigned to events, leading to increased rather than decreased confidence in an erroneous model.[19] A police watch commander may conclude that citizens and news media are obstacles to swift disaster response because of an event like the air crash described earlier. In planning for future crises, he decides his unit will protect itself by minimizing information sharing and he opposes detailing personnel to deal with spontaneous public helping behavior.

When these strategies aggravate rather than solve problems in the next event, he is likely to conclude that his model has been vindicated. Indeed, he may conclude that citizens and news media are even greater obstacles than he had previously imagined. This is also a maladaptive process because an erroneous cause has been attributed to the problem leading to ineffective preparedness strategies.

Planning activities can create a shared cognitive domain by expanding the range of disaster attributes considered meaningful (e.g., disasters do involve changes in effective authority and new interdependencies with community sectors). Cognitive pathways for creation of this shared domain have been suggested by research on the use of heuristics and biases in judgment under uncertainty. When evaluating the likelihood of an event, people tend to be influenced heavily by the information that is most readily accessible or "available" in memory.[20] Choice by availability can also be based on whether an option is merely associated with some *other* information, situations or persons that are already frequent in experience.

Experiments on inductive thinking have further shown that individuals are less influenced by abstract (written or numerical) information relevant to a judgment task than they are by concrete, and, especially, vivid information such as pictures, face-to-face conversations and the like. In fact, instructions to imagine an event have been found to be sufficient to increase expectations for that event.[21] Individuals are especially likely to be strongly influenced by information about disaster demands imbedded in frequent and concrete interaction with trusted colleagues or as part of organizationally sponsored activities such as simulating, debriefing, preparing plans or training.

In the process of identifying and anticipating disaster demands, organizations with frequent and concrete planning activities can be expected to adopt strategies addressing a wider range of (response-generated) demands than organizations with limited planning behavior. When planning activities are infrequent and participation is narrow, units are more likely to have diverging schemas of disaster attributes. Consensus on anticipatory coping strategies to be adopted by the organization is difficult to achieve, due to "mutual ignorance" of the disaster demands anticipated by other subunits and conflicts over the setting of priorities for the proposed disaster response strategies. In addition, fewer disaster response actions are likely to be feasible for adoption since the resources (e.g., trained personnel, specialized equipment and facilities) required for their implementation will be lacking.

This hypothesis is not restricted to organizations with direct disaster experience. Because of opportunities for vicarious learning, it applies also to those organizations that have learned about the experience of others. The content of planning activities (such as training, simulations, or multidisciplinary discussion) can include information about disaster situations with which the organization has no direct experience. Vicarious learning permits an organization to learn from other organizations' responses and their consequences. Of course, vicarious and, especially, direct experience can also influence organizational disaster preparations even in the absence of an effective planning process. These *ad hoc* pathways are expected to be less influential, however, because the organization will not have developed a shared schema, and, thus, would not have reached consensus on what to plan for.

Propositions

The literature reviewed in previous sections supports four general propositions that relate experience to planning activities and the adoption of preparedness practices via the development of individual and shared schemas of disaster demands. These propositions form the core of the model proposed here.

First, because disasters are infrequent events, lack of direct experience tends to prevent the development of both individual and shared disaster schema. When direct experience does occur, it tends to create an expectation that observed demands could occur again in the future, although the evidence from research on social cognition, as supported by observations of disaster researchers, indicates that the correlation between direct experience and expectations is not likely to be high. Differences among individuals in the interpretation of direct experience makes it difficult to develop a shared schema of disaster demands.

Second, expectations that emergency demands could occur in the respondents' jurisdictions would, in turn, be expected to stimulate planning activities that will promote a productive interaction among those who will be responsible for responding to an emergency. Such efforts include:

- assessing vulnerability to hazards other than the one(s) that produced that experience,
- identifying emergency demands (especially response-generated demands) other than those directly experienced,
- defining appropriate roles for private and public sector organizations that can contribute to an effective response,
- training response personnel in methods for recognizing and responding effectively to emergency demands, and
- testing the ability of emergency response organizations to respond in a coordinated manner through special emergency exercises and drills.

Third, these planning activities, in turn, would be expected to stimulate the development of a shared schema regarding emergency demands, and appropriate roles and coordination mechanisms for emergency response. Such a shared schema would tend to increase the adoption of strategies that would be effective in coping with the "response-generated" demands of an emergency. The adoption of these strategies is indicated by the commitment of resources (time and funds) to establish procedures, train personnel and purchase equipment.

Fourth, adoption of the good practices does not necessarily require that such a consensus exist. For example, it is possible that experience in issuing evacuation orders could lead directly to the development of training in warning mechanisms and identification of resources for evacuation transportation support without any intervening development of a shared disaster schema. But while this "short-circuited" pathway to adopting a single disaster preparation may exist, it is less likely to lead to a large number of different strategies being adopted in the absence of the organization's schema of disaster created by an effective planning process.

The relationships among the variables described in these propositions— experience, planning, and strategies—are portrayed in Figure I-1. The concept of planning has several specific dimensions. The planning process can vary with respect to the types of activities that are carried out. As already discussed, differences may exist between a jurisdiction that relies solely on the writing of plans as its major planning activity and a jurisdiction that conducts activities like simulated emergencies or meet-ings of interdepartmental working committees, which involve more face-to-face communication. More frequent use of a planning activity is likely to have a different effect than infrequent use. This dimension, the type and frequency of different planning activities, is of main interest here.

However, other attributes of the planning situation may also have effects that need to be accounted for. A planning process in which activities are attended by a narrow range and small number of personnel is likely to differ in its effects on disaster preparedness from a process in which the same activities are attended by personnel from a wide range and large number of units. The diversity of viewpoints and experiences that are available when participation is broad is likely to lead to a broader range of preparedness actions being adopted. Therefore, the scope of participation in planning by various departments of a local government must be accounted for, as shown in Figure I-1. Likewise, when the content of planning activities such as exercises and training sessions fails to include a broad range of different types of disaster tasks, a narrow range of preparedness actions may result.

The visible support of the chief administrative officer of the jurisdic-tion is also likely to influence the range of units that participate in planning activities and the actions taken as a result of planning efforts. As one police chief in a city of 650,000 put it during exploratory case studies we conducted in 1984: "My number one priority is getting the uniforms out in response to calls. The public judges me on that perform-ance, not whether I'm planning for an earthquake that may never happen. If left alone, disaster planning would get even less attention from my office. It requires that the executive clearly make this a priority." A lack of chief administrator support may result in little enthusiasm among personnel for implementing preparedness practices suggested in the planning process, and therefore must be taken into account in our model.

Methods

A test of this conceptual model requires measuring how a local government's adoption of effective disaster response preparations is influ-enced by experience and planning behavior. Reports of an organization's behaviors (including instances of specific experiences) are much more readily obtained and are likely to be more reliable than data on individ-ual cognitive structures. Therefore the model, as tested here, assumed

FIGURE I-1

A PROCESS MODEL OF DISASTER PREPAREDNESS

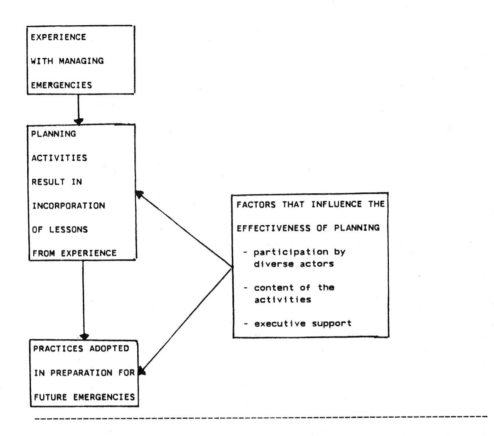

that the extent to which an organization has opportunities for developing an organization-wide disaster schema is indicated by available experiences and the characteristics of the planning process. One way to state the major hypothesis is to ask, "Is it experience with a disaster that plays the major role in spurring the adoption of effective disaster response preparations, or does the planning process also play a significant role in linking experience to action?" A preliminary test of this hypothesis conducted in 1986 showed some evidence that planning mediates between experience and effective preparedness actions.[22] That study was limited in several respects. It utilized a small sample drawn from only three states, and it addressed only a small number of types of experiences, planning activities, and effective preparedness practices. In addition, this preliminary study did not account for the effects of multidepartmental participation in planning and the presence of chief executive support for planning, perhaps resulting in an overstatement of the effects of planning activities on preparedness.

Study Design

Expert informants from 450 municipal governments were asked to complete a mail questionnaire about their organization's disaster management experiences, planning processes, and disaster preparedness practices. Informants were selected within organizations by routing the survey through the chief administrative officer (mayor or city manager) with a request that an appropriate staff member respond.

Cities were selected from those responding to a 1982 International City Management Association (ICMA) Baseline Survey of disaster planning organization. They were chosen for two reasons. These cities had demonstrated interest in disaster planning problems by responding to the earlier survey, one which achieved a 39 percent response rate. Second, cities within this group had a higher incidence of disaster experience than is true nationally, thus providing appropriate cases for testing our main hypothesis. The ICMA survey only touched superficially on topics of the present study. Specifically, it queried cities about the severity of past disasters, but not about the nature of the city's response to the event. The survey instrument used here delves into more detail concerning a specific range of emergency tasks, planning activities and good preparedness practices.

All large cities (over 50,000 population) that responded to the ICMA survey are included in the present sample; an equal number of medium-sized cities (20,000–50,000) was randomly selected from the ICMA respondents. The 450 sampled cities include half of all large and about one-fifth of all medium-sized cities in the United States. Smaller cities were not included as they are less likely to have disaster planning personnel. Fully or partially completed questionnaires were returned by 88 percent of the cities surveyed. Deletion of partially completed questionnaires yielded an effective response rate of 76 percent of the original sample. There were slightly more medium sized cities (55%) than large cities (45%) in the final sample of respondents. Only 16 percent of the responding jurisdictions had not experienced a major emergency or disaster in the preceding ten years.

Survey Instrument

All informants used identical lists to report on their organization's experiences, planning behaviors, and development of disaster response resources. The experience items cover task attributes of disaster defined as "response-generated demands" because, as discussed earlier, these are considered most underemphasized in local plans. Each city representative in the sample was asked if they had direct EXPERIENCE with each task as the result of either a major emergency or a legally declared disaster in the last ten years. In addition, each was asked if it has vicarious experience with each task as a result of that task being included in the CONTENT of simulations, training, or other planning activities. Positive responses were summed to form one variable for direct experience and another for planning CONTENT.

The planning process items include mandated activities (writing plans and standardized procedures, holding exercises) as well as those which increase communication between units within the organization, and between the organization and other community sectors (e.g., the news media, voluntary organizations, and other governments). These activities were scored according to their reported frequency of use: least frequent = 1; in last 2–3 years = 2; annually = 3; 2–3 times per year = 4; more frequent = 5). The sum of the item scores was used as the index of PLANNING activities. A separate measure of PARTICIPATION in planning was constructed from the total number of departments that were reported to regularly participate in planning (out of a predetermined list of twelve).

Cities were rated on an index of planning outcomes, which is the total number of good PRACTICES that have been adopted in disaster preparations. The list of practices, shown in the last column of Table I-1, is not exhaustive of all possible municipal preparations for response-generated demands. However, this list is representative of important resource requirements which have frequently been mentioned in reports of local response in emergencies and in literature that attempts to provide guidance to local planners. EXECUTIVE support for disaster planning was assessed by the question about actions by the chief administrative officer (CAO): "In the last two years, has the CAO made any special directives to departments that require them to participate in emergency planning, training, or exercising?" Positive responses are coded as 1 and negative responses as 0.

TABLE I-1

ITEMS FOR EXPERIENCE, PLANNING, OUTCOME VARIABLES

EXPERIENCE	PLANNING Activities	Response PRACTICES
----------------------	----------------------	------------------------
Issuing an evacuation order to citizens.	Updating written plan.	Communication link with radio/TV stations.
Searching for outside (mutual aid) resources.	Updating each unit's standard operating procedures.	Establish emergency fee and rate agreement with vendors.
Using untrained citizen volunteers who appear at time of disaster.	Multi-unit emergency simulations/exercises.	Install equipment and task staff to operate public information phone bank (not 911).
Provide emergency public information via radio or TV news media.	Multi-unit critiques after minor/moderate emergencies.	Train citizen members of Block Watch & other neighborhood groups for emergency self-help.
Using amateur radio volunteers from the organized associations.	Review disaster roles with legislative body.	Establish site & staff for a media information center for face-to-face communication with TV and radio reporters.
Restricting residents from returning to homes in hazardous areas.	Meetings of multi-unit standing task force for disaster planning.	Assign & train staff to organize citizen volunteers who appear at time of emergency.
Working jointly with personnel from a nearby city/county.	In-city emergency training events, beyond normal unit training.	Set out open purchase orders for units to make and document crisis expenditures.
Providing shelter to evacuees and responding to mass casualties.	Meetings with a local disaster council that includes voluntary and industry groups.	Train staff in methods of evacuation warning, besides siren use.
Working jointly with private voluntary groups during emergency.	Preparation of a "Most Likely Hazards" analysis.	Establish evacuation transit for mobility-impaired citizens.
Giving emergency public information to citizens directly via phone banks or other methods.	Meetings with radio/TV station managers to review emergency procedures.	Form multiple casualty plan with hospitals for the routing of patients.
Providing evacuation transit to citizens citizens ordered out.	Meetings with nearby cities or counties to review mutual aid plans.	Agree on agency or voluntary group to shelter evacuees.

ANALYSIS

Table I-2 shows the percentage of responding cities that have had any actual experience with the 13 emergency response tasks included in this study. Experience in working with other units of government (72%) and organized voluntary groups (71%) is much more prevalent than experience in working with untrained citizens, although one-third of all cities have had experience with the latter. Communicating with the public through the organized news media is more likely (61%) than direct communication with citizens through phone banks or other means (47%). As disaster researchers have been insisting for some time, actual experience with antilooting curfews is not very prevalent in the United States. Only one-tenth of these major cities surveyed have encountered this need in the last ten years.

In general, at least one-third of sampled cities have performed each of the emergency tasks listed, excluding antilooting preparations and the management of massive casualties. The proportion of cities that include these tasks (see Table I-2) in training and exercises is similar to the proportions that have experience, with some notable exceptions. Fewer cities have emergency training involving direct contact with the general citizenry than have had experience with these kinds of tasks. These tasks include managing untrained volunteers and persons who wish to return to damaged neighborhoods, and the provision of direct public information to citizens. Yet, almost four times as many cities train for mass casualty events as have had experience with them.

In reviewing how often certain planning actions are taken (see Table I-3), it is apparent some planning areas are much overlooked. These include communicating and planning with elected officials, with community groups, and with the commercial news media. Not surprisingly, case studies of disaster response often cite failures of local government to work effectively with all three of these groups. This pattern is also reflected in Table I-4; it lists the proportions of cities which have adopted thirteen practices for improved response preparedness. Least likely to have been adopted are provisions for communicating directly with the population, and for working with neighborhoods and untrained citizen volunteers.

To test our main hypothesis about the relative effects of experience and planning on preparedness, the cities were split into equal-sized, low versus high experience groups and low versus high planning groups. These categories were created by dividing the cities into groups around

TABLE I-2

EXPERIENCE WITH SELECTED EMERGENCY TASKS VS. COVERAGE OF THESE TASKS IN TRAINING AND PLANNING

N=370 cities

	% with experience	% coverage in training
X1 Issuing and evacuation order to citizens.	53	45
X2 Searching for mutual aid resources (personnel and equipment).	59	66
X3 Using untrained citizen volunteers who show up at time of emergency.	34	22
X4 Providing emergency public information through the broadcast media (radio/TV).	61	61
X5 Using amateur radio volunteers (RACES, CB) to expand city emergency operating staff.	43	64
X6 Restricting residents from returning to their homes in a dangerous area.	52	27
X7 Working jointly with personnel from a neighboring local government.	72	69
X8 Providing a facility for reception and care of citizens evacuated from their homes.	57	50
X9 Working jointly with private sector voluntary groups during an emergency (e.g. Red Cross).	71	69
X10 Giving direct public information to citizens by public address systems, phone banks, etc.	47	38
X11 Declaring a curfew to prevent looting.	9	12
X12 Providing transportation to citizens advised to evacuate their homes.	36	36
X13 Responding to mass casualties.	18	72

TABLE I-3

FREQUENCY OF EMERGENCY PLANNING ACTIVITIES

N=370

Planning Activities:	Less Than Yearly or Never (%)	Once Each Year (%)	More Than Yearly (%)
P1 Updating the city's written disaster plan	58	38	4
P2 Updating each unit's SOPs or annexes	55	35	10
P3 Multidepartmental critiques after small multi-unit emergencies	60	14	26
P4 Multidepartmental emergency exercises	45	40	15
P5 Review emergency roles with legislative body	72	23	5
P6 Interdepartmental task force/planning meetings	47	19	33
P7 On-site training, beyond usual departmental training	52	29	19
P8 Meeting with a disaster assistance council that includes private and voluntary sector participation	65	11	24
P9 Preparation of hazard vulnerability analysis	57	35	8
P10 Meeting with local radio/TV station management to review emergency broadcast procedures	72	19	9
P11 Meeting with nearby localities to review mutual aid agreements	45	25	30

TABLE I-4

PERCENT OF CITIES ADOPTING GOOD PRACTICES

N=370

	Percent Adopting
S1 Establish emergency equipment rate and use agreements with contractors/industry.	49
S2 Establish communication link to a major area radio/TV station, such as protected phone lines or dedicated radio channel.	56
S3 Install rotary phone connections and establish staff procedures to operate a citizen emergency information phone bank (other the 911).	40
S4 Train citizen members of Block Watch or other neighborhood groups for emergency self-help.	42
S5 Establish agreements with RACES, CB or other radio amateurs for assisting city staff in an emergency or warning situation.	78
S6 Assign location and staff responsible for a "media information center" at which reporters will be given frequently updated information in an extended emergency.	90
S7 Assign and train city staff to take responsibility for organizing untrained citizen volunteers who may show up in a major emergency.	39
S8 Establish a procedure (multiple casualty incident plan) with hospital and ambulance managers for coordinating reception of casualties in a major emergency.	86
S9 Establish open purchase orders or other means for city departments to make and document necessary emergency expenditures.	70
S10 Develop methods and staff trained to make public evacuation warnings, besides fixed outdoor sirens.	71
S11 Designate usable vehicles and drivers to carry transit-dependent and mobility-impaired persons in an evacuation of a neighboorhood or institution.	65
S12 Designate voluntary group or agency responsible housing citizens temporarily evacuated from a hazardous area.	83
S13 Establish an incident command system that identifies staff who will provide needed command post services in a multi-agency emergency response (joint communications, food, media relations, etc.).	95

the median values on the experience scale and the planning scale respectively. The average number of preparedness practices adopted was then computed for high versus low experience group, and high versus low planning groups (see margins of Table I-5). Experience and planning were considered together in the cells of Table I-5.

TABLE I-5

EFFECTS OF EXPERIENCE VS. THE PLANNING PROCESS
ON THE ADOPTION OF GOOD PREPAREDNESS PRACTICES

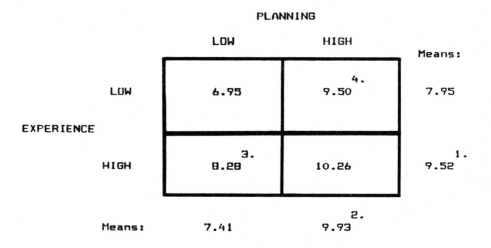

N=370

PLANNING

		LOW	HIGH	Means:
EXPERIENCE	LOW	6.95	4. 9.50	7.95
	HIGH	3. 8.28	10.26	1. 9.52
	Means:	7.41	2. 9.93	

1. t = 5.55, p < .001 for difference in means due to experience

2. t = 9.60, p < .001 for difference in means due to planning

3. F = 15.28, p < .001 for effects of experience in analysis of
   variance

4. F = 74.00, p < .001 for effects of planning in analysis of
   variance

The margins of Table I-5 show that more experience and more planning effort each have a significant effect on the number of practices adopted. High experience cities adopt about 1.5 more practices on average (9.52 vs. 7.95) than do low experience cities. High planning cities adopt about 2.5 more practices on average (9.93 vs. 7.41) than do low planning cities. Both of these differences are significant at the .0001 level.

The cells in Table I-5 reveal the results of classifying cities with respect to both experience and planning effort. Low experience and planning cities only adopt about 7 good practices on average, compared to an average of 10 adopted among the high experience and planning cities. Of particular interest, however, is that low planning cities only gain about 1.3 more practices adopted by having more disaster experience (6.95 vs. 8.28 practices), while low experience cities adopt about 2.5 more practices when planning effort is high compared to when it is low (6.95 vs. 9.50 practices adopted).

What this suggests is that cities gain more in terms of improved preparedness from an increase in planning effort (even without further experience) than from actually experiencing an emergency but neglecting planning. This is consistent with our proposal that cities fail to learn from experience when there is a failure to follow through with planning activities that build a schema—a model—of what exactly they should prepare for. Even high experience cities adopt 25 percent more good practices on average when planning effort is high rather than low, and this further supports the proposition.

TABLE I-6

REGRESSION ANALYSIS FOR MODELS 1, 2, AND 3
DEPENDENT VARIABLE   NUMBER OF PRACTICES ADOPTED

Predictors:	Standardized Regression Coefficients:		
	Model 1	Model 2	Model 3
EXPERIENCE	.35 **	.20 **	.17 **
PLANNING		.50 **	.33 **
CONTENT			.18 **
PARTICIPATION			.15 *
EXECUTIVE			.11 *
Adjusted R^2	.12	.35	.41
Model F	93.4	50.1	49.8
N = 350			

Significance of coefficients: * = p < .01, ** = p < .001

To examine the relative effects of all five of our predictors on the number of good preparedness practices adopted, multiple regression analysis must be used (see Table I-6). Standardized regression coefficients have been estimated to allow comparisons of different predictors.

First, we can again examine the relative effects of experience and planning in the first and second regression models estimated (the first two columns of Table I-6). Model 1 shows the effects of disaster experience on adoption of preparedness practices to be statistically significant (i.e., very unlikely to be a matter of chance) and explains about 12 percent of the variation in practices adopted. In Model 2, both the effects of experience and the planning activities are estimated. Both experience and planning are significant influences on preparedness practices adopted, and together they explain more than one-third of the differences in preparedness decisions among the sampled cities (R^e = .35). Planning is a significant predictor of preparedness even after differences in experience have been accounted for. In fact, planning accounts for two and one-half times more of the explained differences in preparedness among cities than does experience (i.e., a standardized coefficient of .50 versus .20). This, of course, is another way of reaching the conclusions drawn earlier from the analysis of Table I-5.

The final model (Table I-6) shows the effects of experience and of all the organizational variables together: planning activities, planning content, participation, and executive support. Because the standardized coefficient for planning activities drops from .50 to .33, we conclude that some of the effects of these activities are due to their content, to multidepartmental participation, and to visible executive support for emergency management. The effect of planning activities is still, however, about twice that of any other factor, and much greater than the effect of experience.

Clearly, cities that have had disasters but neglect building an organizational consensus on what was learned, are very unlikely to make improvements in response preparations. Cities that have active planning processes are more likely to adopt the good practices, regardless of actual experience. In addition, those cities whose planning processes also reflect important emergency tasks in exercises and training seem to enjoy multidepartmental participation and executive support. They are likely to have adopted the largest number of good preparedness practices.

Management Implications

Multivariate analysis techniques are useful in making a broad test of the hypothesis that emergency planning processes are the bridge between disaster experience and actions to improve preparedness. Now that we have some general support for this conclusion, what findings are of practical use for managers? The research questionnaire was designed to provide some detailed management information as well as data applicable in broad research measures. In fact, these data are now being applied in at least one state government emergency agency. Here we draw examples of implications for the practice of emergency planning in local government.

First, our analyses have shown that the activities making up the emergency planning process exert a strong influence on the quality of preparedness actions. But which activities are most important, and are these the same activities emphasized by federal and state level requirements for local emergency planning? Table I-7 shows how differences in the number of good practices adopted are associated with the frequency with which localities conduct each of the eleven planning activities. The data on frequency of planning activities have been divided into two groups representing high usage (at least once a year) and little or no use (in the last two or three years or never).

There is a statistically significant difference between the number of practices adopted by high and low users of every activity (p. < .001), but some planning activities are associated with greater improvements (practices adopted) than others. It is that pattern which is of interest here. Use of three planning activities—plan updates, standard procedure updates, and reviews of mutual aid procedures—lead to substantially fewer practice adoptions than did other planning activities. All three of these activities primarily involve codifying procedures, rather than learning about what the procedures may not cover. They also involve communication between governmental personnel who more often than not share similar backgrounds and job knowledge.

In the terms of the conceptual model presented in this chapter, these activities may contribute little to either broadening a local government's disaster schema or to gaining agreement between personnel who may have quite different views about what to plan for in a disaster response. In addition, two of these three activities (plan and procedure updates) are major requirements of federal and state programs for the financial

TABLE I-7

EFFECT OF FREQUENT VS. INFREQUENT USE OF PLANNING ACTIVITIES ON PRACTICES ADOPTED

Planning Activity:	At Least Annual Use (A)	Less Frequent or Never (B)	(A-B)	t-ratio for difference
P1 Plan Updates	9.4	8.1	1.3	4.67
P2 Procedure Updates	9.3	8.1	1.2	4.29
P3 Critiques	9.7	8.0	1.7	6.07
P4 Exercises	9.5	7.7	1.8	6.26
P5 Reviews with elected officials	10.2	8.1	2.1	6.86
P6 Task Forces	9.6	7.6	2.0	7.26
P7 Training	9.8	7.6	2.2	7.79
P8 Community Disaster Assistance Council	10.0	8.0	2.0	7.04
P9 Vulnerability Analyses	9.7	7.9	1.8	6.56
P10 Meeting with Radio\TV Managers	10.0	8.2	1.8	5.84
P11 Review Mutual Aid With Neighbor Cities	9.3	7.9	1.4	4.91

support of local emergency programs. (Annual exercises are a third widely stressed requirement.)

Plans and Standard Operating Procedures (SOPs) are easily measured milestones in evaluating local performance, since at the very least they result in a physical document. Our analysis, however, suggests that an over-emphasis on these product-oriented efforts, at the expense of less easily monitored activities that create more learning and interagency communication, does not lead to great improvements in preparedness. This is not to say that plans and procedures are unimportant. They define basic roles of relevant public agencies and even other community sectors, and establish necessary legal and administrative authorities for carrying out emergency operations. However, when local governments must make a choice between using scarce emergency planning resources to produce documents for federal and state funders at the expense of improving the process, the real aims of the funds involved are not well served.

The analyses also have shown that the content of training and exercises has an effect on the preparedness practices adopted even after accounting for the type and frequency of planning activities. As shown in Table I-2, localities do not cover key emergency tasks in training and exercises much more frequently than they have actually experienced these tasks. Localities utilize training curricula and technical assistance materials for conducting exercises that are provided by the Federal Emergency Management Agency (FEMA) and many of the state emergency agencies. But some private sector emergency management trainers have recently pointed out that those materials do not always reflect the community-oriented tasks that emergencies actually require.[23]

Our analyses demonstrate that preparedness improves when a larger number and variety of local government departments participate in planning, and when chief administrators visibly support emergency planning. When these conditions do not exist, cities run the risk of confronting the problem Santa Cruz County, California experienced after its devastating storm-driven floods in 1982. A Grand Jury evaluating the county's execution of emergency responsibilities concluded that: "The emergency services organization . . . existed on paper only, was not generally known, was not used, and the *ad hoc* organization which arose was a poor substitute." This outcome resulted directly from an emergency planning process that had only narrow support and that yield only limited participation within county government.

Which departments are most or least likely to participate? Executive support is likely to strongly influence departmental willingness to participate in emergency planning, but what exact effect does this have? Table I-8 shows the extent to which each city's emergency planning effort involves personnel from among twelve different municipal departments

under two different conditions: cities in which executive support for
emergency management is visible, and cities in which such support is
not obvious.

TABLE I-8

MULTIDEPARTMENTAL PARTICIPATION AS A FUNCTION OF SUPPORTIVE ACTION BY CHIEF ADMINISTRATOR IN LAST YEAR

(Percent of each department type that participates
in emergency planning activities is shown)

Action by Chief Administrator:

Depts:	None	In Last Year
FIRE	89%	98%
PARKS	24	42
FINANCE	17	44
FLEET	14	30
POLICE	82	95
EMGMEDICAL	58	73
PERSONNEL	14	36
CAO	41	76
PUBWORKS	59	77
PUBHEALTH	25	41
ATTORNEY	7	27
PLANNING	14	35

It is quite apparent that the public safety disciplines (police and fire)
are likely to be involved regardless of the organizational climate for
emergency planning. Notable, in cities where chief executives support
emergency planning, is the participation by other key municipal agencies,

most particularly those that control much of a city's physical resources: the public works and parks departments. In addition, chief executives themselves are more likely to participate in planning in cities where emergency management is visible.

In summary, these examples send a message to federal and state agencies that attempt to evaluate local emergency preparedness efforts and that provide resources and standards for training and practices. Local governments which allow planning only in a narrow domain of departments and functions will fail to succeed at preparedness. The emergency planning process can be designed to promote adaptive preparations for emergency response rather than preparations that merely satisfy funders or represent habitual ways of doing things.

Unfortunately, until recently, local governments have not been asked to look introspectively at their approach to emergency response planning. This situation has begun to change. In 1986, the Tennessee Emergency Management Agency (TEMA) developed an expanded version of the questionnaire used in this study and asked all local emergency agencies in the state to evaluate their own programs.[24] The results will be used to both refine state assistance programs and to monitor local performance. In 1987 the Federal Emergency Management Agency's National Emergency Training Center began a review of these findings to explore possible changes in training curricula. In addition, hundreds of cities and counties have requested a brief summary of these results and, presumably, are conducting their own self-assessment of planning needs.

CONCLUSION

In conclusion, all the reasons why local governments fail to be prepared seem to be important, but they should not be viewed in isolation. Lack of experience with disaster is an impediment, but not one as great as might be expected. Failures to apply what was learned from experience can take place when there is no planning process to imprint those lessons within the organization's model of disaster needs.

Finally, although different approaches to emergency planning all have some positive impact on preparedness, the payoff is greater when planning is not merely a technical exercise but is more a face-to-face learning process. When a broad set of planning activities enjoy wide participation from local agencies, a local government is most likely to prepare strategies that are adaptations to the disaster environment instead of ineffective attempts to impose routine solutions on nonroutine problems.

Notes

This is an account of work supported by National Science Foundation Grant ECE-8217550. Opinions are solely those of the authors.

[1]See: G. Hoetmer, *Emergency Management,* Baseline Data Reports Vol. 15, No. 4. (Washington, DC: International City Management Association, 1983). The quote is from: Hoetmer, "Interorganizational Relationships in Emergency Management," Paper prepared for the NASPAA/FEMA Public Administration Faculty Workshop on Emergency Management, National Emergency Training Center, Federal Emergency Management Agency, Emmitsburg, Maryland, May 20–June 2, 1984.

[2]Studies demonstrating this include: W. A. Anderson, *Disaster and Organizational Change: A Study of the Long Term Consequence of the 1964 Alaska Earthquake* (Columbus, Ohio: Disaster Research Center, Ohio State University); J. Weller, *Organizational Innovation in Anticipation of Crisis* (Columbus, Ohio: Disaster Research Center, Ohio State University, Report Series No. 14, 1974); and D. C. Wenger, C. Faupel and T. James, *Disaster Beliefs and Emergency Planning* (New York: Todd Publications, Inc., 1980).

[3]See: R. W. Perry, "Incentives for Evacuation in Natural Disasters: Research-Based Community Emergency Planning," *Journal of the American Planning Association* 45 (1979): 440–447.

[4]J. Kartez, "Adaptive Planning for Community Disaster Response," *Hazard Monthly* 7 (1986): 8–10.

[5]C. Fritz, "Disaster," in *Contemporary Social Problems,* edited by R. Merton and R. Nisbett (New York: Harcourt, Brace, and World, 1961), p. 682.

[6]This is drawn from the workshop presentation by Gerald Fox, former city manager of Wichita Falls, Texas, at the conference on "Managing the Disaster Response: A Search for Theory," National Emergency Training Center, Federal Emergency Management Agency, Emmitsburg, Maryland, August 21, 1984.

[7]See: J. Kartez, "Crisis Response Planning: Toward a Contingent Analysis," *Journal of the American Planning Association* 50 (1984): 9–21.

[8]T. Drabek, "Alternative Patterns of Decision-Making in Emergent Disaster Response Networks," *International Journal of Mass Emergencies and Disasters* 1 (August 1983).

[9]These terms originate from: R. Dynes, E. Quarantelli, and G. Kreps, *A Perspective on Disaster Planning* (Columbus, Ohio: Disaster Research Center, Ohio State University, 1972).

[10]E.L. Quarantelli, *Organizational Behavior in Disasters: Implications for Disaster Planning* (Emmitsburg, Md.: National Emergency Training Center, Federal Emergency Management Agency, 1984).

[11]J. Weller, *Organizational Innovations in Anticipation of Crisis.*

[12]See: T. Caplow, H. Bahr, and B. Chadwick, *Analysis of the Readiness of Local Communities for Integrated Emergency Management Planning* (Washington, DC: Fed-

eral Emergency Management Agency, 1984); and, J. Labadie, "Problems in Local Emergency Management," *Environmental Management* 8 (1984): 489–494.

[13]L. McCoy, "What Happened to the Total Emergency Response System?," *Natural Hazards Observer* VI (1982): 6–7.

[14]R. Wolensky and E. Miller, "The Everyday Versus the Disaster Role of Public Officials: Citizen and Official Definitions," *U rban Affairs Quarterly* 16 (1981) 483–504; M. Meyer and P. Belobaba, "Contingency Planning for Response to Urban Transportation System Disruption," *Journal of the American Planning Association* 48 (1982): 454–465.

[15]National Research Council, *The U.S. Government Foreign Disaster Assistance Program* (Washington, DC: The Council, 1978).

[16]S. Kiesler and L. Sproull, "Managerial Response to Changing Environments: Perspectives on Problem Sensing from Social Cognition," *Administrative Science Quarterly* 27 (1982): 548–570.

[17]D. Wenger, E.L. Quarantelli, and R. Dynes, "Disaster Analysis: Emergency Management Offices and Arrangements (Final Report on Phase I), FEMA Contract #EMW-85-C-1981 (Newark, Del.: Disaster Research Center, University of Delaware, 1987).

[18]D.J. Isenberg, "Thinking and Managing: A Verbal Protocol Analysis of Managerial Problem Solving," *Academy of Management Journal* 29 (1986): 775–788; A. Tversky and D. Kahneman, "Causal Schemas in Judgments Under Uncertainty," in *Judgment Under Uncertainty: Heuristics and Biases,* edited by D. Kahneman, P. Slovic, and A. Tversky (New York: Cambridge University Press, 1982).

[19]H. Einhorn, "Learning from Experience and Suboptimal Rules in Decision Making," in *Judgement Under Uncertainty;* E. Hamilton and T. Rose, "Illusory Correlation and the Maintenance of Stereotypic Beliefs," *Journal of Personality and Social Psychology* 39 (1980): 832–845.

[20]A. Tversky and D. Kahneman, "Availability: A Heuristic for Judging Frequency and Probability," *Cognitive Psychology* 5 (1973): 207–232.

[21]E. Borgida and R. Nisbett, "The Differential Impact of Abstract Vs. Concrete Information on Decisions," *Journal of Applied Social Psychology* 7 (1977): 258–271; J. Carroll, "The Effect of Imagining an Event on Expectations for the Event: An Interpretation of the Availability Heuristic," *Journal of Experimental Social Psychology* 14 (1978): 88–96.

[22]J. Kartez and M. Lindell, "Planning for Uncertainty: The Case of Local Disaster Planning," *Journal of the American Planning Association* 53 (1987).

[23]These points were made in an unsolicited 1986 proposal to the Federal Emergency Management Agency by the Emergency Response Institute of Olympia, Washington, a firm which currently has emergency training contracts with a number of state government emergency agencies that have chosen to shop for these services.

[24]See: "Tennessee Community Emergency Management: Strategies Workbook," (Nashville: Tennessee Emergency Management Agency, Military Department of the State of Tennessee).

Chapter II

DISASTER ASSISTANCE
SECURING PRESIDENTIAL DECLARATIONS

Allen K. Settle

INTRODUCTION

A presidential disaster declaration is essential to U.S. state and local officials if they seek disaster assistance from the federal government. Sound methods and accurate documentation are critical in securing aid in a timely manner. Local governments that need help after a disaster often have leaders who fail to recognize the importance of sound damage assessment methods and valid estimation of replacement costs. Public and private property damage repair costs are used at the federal level to determine if a community can recover economically from a disaster. Community economic recovery capacity, in turn, helps decide the level of need an afflicted community has and correspondingly how much help it will get if a presidential disaster declaration is made. In any disaster there is no guarantee of federal or state assistance and there is no automatic way that a city or state can get a declaration from the president.

History shows that 41 percent of all states and localities that have requested presidential disaster declarations have had their request denied. It remains unclear to many state and local officials, as well as to citizens in general, what the decisive factors are in obtaining federal disaster aid. For example, residents of the Love Canal area of Niagara Falls, New York, aided by state and local officials, had sought federal help for many years. Homeowners wanted the federal or state government to purchase their chemically contaminated properties. They hoped to move into new homes and thus escape the toxic pollution of their former neighborhood. Even after evidence of genetic damage to Love Canal area residents was discovered and publicized, there was still no federal disaster declaration. National relief finally became available as a grant to New York State, not as a direct federal grant to the affected community.

Another example is Portugese Bend, an area near Los Angeles,

California. There local government and citizens were denied federal aid that could have helped compensate for damage caused by a slow moving but destructive landslide that had destroyed homes and public facilities over a period of years. Yet, in Times Beach, Missouri, the federal government quickly purchased the property of the entire flood-prone community because of the threat posed by dioxin contamination and flood damage.

The purpose of this paper is to examine criteria that may serve as guidelines in determining which states or communities are entitled to a presidential disaster declaration and a commensurate amount of federal financial help. The focus is on a proposal put forward by the Federal Emergency Management Agency (FEMA), the agency that establishes federal rules for disaster aid decision making. The proposal was FEMA's attempt to set out criteria that made state and local governments assume greater responsibility and cost sharing for emergency management and planning, before disaster struck and before federal aid was sought. The original Gramm-Rudman-Hollings antideficit law of 1985, among other things, forced FEMA to find ways to reduce federal disaster relief spending. FEMA is involved in the declaration process and in community damage assessment. The agency tried to win approval of criteria under which presidential declarations would link federal support to funding eligibility evidenced in community recovery efforts. So, the more prepared a community was to undertake its own recovery effort, the easier it would be to judge whether a federal disaster declaration was warranted.

In this process, FEMA officials collected background information regarding general procedures and methods state and local governments use in requesting a presidential disaster declaration. They also analyzed the types of aid offered by the FEMA itself. Much of this was published in the *Federal Register,* in General Accounting Office reports, and in FEMA publications. Besides federal sources, there were state publications such as the *Disaster Assistance Procedure Manual* of the Governor's Office of Emergency Services in California.[1]

POLICY ISSUES

A major policy problem of federal disaster declarations involves damage assessment. City, county, and other local governments seldom have good fixed asset accounting systems. Valid budget and depreciation figures are essential in calculating revenue and property losses. Dollar loss estimates are used in determining the percentage of total loss government should pay. When there are differences between federal loss figures and state loss figures, controversy often results.

Questions emerge constantly over the degree of federal participation in disaster relief. Should communities be warned that failure to plan may result in reduced federal aid or worse, a denial of all federal relief? What land use planning performance standards should the federal government hold local governments to? Should the federal government withhold financial help simply because local communities fail to comply with certain federal contracts, like those embodied in federal flood insurance performance standards? There have been lawsuits to seek what is known as "subrogation." FEMA uses subrogation when it sues to force local compliance with FEMA's floodplain regulations. When reviewing repeated requests for Presidential declarations or other forms of emergency aid, FEMA might take into account the claims it has made against local governments that have violated FEMA requirements by permitting urban reconstruction in floodplains. If a disaster is compounded by a community's negligence in emergency and land use planning that community is, in effect, receiving an open subsidy from the U.S. Treasury at the expense of the nation. Admittedly, planning may be difficult in some types of disasters. For example, tornados cannot be easily predicted, so it is extremely difficult to insure adequately against loss of life or property from tornado destruction. Nonetheless, when disaster damage does occur the problem remains, what is the best way to ascertain the dollar value of losses? When local damage and loss assessments differ markedly from federal damage and loss assessments, disputes arise over whose estimates are correct. This often causes delay in the delivery and distribution of aid.

This study presents case illustrations to show how difficult it is to achieve a workable and easily understood declaration standard for all to follow. Before this, a review of general declaration procedures and sources of federal help is in order.

PROCEDURES AND DIRECT FEDERAL ASSISTANCE

When local officials ask the governor of a state to request a federal disaster declaration, the Federal Emergency Management Agency is usually the first federal agency to inspect the extent of damage and to gauge local financial consequences. FEMA has regional offices in each standard federal region and within each region there are other FEMA offices, most of which can conduct damage assessment. The damage assessment and the estimation of recovery costs help the president decide whether to issue a declaration. The president cannot issue a declaration unless the governor of the affected state requests one.

Damage assessment begins as soon as it is clear state or federal help may be requested. For example, in California these data are reported to the State Office of Emergency Services (OES) along with a request for a Gubernatorial proclamation. Table II-1 presents a flow chart of expected local, state, and federal decision-making stages after a disaster in California. The damage review takes into account losses in both the public and private sectors.

Local officials accompany state support teams on field trips to damaged areas. The FEMA regional director is responsible for dispatching federal staff to the field. They assess public sector damage. Aided by federal support teams, the regional director reviews and evaluates requests for federal assistance submitted by the California OES. When federal relief is requested, county government must submit true records of loss compiled from the onset of the disaster through the duration of the event, with secondary consequences of damage included.

If local and state governments are incapable of effective recovery and mitigation in the wake of a disaster, the governor ordinarily asks the president to make determination of an Emergency or to declare a Major Disaster under Public Law 93-288, the Disaster Relief Act of 1974. Under this law what constitutes, "beyond the capability to mitigate effectively," is unclear. Yet, the governor's request must document that: (1) the state emergency plan has been implemented; (2) an estimate of damage by type, public and private, has been made; (3) effective response is beyond the capability of state and local government; (4) a damage assessment report indicating the amount of federal aid required by public and private entities and persons has been completed; (5) supplementary justification data has been submitted for review. Table II-2 presents categories of state damage assessment information that must be provided to FEMA if a request for a major disaster declaration is sought.

The presidential determination of an Emergency makes available specific assistance to meet a particular need in the affected area. The type and extent of federal help to be provided is set forth in a Federal-State Agreement, executed by the governor for the state and by the FEMA regional director for the federal government. Sometimes the Federal-

TABLE II-1

DIAGRAM OF LOCAL ACTIONS FOLLOWING A DISASTER

CALIFORNIA EXAMPLE

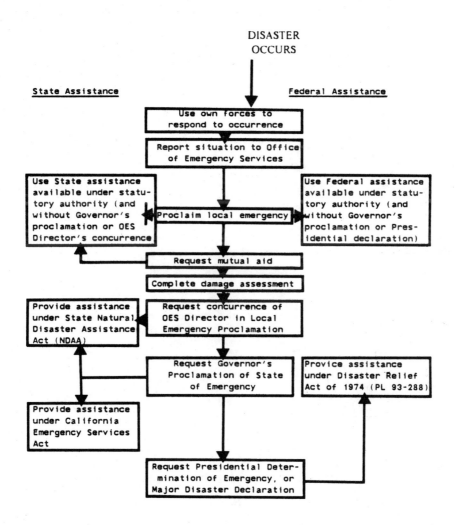

State Agreement is not fully developed or signed until after a presidential declaration has been issued.

Once a disaster declaration is issued, FEMA authorities appoint a Federal Coordinating Officer (FCO) who operates in the affected area and makes the initial appraisal of damage and types of relief most urgently needed. At this point differences of opinion often arise about

TABLE II-2

SUPPLEMENTARY JUSTIFICATION
STATE DAMAGE ASSESSMENT

REQUEST FOR A MAJOR DISASTER DECLARATION

    I. <u>BACKGROUND</u>. Provide brief narrative description of predisaster conditions covering, where applicable, factors such as:
- General economic conditions in affected area(s)
- Income level(s) of affected persons
- Special language or ethnic conditions
- Availability of vacant housing in the affected area(s) into which homeless people could be placed.
- Extent, types and provisions of insurance to cover losses and description of uninsured damages
- Unemployment
- Other relevant factors

    II. <u>IMPACTS</u>. Provide a narrative description of impacts to document a clear picture of the magnitude and severity of the disaster as reflected by losses or damages, effects on people, and effects on State and/or local government. The resultant hardships, economic and social consequences should be addressed. The following factors should be addressed only when applicable.

A. General Impact
- Deaths
- Injuries
- Missing persons
- Continuing public health and safety problems
- Extent of damages to homes
- Continuing occupancy of mass shelters
- Additional unemployment in the affected area(s) resulting from the major disaster
- Other significant personal property losses
- Extent, types, and provisions of insurance coverage of losses or damages (describe nature and extent of uninsured damages)

B. Significant effects on State or local governments
- Isolated families or communities
- Interruption of essential public services
- Search and rescue efforts
- Continuing public health and safety problems
- Extent, types of provisions of insurance coverages
- Loss of tax base
- Financial hardships
- Loss of governing capabilities (deaths or injuries to key officials, loss of records, etc.)

C. Significant effects on private, non-profit organizations (educational, utility, emergency, medical or custodial care facilities)
- Same as II. B above
D. Significant effects on businesses
   - Extent of disruptions in services or closings
   - Financial hardships
   - Employees
   - Losses or damages to facilities or inventories and their importance to the area(s)
E. Significant effects on agriculture
   - Major crop/livestock losses
   - Extent of insurance
   - Financial hardship
   - Losses or damages to facilities and their importance to the area(s)
   - Outlook for future plantings
F. Significant factors not otherwise covered under paragraph A through E above.
III. STATE AND LOCAL RESPONSES
A. State
   1. State Emergency Plan. (Specific assistance provided as a result of this plan—number of personnel, equipment, State departments involved and days of utilization, etc.)
   2. Other. (Details on other State resources which have been or will be used. Also indicate disaster/emergency history within past 12 months.)
   3. Restrictions. (Indicate resources which canot be used due to any type of restrictions, such as State constitutional prohibitions or debt or borrowing limitations. Also indicate which steps have been taken by the Governor to remove or avoid the impact of such restrictions.)
   4. Financial Data. (Furnish information concerning the availability now of any State emergency fund money or money from the Governor's discretionary funds. Provide general fund balance and status of applicable budgets for damage involved: e.g., road and bridge budget if State road and bridge damage is shown.)
   5. Hazard Mitigation. (Indicate any actions or plans currently underway. Where similar major disasters have been declared previously, discuss the status of hazard mitigation activities which resulted from the plans which FEMA reviewed.)
B. LOCAL
   1. Local Response. (Specific assistance provided by the local government(s) as a result of the incident—number of personnel, equipment, departments involved and days of utilization.)
   2. Other. (Details on other local resources which have been or will be used, if not described in detail in the letter. Also indicate assistance provided by community or private volunteer organizations. Indicate disaster/emergency history within past 12 months.)
   3. Restrictions. (Provide similar information to that provided by the State in A [3] above.)
   4. Financial Data. (Provide similar information to that provided by the State in A [4] above.)

damages and recovery costs. After Coalinga, California's earthquake in 1983, media coverage of damage aftermath helped local officials contend that the scale of damage was beyond the recovery capability of both state and local government. Nevertheless, loss figures and estimates were disputed and delays in receipt of disaster funds resulted. Had there been explicit federal criteria that took into account the percent of community damage and loss relative to community size or community per capita income, federal aid might have come sooner. An updated city government accounting of municipal facility values, replacement costs, and depreciation would have helped in the mutual determination of dollar losses and in evaluation of the community's ability to recover financially. Also useful in gauging recovery capacity is comparison with adjacent localities that also may have experienced the disaster's effects.[2]

FEMA's enabling authority resides in the Disaster Relief Act of 1974. The agency is empowered to organize and coordinate federal activities regarding major emergencies. Since 1979 FEMA has organized and divided disaster relief programs into the general categories of public and individual aid. Repair of bridges, buildings, and other facilities owned by state or local governments may be eligible for federal subsidization of 75 percent of cost. State and local governments that qualify are reimbursed once repair or restoration is completed. Local governments must find the 25 percent matching share from their own resources, from state grant underwriting, or from loans they might secure. FEMA will not pay for replacement or repair of public facilities that were not properly maintained before the disaster. Inadequate maintenance may result in rejection of federal financial help and in a lawsuit against the party responsible for operating the facility. Moreover, FEMA does not pay for the costs of facility improvements, only for the costs of replacement. So if a bridge was originally built too low and was later destroyed in a flood, no extra federal funding is provided to rebuild the bridge at a clearance that is likely to avert future flood damage. So, the added costs to improve public facilities over what they were before a disaster must be absorbed by state and local government.

Other federal help is offered by the Army Corps of Engineers, the Soil Conservation Service (SCS), the Federal Highway Administration, and the Department of Education. The latter helps repair or rebuild elementary and secondary public school buildings. The Army Corps, the Highway Administration, and SCS each provide grants to flood control districts intended to promote mitigation and preparedness. Except for some soil conservation programs funded 80 percent federal and 20 percent local, disaster relief programs of these agencies are 100 percent federally subsidized.

FEMA coordinates, but does not subsidize, benefits made available by the Small Business Administration (SBA) and the Farmer's Home (Loan) Administration (FHA). The FHA provides emergency loans to those who own or operate a farm business. This program is one of the few that offers help to victims in isolated areas when a disaster does not qualify for broadly dispersed federal aid. SBA offers homeowners loans of up to $50,000 for structural repairs, loans to $10,000 for personal property losses, or a combined maximum loan of $60,000. Residents of rental property may apply for loans up to $10,000 for damaged or lost personal property. Business loans up to 75 percent or a maximum $500,000, can be used to cover losses of real property, equipment, and inventory. Under the Economic Injury Disaster Loan Program, SBA can also extend a loan of up to $500,000 to a single firm. Money is also available from the Department of Housing and Urban Development and offices of the Department of Transportation besides the Federal Highway Administration.

Federal funds are available from these sources but FEMA serves as the primary repository of federal aid under a presidential declaration. As mentioned previously, FEMA can extend public and individual disaster aid or grant-in-aid funds to help cover losses. What then should be the criteria for determining if a community deserves federal help or not?

BASIS OF PRESIDENTIAL DECLARATION

Remember, the cost shares absorbed by federal, state, and local government in disaster recovery is based on damage assessment. Without clear damage assessment figures it becomes difficult to judge whether a state or community could recover independently after a disaster. Lack of clarity can either delay or block issuance of a presidential declaration and the federal aid that the 1974 Disaster Relief Act conveys. Under this law, FEMA must make available necessary disaster funds but within the limits of budget authority made available to the agency.

Since governors must ask the president to issue a disaster declaration, a state-level damage assessment becomes the initial criteria for measuring disaster losses. The severity and magnitude of disaster damage must be beyond the recovery capability of the state and the affected local governments such that federal aid is essential to the preservation of life, to the protection and restoration of property, and to the aversion of possible greater damage. Therefore, the governor's request must emphasize: (1) how state and local effort and resources have been used to address the emergency; (2) what specific types of federal aid are needed; and (3) how state and local capabilities and resources have been committed to cope with the disaster.[3]

The Disaster Relief Act stipulates that state and local governments are obligated to meet their responsibilities through public expenditures aimed at alleviating damage effects, losses, hardship, or suffering resulting from disaster. This includes provision for assisting the public and for restoring the government's own facilities. State government can commit local government to pay the matching money required to secure federal aid. Local officials may oppose this state mandate because disasters and their effects are often hard to predict and because it is therefore difficult for them to know how much the community needs to hold in reserve for disaster recovery costs. Sometimes local governments may not need as much federal support as is made available. Also, the 75-25 match of federal to state-local disaster relief may over-benefit some state or local governments. Table II-3 depicts FEMA help to state and local government in temporary housing, unemployment aid, individual and family grants, and flood insurance.

When they examine a request for an emergency or disaster declaration, FEMA officials rely on information provided by the governor and on preliminary damage estimates compiled by FEMA region staff. In the past, FEMA authorities have tried to negotiate agreements with governors of disaster-prone states to get them to commit a portion of state and local resources to disaster recovery before disaster strikes. Some agreements commit the state to pay recovery expenses that the Disaster Relief Act cannot by law reimburse. Some agreements obligate states to pay for the administrative costs incurred in handling disaster. Some require states to pay for mitigation measures needed to minimize the threat of future damage. Apart from these agreements, FEMA once tried to win approval of a plan that combined the 25 percent state and local matching share of disaster recovery cost. This would have allowed local government officials to fall back on state subsidization of the required local cost share if they were unable to provide enough local matching money in the aftermath of disaster. This plan was not proposed as a prerequisite of federal relief eligibility.

TABLE II-3

TYPES OF FEDERAL ASSISTANCE
TO STATE AND LOCAL GOVERNMENTS

FEMA ASSISTANCE TO STATE AND LOCAL GOVERNMENTS

Cost-sharing grants for repairs to public facilities and certain non-profit facilities:
- Debris removal
- Emergency protective measures
- Streets, roads, and bridges
- Water control facilities
- Public buildings and equipment
- Public utilities
- Public parks, recreational facilities
- Public facilities under construction

Emergency Communications
- Emergency public transportation services

Vector control to prevent spread of communicable diseases by animals or insects

Community Disaster Loans

TEMPORARY HOUSING (Federal Emergency Management Agency [PL 93-288])
Provide for temporary housing for up to 12 months for persons whose homes have been made uninhabitable by a disaster, in the form of:
- Government owned housing resources
- Private owned/commercial housing resources
- Government owned mobile homes
- Emergency repairs to primary (owner occupied) residences

Provide for mortgages or rental payments for persons faced with loss of their residence because of disaster-caused financial hardship.
(Implemented by Presidential declaration only)

UNEMPLOYMENT ASSISTANCE (U.S. Department of Labor and Federal Emergency Management Agency [PL 93-288])
- Disaster unemployment compensation payments to those out of work because of a major disaster and not covered by regular unemployment insurance programs.
- Provides job placement services. "This program includes self-employed individuals."
(Implemented by Presidential declaration only)

INDIVIDUAL AND FAMILY GRANTS (State Administered but Federal Emergency Management Agency funded [PL 93-288])
- Grants up to $5000 (75% Federal/25% State) [raised to $10,000 under the Stafford Act of 1988 presented below] for individuals or families who have disaster-related serious needs and necessary expenses that cannot be met through other means.
(Implemented by State application following a Presidential declaration)

FLOOD INSURANCE (Federal Emergency Management Agency and Federal Insurance Administration)
  - Insurance against physical loss to buildings and contents caused by floods or flood-related mudslides.

Section 1362

THE STAFFORD ACT OF 1988

The Robert T. Stafford Disaster Relief and Emergency Assistance Act of 1988 amends the Disaster Relief Act of 1974. Below is a partial list of its provisions.

PUBLIC ASSISTANCE

-A 75%/25% federal/state and local cost share formula has been established as the legal minimum. The president is allowed to advance the 25% state and local share if necessary (Section 403, 406, 407). The non-federal share may be advanced in cases of concurrent, multiple, or catastrophic events. The advances must be repaid and will bear interest at Treasury rates (Sec. 319).
-Eligible costs for Public Assistance Grants have been expanded to include:
  - hazard mitigation measures required by FEMA (Sec. 406-e),
  - fringe benefits for force account labor (Sec. 406-f),
  - costs of mobilizing the National Guard,
  - costs of prison labor,
  - administrative costs (Sec. 406-f)
-It is now easier to administer individual projects as long as they are less than $35,000 to run. A vast majority of FEMA individual projects are less than this amount of money and should therefore make it easier for FEMA officials to respond quickly to this type of request.
-Payment of any assistance shall be completed within 60 days after the date of approval (Sec. 601-a).
-There is a new definition of "eligible private non-profit facility"; it includes all those facilities providing essential services of a governmental nature (Sec. 102-9).
-Reasonable expenses incurred in anticipation of, and immediately preceding, a declared event are eligible for assistance. This reaffirms the current practice of paying for emergency work performed in anticipation of a disaster (Sec. 424).
-For insurable public structures within an identified base floodplain, the maximum amount of insurance recovery that could have been obtained must be subtracted from otherwise eligible costs. Special exception is made for eligible private non-profit facilities in communities not participating in the National Flood Insurance Programs (Sec. 406-d). Once a disaster occurs and the federal government helps to restore facilities, insurance must be purchased. If this is not done, or if the insurance coverage is not maintained, the federal government will refuse to pay the first $200,000 of loss. This applies to the Federal Disaster Protection Act. Under that Act, a government with facilities in a flood hazard zone is not required to have flood insurance before an emergency or disaster. However, under the new law [Stafford Act] insurance is required or else the local government must pay the first $200,000 of rebuilding cost for its damaged facilities.

-Flexible funding is now available to applicants. If restoring the facility is a necessary public good, a federal contribution is allowed, but is held to no more than 90 percent of the total federal share and is based on estimates of repair or replacement costs.

-Any appeal by an applicant must be submitted within 60 days after notification of a FEMA decision regarding assistance. If an appeal is submitted after a state or local damage claim has been rejected, FEMA has 90 days in which to render a decision on the appeal.

HAZARD MITIGATION

-The federal government offers 50/50 federal/state matching grants to underwrite hazard mitigation projects. These grants must be federally approved but are not a requirement of federal disaster assistance. Ten percent of the total cost of all restoration projects represents the ceiling for federal hazard mitigation grants.

DECLARATION PROJECT

-The use of resources from the Department of Defense has been made available under a cost sharing scheme of 75% federal/25% state and local, up to a period of ten days. This can be extended to cover the cost of life-saving and property-protection done by the military before the federal disaster declaration was issued.

-An arithmetic formula based on population or income may not be used as the sole basis to deny a geographic area federal assistance. Such a formula may be used to assist FEMA in eligibility determinations, along with other factors.

-Emergency Assistance (Title V) declarations are intended to apply to events not normally considered Major Disasters. The president may declare unilaterally any event an emergency as long as the subject of concern involves primary federal responsibility. Assistance will be cost shared at no less than 75% federal share. Total federal assistance is limited to $5,000,000 per event except in extraordinary circumstances (Sec. 501-503).

-A new definition of emergency includes any event determined by the president to require federal assistance. It will be used within new Title V (Sec. 102-1)

INDIVIDUAL ASSISTANCE

-Individual and family grants are increased to a maximum of $10,000 from $5,000, with annual adjustment for increases in the Consumer Price Index (Sec. 411).

-Some parts of the Federal Temporary Housing and Disaster Employment Assistance programs have been changed and clarified. These include housing assistance for up to 18 months at 100% federal funding except for construction of mobile home group sites, which will be supported at a 75% federal/25% state share. Applicants must be informed of the types of assistance available, eligibility criteria, and any limitations, when they apply (Sec. 408).

-Benefit period for Disaster Unemployment Assistance (DUA) is charged to twenty-six weeks after declaration. FEMA will not pay for waiting week credit nor will it supplement regular unemployment compensation (Sec. 410).

-Duplicate benefits may be paid to a person if one of the two sources of benefits is late. However, the recipient must agree to repay duplicative assistance (Sec. 312)

-In crisis counseling assistance, FEMA is no longer required to provide such assistance through the National Institute of Mental Health (Sec. 413).

OTHER ASSISTANCE

-Disaster Preparedness Improvement Grants are increased to $50,000 per year (Sec. 210-d).
-There will be a one time planning assistance grant of up to $250,000 for the eight Great Lakes States. The states will match with a contribution equal to one-fourth of the federal grant. Separate appropriations are required since this federal money must not come from the President's disaster fund (Previously Title II or H.R. 2707).

ADMINISTRATIVE AND PROCEDURAL CHANGES

-FEMA will establish standards to assess the efficiency of assistance programs and will annually review disaster activities (Sec. 313).
-FEMA may institute recovery action in court against any person who intentionally causes a condition for which Federal assistance is provided (Sec. 317).

FEMA CRITERIA DEVELOPMENT EFFORTS

In December 1981, the General Accounting Office (GAO) issued a report that called for a better system to evaluate requests for federal disaster aid.[4] The report claimed that FEMA's policies, procedures, and guidelines for evaluating requests were not widely known. It maintained that more information on assessment processes would help state and local officials decide whether they had a valid basis for requesting aid. The report alleged that since FEMA uses a wide range of information in making emergency or disaster declaration requests, there is a lack of consistency in the quality and method of assessment. It also concluded that Congress had to clarify disaster assistance issues.

FEMA later published new formats and procedures for processing emergency and disaster declaration requests.[5] The proposal required state governments to submit damage assessment information through the supplemental justification procedure. The agency wanted more information about economic conditions in damage areas. FEMA sought information regarding income levels of affected people, provisions of insurance coverage for their losses, and description of uninsured damages.

In another study of FEMA, GAO published a report about federal disaster relief furnished to victims of a major flood in Virginia in 1985.[6] The report focused on the adequacy and timeliness of federal disaster aid provided to flood victims. When widespread and severe flooding occurred in the Roanoke, James, and Potomac river basins of Virginia in early November 1985 about 8000 homes and businesses were either destroyed or seriously damaged. The disaster killed 22 people and resulted in property damage exceeding $700 million. The presidential declaration issued for this disaster encompassed 52 counties and many municipalities.

The GAO investigation was prompted by numerous complaints about the time it took to get federal help. Within two weeks of the start of the flooding FEMA began placing families into temporary housing and two weeks after that FEMA began issuing individual and family grant checks. The report found that disbursements of funds under FEMA's National Flood Insurance Program was generally prompt. It also concluded that FEMA housing and road repair assistance was timely. But, the report criticized FEMA's individual and family grant program and SBA's Physical Disaster Loan Program for slowness. SBA did not begin distributing home and business loans until January 17, 1986, almost ten weeks after the disaster occurred.

In this flood some communities were damaged far more than others, but no precise criteria were in place to help differentiate levels of local need or to apportion aid on the basis of local need across the federally declared disaster area. Presidential declaration aid distribution criteria needed refinement. After a major flood in West Virginia, also in November 1985, FEMA officials concluded that even with only a 25 percent matching contribution, response and recovery costs may be beyond the financial capability of governments that suffer catastrophic losses.

FEMA policy analysts considered using a sliding scale cost sharing formula under which each applicant would have to pay a small portion of its claim or a deductible. Once the state or local government paid the deductible, a sliding scale cost sharing formula would take effect permitting the federal share to rise as high as 90 percent when recovery costs exceed $10.00 per capita in the jurisdiction. This plan would allow FEMA to draw money from a pool of state and local deductible contributions enabling the agency to cover the added increment of funding between the standard 75 percent share and the new 90 percent ceiling. In 1986, FEMA leaders proposed reducing the federal contribution to state and local governments for major disaster and emergency-related public assistance from 75 percent to about 50 percent of total eligible cost.[7] FEMA officials believed these measures would save money thereby helping to reduce a fraction of the federal deficit as called for in the Gramm-Rudman-Hollings Act of 1985.

In designing a more uniform and consistent measure of state and local disaster recovery capability, FEMA leaders assumed that the chief consequence of disaster for government is financial. They insisted that financial capability is best measured by analyzing state and local government ability to raise the money needed to respond to emergencies and disasters. Using this logic, the existing declaration process appears biased in favor of state or local governments that choose not to tax themselves as heavily as other state and local governments. To correct this, the declaration process had to factor in local financial viability. But, tax effort was not to be considered in the declaration process. For review of petitions for presidential disaster declarations, FEMA officials proposed rules that measured ability-to-pay, not willingness-to-tax.

FEMA's proposal presented several ways to measure state and local financial capacity. They included per capita income, the Representative Tax System (RTS), the Gross State Product (GSP), and Total Taxable Resources (TTR). FEMA officials advised against using the RTS because of its complexity and disputed validity. The GSP and TTR systems were examined, but agency leaders preferred the per capita income measure of financial capability. The FEMA proposal also advocated review of applicant government budgets as another indicator of financial capability, however, this was rejected by the Reagan administration because the size of the budget is more closely related to willingness-to-tax than ability-to-pay.

A congressional report entitled, "General Explanation of the State and Local Fiscal Assistance Act of 1972," examined use of per capita income as a major criteria to use in determining the financial recovery capability of a community after a disaster. The report declared, "population weighted by United States income divided by that of the state recognizes that poorer" jurisdictions "have greater difficulty in providing adequate services than rich" jurisdictions. According to the study, communities with low per capita income usually have a small tax base. A small tax base or limited tax assessment capacity suggests that a community will have greater difficulty providing public services, most particularly in the aftermath of a disaster. The report noted that per capita income analysis is used in other federal programs as an indicator of financial capability, most particularly in programs of the Department of Commerce.

Average per capita income for the United States was $14,592 in 1986. Based on this figure, FEMA staff analysts deduced that each state should be able to provide at least $1.00 for each state resident to cover the cost of state disaster response and recovery. The state dollar per resident system dedicates a sum that is about one-tenth of one percent of the estimated

General Fund expenditures of all 50 states. By multiplying state per capita income by state population and then multiplying the result by the ratio of state per capita personal income to national per capita personal income,[8] an objective indicator for each state is generated. The indicator can be updated annually and a per capita base year can be adjusted for inflation or changing income levels to reflect the state's changed financial capability.

The FEMA proposal took into account that local governments collectively had a per capita income close to the national average. FEMA estimated that local governments should be responsible for disaster response costs up to $2.50 per capita. So if a community had 100,000 residents it should have the financial capacity to pay up to $250,000 in recovery costs from its own resources. FEMA has always considered the capability of local governments to pay disaster recovery costs, but the agency has never used per capita income to gauge this capability. When local per capita personal income is measured for local governments across-the-board, figures of local financial capability ranged from $3.50 to $10.00 per capita times local population. By setting a floor of $2.50 times population, any local government would have to set aside less than one-half of one percent of its budget for disaster response cost as a condition of federal disaster aid eligibility.

Eligibility Thresholds

The per capita sliding scale contained thresholds to be used in determining percentages of federal funding once a declaration was issued. The Level 1 Threshold was $1.00 times population for states and $2.50 times population for local governments. These amounts were presumed to be within the financial capacity of each government that might apply for federal disaster aid. The money would be reserved for local public emergency response and recovery activities. If an applicant government was below Level 1 Threshold, FEMA proposed that no federal financial relief be provided. To qualify for a Presidential declaration a local government had to meet the a minimum $2.50 per capita expenditure. If the local population was 80,000, the locality had to be prepared to spend $200,000 on disaster recovery. For example, in California the $1.00 per capita minimum expenditure meant that about $22 million had to be reserved for state disaster spending.

The Level 2 Threshold of $10.00 per capita yielded a larger percentage of federal funding because it was based on a higher level of fiscal effort than under Level 1. Local policy makers might have preferred maintaining eligibility for Level 2 if they wanted increased federal disaster aid [as much as 90 percent federal reimbursement] and were willing to hold more local funds in reserve. This could expedite disaster recovery and restoration of governmental functions. Between levels 1 and 2, FEMA would reimburse up to 75 percent of eligible public relief costs. Above Level 2, FEMA could reimburse as much as 90 percent of eligible cost.

FEMA Proposal Rejected

These FEMA proposals were put forward in 1983 but were rejected by Congress after state and local officials expressed great opposition to them. As late as 1988 FEMA had no single method for measuring local government capability, but still relied on per capita income measures in one method. FEMA's old public assistance capability indicators were still used in the agency's decision making. FEMA has been prevented from bringing greater consistency into its declaration criteria. Consistency may only be realized in future FEMA reforms or in future law.

The FEMA proposal made it obvious that damage costs, calculated through the Federal/State preliminary damage assessment, would not displace FEMA's capability indicators in the presidential disaster declaration process. This is because state and local differences over the value of losses have often led to disputes about damage assessment.

But recall, communities using fixed asset accounting systems are usually better prepared to assess replacement or repair costs of their damaged facilities. Fixed asset accounting, or other accepted accounting techniques, produce good documentation of maintenance thereby attesting to appropriate predisaster maintenance of the facility. Communities applying such accounting systems are sometimes better able to calculate accurate dollar losses than FEMA itself. This permits local officials to better defend their estimates. FEMA staff can either accept or reject the compiled damage estimates of local governments. A decision to accept is more likely if localities use sound accounting methods.

The FEMA proposal included additional factors that could have been used in judging need for a federal declaration. Hazard mitigation activities of state and local governments were to be taken into account. Also, significant loss of tax base was to be another criterion. If the state had experienced one or more governor declared emergencies during the current, or in a recent, fiscal year, this too was to be considered by FEMA. This would take disaster frequency into account and would be fairer to areas of multiple disaster. Also, if there was an imminent threat to public health and safety, FEMA would have weighted this heavily in its review of the presidential declaration request. These need factors were to be incorporated into FEMA decision making so that no single factor would take priority.

If damage assessment showed that a community could recover on its own, FEMA could have recommended against issuance of a major disaster declaration. Moreover, a declaration request could be turned down if: (1) assistance was available from other federal programs that would alleviate satisfactorily the disaster's effects, (2) the damage did not involve a "sufficient" number of essential facilities, (3) insurance was available to provide adequate compensation for losses, and (4) damage was such that the impact on applicant governments was deemed minor.

The most controversial feature of the FEMA proposal was reduction of the 75 percent federal contribution to an across-the-board 50 percent federal share with 50 percent state or local matching. The proposal also included a sliding scale of federal aid that ranged from no federal funding for governments sustaining minor damage to a 90 percent federal share for truly devastated jurisdictions. This strategy had the effect of bringing federal government contributions down to about 50 percent of total relief and repair costs for all federally-declared disasters. It would have forced governors seeking presidential declarations or determinations of emergency to meet state subsidization requirements set out by FEMA.

The proposal tried to achieve five objectives. First, it aimed for uniform compliance with statutory requirements so that federal resources were supplemental to, not a substitute for, state and local government resources. Second, applicant governments that were more heavily damaged would receive proportionally more federal aid than applicant governments with less damage. Third, federal outlays would be reduced to about half of total eligible public costs, rather than the three quarters total they now represent. Fourth, cost sharing and the new declaration criteria were expected to encourage more prudent decision making by state and local officials during the rebuilding or repair of public facilities. The proposal furnished incentives and penalties intended to get state and local officials to minimize damage from future disasters. Fifth, the proposal encouraged states and communities to better plan their response to future disasters and emergencies.

Rejection of FEMA's proposal meant that the suggested criteria could not be used, but FEMA's experience and research in this matter may be of benefit in future agency efforts to achieve sound criteria. The two-threshold sliding scale may never be adopted because state and local officials so vehemently opposed FEMA's elimination of the fixed 75/25 ratio of funding. At this writing, FEMA continues to operate without a set of standard criteria. Consequently, state and local officials remain unclear about what criteria will be used to decide whether their federal disaster declaration request is acceptable. This also means that uncertainty continues about the amount of federal funding applicants are likely to receive even if their declaration request is approved.

REFORM FAILURE CONSEQUENCES

It has not been easy for the FEMA to develop more precise criteria through which to better advise for, or against, issuance of a presidential disaster declaration. Nor have FEMA officials found it easy to estimate appropriate levels of federal disaster relief. Yet, the FEMA reform effort reviewed here suggests that several items would help federal, state, and local officials better determine their disaster recovery needs. First, the economic ability of a community to recover from a disaster needs to be measured in a more precise and uniform way. Second, calculation of state and local recovery capability should control for the per capita income of residents of the respective jurisdictions, to get a better indication of need. Third, these calculations should adjust for the size of the community tax base. Fourth, factors should be used that control for types of damage and degree of damage. Fifth, local government officials should be encouraged or instructed to use an appropriate local accounting system, especially one with a depreciation schedule.

While these items will help distribute federal financial relief to where it is needed most, few local officials are likely to agree to restrictions they do not think are in their own best interests. Local officials also worry that new FEMA regulations will require them to set up more sophisticated emergency management programs that address preparedness, mitigation, response, and recovery. Some are unwilling to pay for the costs of these programs. Some have deduced that the less prepared their governments are for disaster, the greater the probability that there will be a generous federal bail-out after disaster strikes.

More research needs to be done on better methods of reviewing disaster declaration requests and on better methods for estimating the financial aid that is warranted. Until this occurs damage assessment will continue to produce conflict between federal officials and their state and local counterparts.

Perhaps the FEMA proposal analyzed here was too ambitious. In pressing their reforms, FEMA leaders failed to build up enough constituency support among emergency managers and among key state and local officials. FEMA people complain that they suffer from a poor image because they often appear unresponsive, slow, and ungenerous to state and local officials who insist, no matter what the circumstances, that their emergency or disaster is truly catastrophic and unquestionably worthy of federal relief and resources. Yet, the imprecision that continues in the wake of FEMA's rejected reforms is the chief reason FEMA cannot be faster, more responsive, and more fair. Even if it can be shown that local disaster planning, preparedness, and mitigation all were inadequate before the disaster struck, federal officials must still meet their obligations in law and extend federal help in disaster recovery. Under existing unreformed procedures, FEMA can do little to induce local government leaders to more seriously plan, prepare, and defend against disaster.

FEMA maintains clear flood insurance policies and procedures. Local governments must meet federal flood insurance performance standards. Federal flood insurance programs have produced high local compliance with federal insurance rules and high local compliance with federal regulations that promote hazard mitigation. Perhaps federal insurance requirements could be a condition applied in reviewing some types of aid requests? This might motivate state and local officials to be better prepared for disasters. For example, in 1987 California mandated that its city governments inventory structurally unsafe buildings, with the suggestion that disaster mitigation measures be applied to them. Private insurance companies and lending institutions can help bring unsafe buildings into compliance by making compliance a requirement of continued insurability or a condition of sale. If state-developed standards for these buildings were used by insurance companies, this might promote the preparedness sought in the rejected FEMA criteria.

THE STAFFORD ACT OF 1988

Recent federal legislation has brought some significant change to
federal disaster assistance programs. In late 1988, the Robert T. Stafford
Disaster Relief and Emergency Assistance Act, named in honor of
Vermont's Republican senior senator, was enacted into law. May 1989 it
took effect. The measure contains information and new sets of requirements that city and county officials must consider when they seek federal
emergency or disaster aid. The law allows the president to underwrite
through grants as much as 50 percent of the cost of maintaining and
improving local disaster relief plans. Disaster Preparedness Improvement Grants were increased to as much as $50,000 per year. Section 403 of
the Act compelled the president to fund the full 75 percent federal share
of Essential Emergency Assistance Program cost, so there was to be no
sliding scale of federal share.

The Act changed other features of the federal declaration process. For
example, Section 320 prohibits any discrimination by the president
when assistance is provided to needy areas. No sliding scales based on
income or population can be used to judge deservedness. Each area must
be assessed apart from any other and each in its own distinct terms. This
means that small and rural areas can no longer be overlooked and will be
just as eligible for federal relief funds as large metropolitan areas.

Added to Table II-3, "Types of Federal Assistance to State and Local
Governments," are the key elements of the Stafford Act. The 75/25
federal/state and local cost sharing formula, mentioned above, is the new
minimum ratio of federal assistance. If applicants cannot meet their 25
percent share and catastrophic or other special circumstances apply, the
president has authority to loan the applicant-government federal money
to cover its share of matching cost, subject to repayment with interest to
the U.S. Treasury. Stafford makes it easier for FEMA to administer
individual projects because any project that costs less than $35,000 to run
can be approved immediately by FEMA people in the field. Moreover,
individual and family grants have been increased from $5000 to $10,000
per year with annual adjustments for increase in the cost of living.

The Stafford Act contains a special requirement that insurable public
structures within an identified base floodplain damaged in a disaster and
restored through federal assistance must, from then on, be insured against
damage. If the local or state government fails to purchase this insurance,
or if the policy is not maintained, the federal government "will refuse to

pay the first $200,000 of loss," in the aftermath of later disasters. Moreover, a government with facilities in a flood hazard zone is *not* required to have federal flood insurance before an emergency or disaster, but those that do not hold either federal flood insurance or private insurance on their facilities will have to absorb the $200,000 federal deductible before they receive any federal subsidy to cover rebuilding their public structures. In a sense, local officials no longer have a "first free bite" of federal disaster monies for public structures they fail to insure.

The Stafford Act clarifies federal disaster policy and programs, promotes hazard mitigation, simplifies FEMA administration in the aftermath of disaster, and is somewhat more generous through lifting federal funding ceilings for some categories of relief. It sets forth clearer criteria to be used in presidential disaster declaration issuance, but it continues to force FEMA to advise on declaration requests case-by-case. FEMA still has no simple or straightforward way to gauge an area's ability to recover economically after a disaster or emergency.

CONCLUSION

Repeating an opening assertion, under current federal policy state and local governments have no guarantee that they will secure a presidential declaration if they should experience a disaster. Moreover, there is no assurance that they will be able to obtain enough federal aid to help them meet their disaster recovery needs. Some legislators prefer this *status quo* in federal declaration decision making because they want federal declaration requests to continue to be reviewed case-by-case. This reasoning leaves unresolved all the problems and inefficiencies of the existing process. It overlooks the possibility that clear disaster declaration criteria might improve local emergency management.

Defeat of FEMA's reforms meant several things. It meant an opportunity had been missed to build up reasonable local financial commitments before disaster strikes and before a federal declaration is sought. It meant that the existing declaration process would continue to function slowly and with delays. Defeat of the reforms meant that FEMA still could not legally differentiate among high-loss and low-loss communities in the rendering of disaster recovery aid. It meant that state and local officials still cannot be sure that enough federal funds will be available to ensure community or area-wide economic recovery after disaster. Maintaining this ill-defined dependency on the federal government in time of disaster is a high-stakes gamble state and local governments may lose.

Notes

[1]See *Federal Register*, July 27, 1983, November 4, 1983, and April 18, 1986; U.S. Comptroller General, Report to the Congress, "Requests for Federal Disaster Assistance Need Better Evaluation," CED-82-4, December 7, 1981 (Hereafter referred to as GAO "Better Disaster Evaluation); U.S. Comptroller General, Report to the U.S. Senate, "Federal Disaster Assistance: Relief to 1985 Virginia Flood Victims—Process and Alternatives," RCED-87-21 BR (October 1986) (Hereafter to as GAO, "Virginia Flood"); U.S. Federal Emergency Management Agency (FEMA), "Program Guide: Disaster Assistance Programs"; and State of California, Governor's Office of Emergency Services, *Disaster Assistance Procedure Manual, 1985*. Other publications on this subject include: J. D. Vinso, "Financial Implications of Natural Disasters: Some Preliminary Indications," *Journal of Mass Emergencies and Disasters*, Vol. 2, No. 4 (December 1977); Howard Kunreuther and J. Wilson, "Disaster Mitigation and Recovery Policies for Natural Hazards," Grant ENV 76-12370, National Science Foundation, Philadelphia, Pa.: University of Pennsylvania, 1976; Howard Kunreuther, *Recovery from Natural Disasters: Insurance or Federal Aid?* (Washington, D.C.: American Enterprise Institute, 1973); James Morentz, "One City's Answer to Funding Hazard Mitigation," *Hazard Monthly* (September 1980), p. 5; "Florida City [Tarpon Springs] Suspended from National Flood Insurance Program," *Hazard Monthly* (December 1983), p. 7, brackets inserted by this author.

[2]This was impossible to do in Coalinga's case because no surrounding communities were damaged by the earthquake.

[3]Although state and local resources do not have to be shown to be fully exhausted.

[4]GAO, "Better Disaster Evaluation," 1981.

[5]See Federal Emergency Management Agency, "Formats for Requests and Processing for Declarations of Emergency or Major Disaster," Part IV, *Federal Register* (July 27, 1983) and Federal Emergency Management Agency, *Program Guide: Disaster Assistance Programs*, DR & R 19 (December 1983).

[6]See GAO "Virginia Flood," 1986.

[7]See *Code of Federal Regulation*, Vol. 44, Part 205, Subpart C, (1986).

[8]Thus providing an adjustment for states that have per capita incomes above or below the national per capita income average.

PART 2

Chapter III

LOCAL FLOOD HAZARD MANAGEMENT: LESSONS FROM NATIONAL RESEARCH

BEVERLY A. CIGLER AND RAYMOND J. BURBY[1]

INTRODUCTION

From the perspective of the national government, floods and other disasters are a serious problem presenting staggering economic losses in property as well as significant losses of life. Since 1925, over 4000 people have lost their lives in floods.[2] The threat to life from flash floods is increasing.[3] In 1985 alone, property losses from flooding were more than $5 billion.[4] Nearly half of all U.S. communities are affected by flooding, this covering an estimated 7–9 percent of the land area of the 48 contiguous states.

If federal, state, and local officials are compared, local government officials are least likely to perceive natural hazards, such as floods, as important problems. Moving from the national to state level and then from the state to the local level, disaster experiences become fewer. The federal government confronts disasters distributed over the land mass of the entire nation. Each state government is preoccupied with disasters and emergencies inside its own borders, and so to state officials only a subset of the nation's disasters are of concern. Correspondingly, each local official is chiefly concerned with disaster events that affect their own government, an even smaller subset of disasters. Consequently, disaster mitigation is a low priority for local governments because any single municipality so seldom experiences disaster.

An "intergovernmental paradox" therefore applies to emergency management. The government officials least likely to perceive emergency management as a key priority—local officials—are at center stage in terms of responsibility for dealing with emergencies.[5] While the states shoulder emergency coordination and informational responsibilities, most disaster mitigation tasks fall to local governments. The Federal Emergency Management Agency (FEMA), the national umbrella agency for coordinating preparedness and response to major disasters, serves a facilitative, not dominating, role. Moreover, the trend in federal postdisaster assistance has been toward decreasing federal subsidies and encouraging more state and local predisaster regulation.

This study assesses local flood hazard mitigation and it uses data compiled from a national survey of local government officials conducted by the authors. The intergovernmental character of flood hazard management is explored because local policy is said to be "driven" by national policies and laws that have mandated various types of local action. Sections that follow describe and review: (1) the data sources used; (2) the national response to the flood hazard problem; (3) the intergovernmental constraints imposed on local flood hazard managers; and (4) key lessons yielded from recent empirical research about local flood hazard management.

Data Collection

Original data were collected by the authors and other members of a research team affiliated with the Center for Urban and Regional Studies at the University of North Carolina at Chapel Hill. Data were obtained through a mail survey of 1219 local officials, one official per community. The survey response rate was 78 percent, 956 of the 1219 community officials contacted. About 25 flood-prone local governments, classified as such by the FEMA, in each of the 50 states were sampled using random selection procedures. Cover letters asked that the survey form be completed by the local government official who knew most about flooding and flood hazard mitigation. More information about each local government was obtained from the FEMA. This included material about flood plain characteristics of local jurisdictions supplied by local officials in the 1980 Census.

Information about state flood management was first gathered through telephone interviews of state flood management officials in 1982. A mail survey in 1983 was directed to 300 state officials, six per state, and this yielded detailed information regarding program organization and management. Of the total approached, 239 state officials returned the survey completed, an 80 percent response rate.[6]

NATIONAL RESPONSE TO THE FLOOD PROBLEM

The national government plays a major role in attempting to reduce hazards to life and property posed by flooding and it seeks to preserve and protect the natural ecology of riverine environments from the damage of flooding. Ever since enactment of the Flood Control Act of 1936, federal policies have focused on structural flood control. This involves physical fortifications, usually public works projects, such as dams, reservoirs, levies, dikes, and other engineered means of flood control. Yet, this type of flood control structure has frequently been criticized for damaging the natural environment. It has also been blamed for making owners of property in flood plains overconfident in the protection such structures provide, so much so that over-development of flood plains results.

Recent federal policies have a new emphasis. They seek to influence local building regulation through provisions of federal flood insurance and through structural projects as well.[7] The National Flood Insurance Program (NFIP) is the premier federal flood program. Its goal is to reduce national flood losses by requiring local communities that want to participate in the program to set forth and enforce land use regulations that will promote safe building practices in flood hazard areas. The use of elevation and floodproofing techniques (site design), rather than discouragement of development (location) in the flood plain, is emphasized. A second purpose of the NFIP is to shift the economic burden of flood losses from the U.S. taxpayer under the federal disaster relief program to those who occupy, and benefit from, flood plains. Residents of communities who do not comply with NFIP requirements cannot purchase federal flood insurance, a federally-subsidized and therefore low cost form of insurance.

The Flood Disaster Protection Act of 1973 required states and local communities, as a condition of future eligibility for federal financial help in property acquisition or construction, to participate in the flood insurance program. Moreover, they had to adopt flood plain ordinances that had effective enforcement provisions aimed at reducing or averting future flood losses. Owners of flood-prone property face severe sanctions if their local government elects not to join the program. Besides being ineligible to purchase federal flood insurance, these property owners cannot receive federal disaster aid for their flood-related damage, loans (e.g., home or business mortgages) from any federally-supervised, regulated, or insured businesses, or grants and loans issued directly by federal agencies (e.g., the Small Business Administration) in the aftermath of flood disaster.[8]

These ineligibility penalties spurred massive local government participation in the federal flood insurance program. In 1973 only 3000 communities held federal flood insurance. By 1986, 17,742 local governments, representing more than 90 percent of all U.S. local flood-prone jurisdictions, participated in the NFIP and 1.9 million properties were insured.[9]

The Reagan administration took a strict approach to local compliance with the NFIP requirements. Reagan officials viewed enrollment as a contract between the national government and the participating community that obligates communities to adopt effective land use measures. Repeated flood loss claims in a participating community were considered a breach of contract under which local officials were held accountable for inadequate flood mitigation. Federal lawsuits against jurisdictions that failed to enforce their land use restrictions induced other local governments to comply with NFIP rules.

The NFIP has been criticized for stimulating development in flood hazard areas, just as structural projects have been criticized for the same reason. The flood fear of owners and lenders tends to dissipate when they know federal insurance is there to protect them. Consequently, NFIP's mandated local regulations may not counterbalance the development stimulus of its insurance program.

STATE AND LOCAL RESPONSE TO THE FLOOD PROBLEM

Most domestic federal programs are not designed to be carried out by federal administrators acting alone. Flood hazard management is no different. State governments are encouraged, and take an increasingly active role. States often provide flood hazard technical help, information collection services, dissemination of data, and land use advice to their local governments. In the realm of flood management, states also engage in planning and coordination, public information, public warning activities, regulation of hazard areas, postdisaster assistance, construction of flood control works, and relocation or land acquisition.[10] The states are pivotal in helping local governments meet the requirements of the NFIP.

The greatest instrument of flood loss reduction is local governmental land use authority. Local government effectiveness, in turn, depends on a complex interplay of government and private actors who possess a share of power over matters of local land use and capital investment. Paradoxically, authority over land affected by flooding is greatest for those possessing the smallest geographical areas: the property owner (e.g., individuals, partnerships, corporations, nonprofit organizations). In many ways, the behavior of other key actors is a reaction to what property owners initiate.[11]

Local response is also affected by the "intergovernmental paradox." In other words, public authority over land use is greatest at the local level even though officials at that level have traditionally been less interested in flood hazard management than their state and federal counterparts. Moreover, local government organization is highly fragmented. It is fragmented vertically in county-local relations, for example. It is fragmented horizontally among the municipalities that share a flood plain or watershed. Also, it is fragmented functionally among the operating units within each government.[12] These divisions weaken the power of public authority in dealing with private self-interest and in imposing specific duties on individual public agencies.[13]

PROBLEM PERCEPTION AND POLICY GOALS

State Government

It should come as no surprise that the policy goals expressed by state officials reflect the flood hazard management priorities of the national program. Of 300 state flood hazard officials interviewed, 6 per state, only 108, 36 percent, think that their governor, and his or her staff, rate flooding as a serious problem. Only 78, 26 percent, believe their state legislature and its staff consider flooding a serious problem. More than a fourth, 27 percent, of the state officials questioned do not think their own personnel consider flooding a serious problem in their state. Given these perceptions, it is not surprising that 55 percent, 165 state flood hazard management officials, see the federal flood program and its administrators as having the greatest effect on flood management activities in their state. Only 21 of the 300 questioned (7%) claim that their governor has the greatest effect on flood management. Only 15 (5%) said their state legislature has the greatest effect on flood management. These opinions suggest the breadth of the NFIP's influence within the intergovernmental system.

By aggregating the responses of officials from each state and using the mean response from each state, the states can be used as the unit of analysis for data reporting (rather than the aggregate of all state officials together). Officials in each state reported that the primary policy goal of flood management was the reduction of flood losses to new development. Those from 45 states mentioned the reduction of flood damage to existing development as a major policy goal. Preservation of natural areas from flood threat was identified as a goal in 38 states. But, only two states reported that increasing development in flood hazard areas was a major concern.

In sum, state officials working directly in flood management rate flooding as a serious concern. They do not, however, think other state officials, especially elected officials, are as concerned.

Local Government

Consistent with the logic of the "intergovernmental paradox," the local official in the national sample—those familiar with their jurisdiction's flood management programs—expressed little concern about flooding as a serious problem. Only 17 percent, 163 respondents, thought flooding was a problem in their locality.

The policy goals of local officials were similar to those of state officials, but local respondents gave their goals lower priority. Recall, each local respondent represents a separate local government. Sixty percent, 631 respondents, mentioned reduction of losses to new development as a goal and 40 percent, 382, listed reduction of losses to existing development as a goal. Three hundred sixty-four, 38 percent, cited preservation of natural areas threatened by flooding as a policy goal. Only 8 percent, 77 respondents, mentioned that their jurisdiction had a policy goal of increasing the development potential of their flood hazard areas.

Flood-prone areas exist in all of the study communities and development continues to increase in each area. According to survey results, 554 of the 956 communities (58%) report flood plains that were developed 10 percent or more. One hundred fifteen communities (12%) reportedly have flood plains that are developed 60 percent or more. However, 400 (42%) were reported to have flood plains that were either undeveloped or less than 10 percent developed.

When asked about expected flood hazard area development or redevelopment over the next 5 years, 640 respondents (67%) said they expected at least light development or redevelopment to occur. Forty-five percent, 430, said their community did not have any formal comprehensive plans or master plans detailing how the government would like to see flood hazard areas used in the future. Nearly half (48%) of the local respondents did not expect flood hazard management measures to affect the amount of new development and construction in their flood hazard zones over the next 20 years. Only 143 respondents, 15 percent, thought such measures would strongly depress future development. Thus, the survey of local officials suggests that flood plain development will continue.

Most officials believe flood hazard management generates detrimental side effects for their communities. Two hundred seventy-seven, 29 percent, thought it would increase costs of construction. Another 152 (16%) believed it would reduce land values. One hundred thirty-four local officials, 14 percent of the respondents, expected flood hazard management to reduce local tax revenue. These presumed negatives suggest that flood hazard management is not a priority in the communities of most respondents.

Fewer than one in five local government respondents rated flooding as a serious problem. These findings dovetail with those of a study by Rossi and associates in which 2000 political and administrative leaders in 20 states and 100 local governments were surveyed.[14] From results of this survey and the Rossi study it can be inferred that development in local flood plains will continue.

STATE AND LOCAL FLOOD PROGRAMS

State Programs

In recent years state governments have assumed a more active role in attacking flood problems than in the past. Our survey of state officials disclosed that 37 states provide flood-relevant technical help to their local governments, 34 states pursue flood control planning and coordination efforts, 33 offer postdisaster aid to their local governments, and 28 have flood warning and public flood information systems. However, few states have taken more ambitious approaches. Only 19, for example, regulate flood hazard areas. Ten are in the business of constructing flood control works and only two or three feature relocation or land acquisition programs aimed at flood hazard management.

Local Program Resources

The survey of local officials yielded considerable information about local flood hazard management and programs. Most local officials reported that little staff time is devoted to matters of flood plain land use management. Three-quarters, 717 of 956, claimed their locality committed less than one person hour per week to the problem.

The types and varieties of positions that local respondents said they held proved enlightening. One-quarter, 239, were city or county managers. Another quarter were building inspectors. Two hundred ten, 22 percent, were planners. Eighteen percent, 172, said they were public works directors or engineers. One hundred five (11%) were in other categories, such as planning board chairs, regional or state technical support personnel, clerks, etc. The diversity of positions of those with flood hazard responsibilities implies that there is a lack of focus in this management area of local government. Sixty-two percent, 593, claimed that flood control was of no, or low, priority in their community. Remember, these are local officials that hold flood management responsibility. This suggests that the exclusive motive for managing local flood plains comes from NFIP benefits and sanctions. It also suggests that local governments revise their existing land use programs to counter flood threat only by including special provisions for areas the NFIP considers prone to flooding.

Types of Local Programs

Communities whose officials responded to the survey use a variety of instruments to manage their flood hazard areas. Table III-1 shows that regulation is the most commonly used instrument chosen to manage the location and character of flood plain development. The most frequently used components of regulation are elevation requirements, zoning, and subdivision rules. A second program category, providing information and advice, is used by almost a third of the responding communities. Instruments such as land acquisition, capital improvement policies and tax incentives were, according to the survey, rarely used.

Four hundred thirty of the 956 reporting communities (45%) undertook flood plain management without first developing a plan for it. So while local governments seem interested in complying with the NFIP,

TABLE III-1

INSTRUMENTS AND METHODS OF LOCAL FLOOD HAZARD MANAGEMENT

(N=956)*

Instrument or Method	Percent of Localities Using	Number of Localities Using
Police Power Regulation		
Elevation requirements	60%	574
Zoning	58%	554
Subdivision regulations	51%	448
Special floodway regulations	44%	421
Floodproofing requirements	41%	392
Septic tank permits	35%	335
Sedimentation and erosion control regulations	22%	210
Wetlands protection regulations	13%	124
Density exchange/cluster development regulations	6%	57
Sand dune regulations	3%	29
Information and Advice		
Public information about hazards	32%	306
Land Acquisition		
Land acquisition for open space, parks, other public uses	17%	163
Relocation of existing hazard area development	2%	19
Capital Improvement Policies		
Location of public facilities outside flood hazard areas	8%	76
Tax Incentives		
Preferential taxation	3%	29

----

*One respondent per community provided information on the methods or instruments of local flood hazard management used in his or her community. Sampling error "+" or "-" 3 percent.

most have exhibited narrowness and a reluctance to experiment with approaches not imposed by the NFIP. For example, truly innovative and lasting answers to the flood problem, such as acquisition of flood property or relocation, were infrequently used by responding local governments. Those approaches are not required under federal programs and they do not receive the support and technical help that building regulation and structural flood control do.

Burby and Kaiser used the instruments contained in Table III-1 to develop the classification of local flood hazard management effort shown in Table III-2.[15] Four program types are set out in Table III-2 and each is based on whether programs meet NFIP and/or local government policy goals:

- *Type 1:* programs designed to meet minimum requirements for participation in the NFIP, but not intended to meet any local goals.
- *Type 2:* programs designed to comply with NFIP requirements and intended to serve local goals by using zoning and subdivision regulations.
- *Type 3:* programs designed to contribute to the local goal of protecting property from flooding by using sophisticated measures such as building elevation requirements or floodway regulations.
- *Type 4:* programs designed both to protect property and contribute to the local goal of protecting natural areas from flood damage, and that use additional measures such as acquisition of properties in flood plains or relocation of existing development inside flood plains.

The Table III-2 classification scheme does not have mutually exclusive categories, but is based on a progression from lower to higher numbered types. So communities classed as Type 2 not only meet the minimum conditions of Type 1 but also use zoning or subdivision requirements to advance an identified local flood control goal. Table III-2 discloses that most responding local governments exceed Type 1, that is, they have adopted programs that go beyond the minimum measures needed to comply with, and participate in, the NFIP. Slightly more than half, 507 communities, had programs that went as far as using building elevation or floodway requirements to protect property from flooding. Yet, only 172 of 956 have reached Type 4 level. That is, only 18 percent of all responding communities meet the conditions of all four types. This highest category involves local government protection of private property, protection of the natural environment, and use of land acquisition and, or, relocation of existing development inside the flood plain.

TABLE III-2

LOCAL GOVERNMENT FLOOD
HAZARD MANAGEMENT PROGRAMS

(N=956)*

Local Program Types	Percent of Localities with Programs that Include	Number of Localities with Programs that Include
Type 1: Minimal compliance with the National Flood Insurance Program	17%	162
Type 2: Any local goal, and use of zoning or subdivision regulations	12%	115
Type 3: Goal to protect property from flooding, and use of elevation or floodway regulations	53%	507
Type 4: Goal to protect and preserve natural values against flood damage, and use of land acquisition or relocation of development	18%	172
Total	100%	956

*One respondent per community provided information on the methods or instruments of local flood hazard management used in his or her community.   Sampling error is "+" or "−" 3 percent.

Private Sector Compliance

Local government's success in flood hazard management depends on its ability to alter the behavior, plans, or actions of land developers, builders, land owners, and residents who own property in, or live on, flood plains. The survey of local officials solicited information about the degree of private sector compliance with local flood control policy objectives. Analysis of survey results were used to compile Table III-3. This documents local officials' responses to questions regarding private sector compliance with local flood control policy objectives.

According to Table III-3, 94 percent or almost 900 local officials say that most new construction in 1982 in their jurisdictions occurred outside the flood hazard areas designated by the NFIP. A total 650 respondents, 68 percent, reported that more than half of all new construction in flood hazard areas between 1978 and 1983 avoided filling floodways. Two-thirds, 631, claimed that at least half of all new construction in flood hazard areas between 1978 and 1983 included elevating buildings to a height at, or above, the level of the 100-year flood. More than half of all responding communities report that most new subdivisions built between 1978 and 1983 have made adequate provision for storm drainage. However, only 200 communities, a scant 23 percent, report that at least half of the existing structures in flood hazard areas have been floodproofed.

Local Program Effectiveness

Local officials were asked to judge the overall effectiveness of flood hazard management in their communities, given the interplay of local goals in general, the effect of programs in operation, and the actions of people outside government. Almost half, 48 percent of the 956 respondents, claimed local flood hazard management in their communities was effective in the prevention of flood losses to new construction. But, only 21 percent, some 200 respondents, issued a "very effective" rating to local efforts aimed at reducing the vulnerability of existing development to flooding. Also, about a third of all respondents thought local actions were effectively preserving natural areas from flood damage.

The data suggest that, in the view of local officials, considerable progress has been made in meeting the central objective of the NFIP, the protection of new construction from flood damage. Respondents judged that considerably less progress has been made in meeting other national objectives. Because nonstructural measures often force changes in the plans or lifestyles of property owners or residents of existing structures, such measures are politically controversial and, therefore, low compliance rates were expected in flood mitigation for existing development.

State officials were asked to rate the effectiveness of flood hazard management programs pursued by local governments in their respective state. Most thought that the bundles of measures used to manage local flood hazards were ineffective. Officials of only 18 states reported that local programs in their states had significantly reduced expected flood loss and damage to future development. Officials of 11 states claimed that local programs had significantly reduced expected flood loss to

TABLE III-3

LOCAL GOVERNMENT RESPONDENT ESTIMATION OF PRIVATE SECTOR COMPLIANCE WITH LOCAL POLICY OBJECTIVES

(N=956)*

Compliance Indicator	Percent	Number
1. the proportion of communities in 1982 in which new construction took place outside of flood hazard areas designated by the NFIP**	94%	899
2. the proportion of communities in which more than half of the new construction occurring in flood hazard areas between 1978 and 1983 AVOIDED FILLING DESIGNATED FLOODWAYS	68%	650
3. the proportion of communities in which more than half of new construction occurring in local flood hazard areas, between 1978 and 1983, was ELEVATED to, or above, the level of the 100-year flood	66%	631
4. the proportion of communities in which half of the new subdivisions developed between 1978 and 1983 made adequate provision for STORM DRAINAGE	53%	507
5. the proportion of communities in which half or more of existing development located in flood hazard areas has been FLOODPROOFED	23%	220

*One respondent per community provided information on the methods or instruments of local flood hazard management used in his or her community. Sampling error is "+" or "–" 3 percent.

**NFIP=National Flood Insurance Program

existing structures. Officials of only six states believed that local programs in their states preserved natural areas from flood devastation and two of these states held this objective as a major state governmental concern.

That state and local officials differ in their perception of program effectiveness is not surprising. An official who is actually working in a local flood management program is likely to overestimate the effectiveness of his or her program. However, state officials may not fully appreciate how effective local flood hazard management programs have been in their state. Is it notable that both state and local officials give higher effectiveness ratings to activities that attempt to reduce flood losses to future development than to activities intended to protect existing structures from flood damage.

Ratings of local flood hazard program effectiveness were correlated with the types of measures local governments employed and the type of community in which they were used. Programs that do more than merely meet NFIP requirements tended to be rated as most effective. However, assessments of effectiveness are influenced by the extent of existing flood plain development and the availability of alternative, flood-safe sites for development. In a general sense, the more existing development in local flood plains the more difficult it is for local flood hazard management programs to be effective. Correspondingly, the more flood-safe land area a local government has available for future development, the more effective the local flood hazard program is likely to be.

CONCLUSION

The intergovernmental character of flood hazard management is evident in the strong mandates of the National Flood Insurance Program. Thousands of local governments have adopted regulatory land use control programs in response to NFIP mandates. Most of these local programs seek to reduce flood losses to future or proposed development. But only a fraction of all responding local officials thought that their local program was successfully protecting existing structures located in flood plains and few thought their program was protecting the natural environment from flood devastation. Responses to the survey suggest that if national and local flood policy goals are weakly defined or of low priority, local program implementation tends to be unsuccessful.

Local governments rarely adopt flood hazard management programs outside the realm of NFIP mandates. Many local governments, as this study shows, adopt regulations to meet NFIP minimum requirements without doing any flood control planning. Bold and innovative approaches to flood hazard management, such as public acquisition of private land or relocation of flood-threatened structures, are seldom taken. Without more effort by federal and state government to protect existing flood-vulnerable structures and the natural environment, U.S. flood losses will continue to mount, and will continue to be unnecessarily high.

Notes

[1] Support for the research was provided by a grant from the National Science Foundation (grant CEE-8209884). The opinions, findings, conclusions, and recommendations expressed are those of the authors and do not necessarily reflect the view of the National Science Foundation.

[2] U.S. Water Resources Council, *Estimated Flood Damages 1975-2000: Appendix B, National Report* (Washington, D.C.: U.S. Government Printing Office, 1977).

[3] Jon A. Kusler, *Regulation of Flood Hazard Areas to Reduce Flood Losses* (Boulder, Col.: Natural Hazards Research and Applications Information Center, Institute of Behavioral Science, University of Colorado, 1982).

[4] Rutherford H. Platt, ed., *Regional Management of Metropolitan Floodplains* (Boulder, Col.: Natural Hazards Research and Applications Information Center, Institute of Behavioral Science, University of Colorado, 1987), p. 3. Hereafter cited as Platt, *Regional Floodplains.*

[5] Beverly A. Cigler, "Current Problems and Issues in Mitigation," *Managing Disaster: Strategies and Policy Perspectives,* Louise K. Comfort, ed. (Durham, N.C.: Duke University Press, 1988), pp. 39–53 + references.

[6] A description of data collection procedures used in each survey can be found in Raymond J. Burby, et al., *Flood Plain Land-Use Management: A National Assessment* (Boulder, Col.: Westview Press, 1985), pp. 15–17. Hereafter cited as Burby, et al., *Land-Use Management.*

[7] Several major laws have strengthened federal flood hazard management and have compelled more flood hazard management at the state and local levels, among these are: the Flood Disaster Protection Act of 1973, the Water Resources Development Act of 1974, the Disaster Relief Act of 1974, and Executive Order 11988, issued in 1977.

[8] Beverly A. Cigler, Raymond J. Burby, and Bruce Stiftel, "Rural Community Responses to a National Mandate: An Assessment of Floodplain Land Use Management," *Publius: The Journal of Federalism,* Vol. 17, No. 4 (Fall 1987), pp. 113–130.

[9] See Platt, *Metropolitan Floodplains,* p. 7.

[10] Burby et al., *Land-Use Management,* pp. 109–133.

[11] See Platt, *Metropolitan Floodplains,* pp. 288–89.

[12]Rutherford H. Platt, M. Mullen, and Jon A. Kusler, *Intergovernmental Management of Floodplains* (Boulder, Col.: Institute of Behavioral Science, University of Colorado, 1980), p. 16.

[13]See: Marion Clawson and Peter Hall, *Planning and Urban Growth* (Baltimore and London: The Johns Hopkins University Press for Resources for the Future, 1973), p. 190 and Platt, *Metropolitan Floodplains*, p. 31.

[14]Peter H. Rossi, James D. Wright, and Eleanor Weber-Burdin, *Natural Hazards and Public Choice: State and Local Politics of Hazard Mitigation* (New York: Academic Press, 1982), pp. 39–67.

[15]Raymond J. Burby and Edward J. Kaiser, "An Assessment of Urban Floodplain Management in the United States: The Case for Land Acquisition in the United States: The Case for Land Acquisition in Comprehensive Floodplain Management," Technical Report #1 (Madison, Wisc.: Association of State Flood Plain Managers, Inc., June 1987).

Chapter IV

CONTRASTING LOCAL GOVERNMENT RESPONSES TO A TORNADO DISASTER IN TWO COMMUNITIES

ROBERT A. STALLING AND CHARLES B. SCHEPART

INTRODUCTION

Natural disasters in the United States are primarily the responsibility of the local governmental jurisdictions in which they occur.[1] That is, operational control of the initial response to damage and destruction rests with a variety of local organizations, most of them agencies of city and county governments. These organizations carry out tasks such as search and rescue, treatment of the injured, security and traffic control, debris clearance, restoration of utilities, and the like.[2] Responsibility for the overall direction of this organized response rests with local government officials. Coordination often begins at an early morning meeting of local officials and the heads of agencies and departments already at the site.[3]

Nonlocal organizations in U.S. natural disasters primarily supplement the efforts of local government. While it is true that organizations such as the state police, the National Guard, and various branches of the armed forces become involved in emergency activities such as security enforcement and debris clearance, most other nonlocal organizations perform tasks that have more to do with long-term recovery than short-term response.[4] These primarily public sector functions are supplemental, not in the operational sense of supporting response activities of local governments, but rather in the sense of providing financial aid and other forms of personal and corporate assistance beyond that available from the private sector (e.g., insurance) or the so-called third sector (e.g., Red Cross disaster aid, donations channeled through religious or welfare organizations, etc.). Historically, most of this extra-local disaster aid consisted of financial assistance from the federal government to repair or replace damaged public facilities such as bridges and civic buildings.[5]

Resources provided by state governments in disaster vary widely, although their main role seems to be the provision of property tax relief and assistance to local jurisdictions applying for federal disaster aid.[6]

This study describes as a comparative case study the disaster response of two communities struck by the same late-season tornado. It focuses on one of two towns that constitutes an exception to this pattern of local responsibility for disaster response. In one community, operational control of response and early recovery efforts was firmly in the hands of the city manager, but in the other community operational control was assumed early by a governor who personally directed the disaster response activities of both local and state agencies.

Our presentation begins with a description of the methods used in the study as well as selected characteristics of the two communities at the time that the tornado struck. We then describe the effects of the tornado in the two communities and the disaster response activities in each. After highlighting the unique features of the governor-led disaster response in one of the communities, we suggest some reasons for disaster response differences between the two. Finally, we conclude with what we feel are the most important lessons learned.

METHODS OF RESEARCH AND CITY FACTS

This study was designed as a comparative case study of local emergency management. Data sources included a variety of observational, interview, and documentary materials. Observational data collection began on the day following the tornado.[7] Extensive interviews were conducted with members of the governor's staff, heads of disaster-relevant state agencies, and regional officials of the Federal Emergency Management Agency (FEMA). Follow-up interviews were conducted with key government representatives and department heads in the two communities approximately eighteen months after the disaster. These were supplemented by telephone interviews with other local officials. Self-administered questionnaires were sent to state and federal agency representatives approximately twenty-four months later. In addition, minutes of city council meetings and the meetings of various local boards such as those for police, fire, and financial administration; disaster reports and releases from agencies at all levels of government; annual reports; budget documents; newsletters; and newspaper accounts were examined for a period of five years following impact. In short, the methods employed were those used conventionally in case studies of local disasters except the design was intentionally comparative from the outset.[8]

The two communities whose responses we compare are located in the State of Connecticut. Their city centers are approximately four miles apart and roughly ten miles from the state capital. At the time of the tornado, Windsor covered an incorporated area of 30 square miles and had a population of approximately 25,000 as reported in the 1980 Census, an increase of 12 percent over the population reported a decade earlier. Demographically, Windsor's residents had a median age of 33.1 years, a per capita income of $8,653, and a median household income of $23,703. Whites made up a majority of the population (88 percent), but a sizable proportion of blacks (10 percent) also lived in the community. Seventy-five percent of the local housing stock was owner-occupied; the median value of those homes was $61,400 in 1980. There were 16,460 people employed in the local labor market, two-thirds of them in manufacturing occupations. Local government in Windsor employed 210 people, with per capita revenues of $715 and per capita expenditures of $706 during the fiscal year before the disaster.

Windsor Locks, the smaller of the two communities, had a 1980 population of slightly more than 12,000 concentrated within its nine square miles. It is very similar to neighboring Windsor in most demographic respects. Its residents had a median age of 33.0 years, a per capita income of $8,035, and a median household income of $22,205. The majority of the population was also white (98.4 percent), with blacks comprising less than one percent of the population. Owner-occupied dwellings constituted 75 percent of the housing stock and had a 1980 median value of $55,900. Fifty-eight percent of the 16,000 locally available jobs were classified as manufacturing. Municipal revenue was $775 per capita while expenditures were $774 per capita. Reflecting its relatively smaller size, the total number of people employed in local government work in Windsor Locks was about half that in Windsor (i.e., 98 compared to 210).

In general, these neighboring municipalities, while very much alike, differed in three respects. Windsor Locks' population was about half that of Windsor's; its public employee work force was about half the size of Windsor's; and, its percentage of nonwhite population was far less than its neighbor's.

Both Windsor and Windsor Locks were hit by the same devastating tornado. It struck in the early fall, a time in New England when damaging tornados are infrequent but not unheard of. Total damage in Connecticut consisted of three killed, 400 injured, and property damage, including direct business losses, in excess of $250 million.[9]

The effects of the tornado were quite severe in both Windsor and Windsor Locks, although the type of loss each sustained was different. It is difficult to say which of the two cities faced the worse problems as a result of the storm. In Windsor, damage to residential property and public facilities was extensive. Two hundred and forty-three homes were damaged or destroyed with 100 families left homeless. Direct losses to residences totaled $15 million. An additional $3 million in damage occurred to public buildings, streets, and bridges. In Windsor Locks, on the other hand, damage was mostly to business and commercial structures. Forty-nine buildings were severely damaged or destroyed with losses estimated to be $140 million. Only 10 homes were damaged with three families left homeless. Damage to public facilities totaled only $40,000 there.

In short, both communities were affected by the disaster but in different ways. The problems confronting each local government following the disaster were similar if not identical. How the two governments responded, however, was not similar.

HOW THE TWO LOCAL GOVERNMENTS RESPONDED

After the tornado, local government response in Windsor was immediate and, for the first several weeks, was like the pattern described in the first paragraph of this chapter. As often occurs in disasters where onset is sudden and unexpected, the first indication that something had happened did not immediately suggest to those at Windsor's city hall that they were dealing with a "killer" tornado. Midafternoon reports that the roof of an auto repair shop had fallen in, activating an automatic fire alarm, and that a senior citizens' minibus had overturned, seemed at first to be two unfortunate but unrelated events. As the city manager and the public works director inspected the sites of the two incidents, however, the severity of the storm and of the flooding accompanying it became vividly apparent—their vehicle stalled in flood waters, stranding the pair for fifteen minutes. After being rescued, the city manager notified both the police and public works departments of the situation and requested that all off-duty personnel be called in to work. A plan of action was soon prepared and implemented that gave the city manager lead responsibility for disaster response. Under his supervision and control, agencies and departments of the city engaged in various disaster-related activities including search and rescue, damage assessment, traffic control, debris removal, provision of temporary housing, and feeding of disaster victims.

Only after inspecting the damage in Windsor from the air did the city manager fully appreciate the scope of the disaster. By then, the city's efforts were well under way. State police and National Guard troops began arriving on the second and third days and assisted local organizations in traffic control, security, and debris clearance. Fire departments from surrounding communities also assisted in response activities under the provisions of mutual aid agreements. For the next two weeks, the pattern of interorganizational relationships remained unchanged. Debris clearance, repair of the city's infrastructure, provision of temporary housing, and advice on financial matters and other forms of counseling were the principal tasks carried out. In addition to the usual presence of military units and extra-local personnel from the utility companies, rehabilitation activities in Windsor were augmented by a large number of volunteer laborers provided through local labor unions and organized under an emergent coordinating structure called the Tornado Emergency Construction Task Force.[10] Just as in the immediate postimpact period, all these groups worked under the control and supervision of Windsor's city manager.[11]

In contrast to Windsor, Windsor Locks responded to this disaster in a nontraditional way and in a way very different from what disaster research literature might predict. For Windsor Locks the disaster began when the storm blew the roof off a local motel and triggered an automatic alarm at the city's fire department headquarters. Observing the severity of damage as he approached the motel, the chief of police called the mayor to report the storm's effects and to ask for his authorization to dispatch public works crews into the area. Sensing that the resources of the small municipal government would be inadequate for such a large-scale problem, the mayor immediately called the director of the state office of civil preparedness and requested assistance. State police arrived within thirty minutes, and within three hours the governor and several state agency heads had arrived as well. By dawn the next morning, the governor was in overall operational control of disaster response activities in Windsor Locks.

Agencies and departments of Windsor Locks' government worked independently and autonomously during the first several hours. The

mayor chose not to assume overall control of the city's disaster response
efforts, stating in a later interview that he had not wanted to interfere
with the operations of his departments since he felt "they knew what to
do without me telling them." Gradually, the efforts of city organizations
were coordinated with those of the state agencies working in the community and, by the morning after impact, both local and state agencies were
under the personal direction of the governor. The mayor surrendered
local control to the governor.

As the days passed, state agencies assumed more and more responsibility for local disaster response activities. Security, traffic control, and
debris clearance were the primary tasks requiring attention. In daily staff
meetings the governor exercised direct supervision over those activities.
The state civil preparedness office set up a disaster assistance center to
coordinate aid and the governor met personally with several victims
during the first few days offering assistance. One week after the tornado
struck, all city departments had ended their disaster response activities.
National Guard and state Department of Transportation personnel,
meanwhile, continued to handle debris clearance for several more days.
The state Department of Labor took charge of processing claims for
temporary unemployment and the Department of Economic Development moved in to assist local businesses in applying for federal loans and
grants that they could use to reopen.

A presidential disaster declaration encompassing both municipalities
was issued the day after the storm, activating the resources of the Federal
Emergency Management Agency (FEMA). Soon, the Small Business
Administration (SBA) issued its own disaster declaration and joined the
list of active participants in the disaster response. The presence of these
federal agencies in Windsor Locks would prove to be a double-edged
sword, a point we will return to.

One additional indicator of the difference in disaster response in the
two communities was the number of formal postdisaster legislative decisions made by each respective city council. In Windsor Locks, where
disaster responsibility was passed to the state, only two storm-related
actions were considered during the three months following the tornado.
One was a resolution authorizing appropriation of municipal funds for
disaster-related expenses and the other was a perfunctory ratification of
an ordinance making possible property tax reassessment for disaster
victims (a local policy that duplicated similar action by the state legislature).
In Windsor, where the municipality assumed full responsibility for disaster

activities, the city council took up ten pieces of legislation (representing 16 percent of its formal biweekly agenda for the period) directly related to the storm during the ensuing three months. These included a major policy change in emergency powers that clarified the authority of the city manager regarding the use of school district resources and in a disaster.

Why The Windsor Locks Response Was Unique

We now offer some propositions which explain why the disaster response in Windsor Locks did not conform to the pattern typically found in other communities in the United States. Using documentary information we obtained about the history of each municipality and recognizing their previous relationships with the state and federal governments, we can identify several factors that account for differences between the two.

The first factor that must be considered is the type and extent of damage caused by the tornado in relation to each municipality's organizational resource capabilities. In the sociology of disaster literature discrepancies between the demands placed upon an organization by a disaster and the organization's capacity for response is defined as organizational stress.[12] A series of hypotheses suggest that the greater the stress, the greater the likelihood that organizational innovation will take place in an effort either to reduce demands or to increase capacity during the emergency period.[13] If one argues that local government can be viewed conceptually as a type of organization comprised of subunits such as departments, offices, and commissions, then this proposition may be applied to evaluate responses by the two municipalities.

The stress hypothesis is supported by the pattern of disaster response in Windsor. However, it does not predict the degree of state involvement in operational matters in Windsor Locks. One reason may be that this proposition is linear, rather than curvilinear, in form. That is, it does not predict a change in the nature of the relationship between stress and organizational innovation at extreme levels of stress. It may be that beyond a certain point increasing amounts of stress resulted in decreasing rather than increasing organizational activity. In Windsor Locks, in other words, the scale of disaster may have been so great relative to the capacity of municipal government that a kind of "organizational resignation" became the official response.[14] We seriously doubt that this was the case, however. For one thing, the overwhelming mass of evidence from social science studies of natural disasters shows that in American culture the response to disaster is universally an active rather than a passive one.[15] Passivity and resignation are uncharacteristic of local governments after disasters. In point of fact, Windsor Locks did not respond passively because its local organizations did at first respond. Soon control and coordination passed to the governor, but Windsor Locks' local government did act.

The second reason why we doubt that extreme and unusual stress is the explanation for the unique response in Windsor Locks has to do with the precision with which levels of stress can be measured. We find it impossible to say, for example, that stress was in absolute terms greater for the municipal government in Windsor Locks than it was for Windsor's government. While the former is only half the size of the latter, the ratios of the number of municipal employees per resident for the respective communities are nearly identical (0.006 for Windsor, 0.004 for Windsor Locks). For this reason, it would be wrong to conclude that the stress level in Windsor Locks was twice as great as that for Windsor.

These are not hypotheses that predict different organizational responses based upon such differences in stress, however. It is not at all clear that our understanding of the variables in these hypotheses is sufficient to allow us to specify such a precise metric (e.g., one set of demands is twice the magnitude of the other). Furthermore, it appears that the type of damage in Windsor imposed more arduous demands than did damage in Windsor Locks. Damage in Windsor was primarily to residences, public buildings, and the infrastructure, while damage in Windsor Locks was primarily to area businesses, with lost income and wages making up the largest share of total economic loss. Moreover, in the first few hours after the tornado struck, the problems in Windsor Locks looked no worse than those in Windsor. A full assessment of damage was not available until days after the storm. We conclude that, while the type of damage produced by the storm differed in the two communities (i.e., residential versus commercial property destruction), the amount of organizational stress experienced by the municipal governments following impact is not different enough to explain why each city government responded as it did to the tornado devastation.

Form Of Government Made A Difference

Differences in each community's government structure seemed to be more important in explaining response differences than were differences in local government response capacity. Windsor's form of government is best described as manager-council, of the type generally associated with the so-called "good government" movement. This form features a separation of powers between an elected city council that meets biweekly to set policy and a professional city manager, hired by and serving at the pleasure of the council, who administers the daily affairs of the city. City departments are headed by full-time, professional administrators appointed by the city manager following national searches. Pay and promotion are based upon a merit system and a formal system of personnel classification is in place.

In terms of its formal government structure, Windsor Locks and Windsor are almost exact opposites. Windsor has a mayor-council government. Instead of the strong mayor version which is characteristic of this type, the powers of the mayor in Windsor Locks have been circumscribed by the assignment of various responsibilities to several boards and commissions. The mayor has direct supervisory responsibility only over public works and general administrative services. Police, fire, and other departments fall under the jurisdiction of separate elected commissions. Windsor Locks has few full-time professional administrators (the chief of police is one notable exception), does not base pay and promotion on a formal merit system, and has no personnel classification system.

We think that one of the principal reasons for the variation in the disaster response of each city lies in differences in local political and governmental structure. We believe this is more important a factor than the magnitude of destruction each city sustained and more important than the relative size of each local government. Both governments manifested a custodial approach to the disaster from the beginning. This means that a minimum of police, fire, sanitation, and other city services were provided and that many problems were left to voluntary organizations or the private sector.[16] Windsor was somewhat more custodial than Windsor Locks. Windsor, more than Windsor Locks, was able to centralize decision making owing to Windsor's more professional city management. For example, certain contradictions and ambiguities in the legal authorizations in Windsor were resolved after the disaster which gave the city manager even greater control over local resources in the event of a future emergency. In Windsor Locks, the structure of local government was such that the mayor shared responsibility with a complex array of boards and commissions. The scope of his authority under both normal and emergency conditions was severely constrained. Hence, both the structure and the past practice of municipal administration meant that a locally coordinated response to disaster would be facilitated in Windsor but inhibited in Windsor Locks.

However, explaining why local control and direction was exercised in one community but not in the other does not necessarily explain why the state would become involved in supervising local disaster response activities. Three additional factors that help explain this unique pattern are the history of local-state relations in local service provision, the history of state and gubernatorial involvement in past disasters, and the difference in organizational demands attributable to differences in the type of damage each community sustained.

Additional Factors

Windsor Locks had a long history of working arrangements with the state, particularly in areas where local government did not attempt to carry out a service or function. In such cases, the municipality would contract with the state to perform that activity. Not long before the tornado struck the city, Windsor Locks had contracted out all of its work in community planning. Disaster preparedness and response, it seems, were also functions that the local government chose not to perform in-house. Windsor Locks in effect "contracted" to have the state assume these functions during the emergency period. The mayor decided almost immediately that the scope of the disaster was beyond the capacity of his government. Governor Ella Grasso and other state officials who converged on the Windsor Locks damage zone, were faced with the need to carry out certain response activities such as traffic control and debris removal, before undertaking more standard activities, such as arranging for federal disaster relief as well as providing financial and other supplemental resources under state law.

While its past history of intergovernmental relations may have predisposed Windsor Locks to rely on the state in this disaster, why did the governor react by picking up the reins, so to speak? Five factors may help account for this. First, state law allowed the governor to take overall control of disaster operations under emergency powers regardless of jurisdictional venue. Second, Windsor Locks is situated only 14 miles from the state capital. But, these conditions apply to both towns. Windsor's authorities could have been preempted by gubernatorial powers just as were Windsor Locks'. However, from the state's perspective, it was Windsor Locks that had first reported the tornado and sought assistance. It seemed initially that the disaster was concentrated in that town and the state moved quickly to establish a presence—including a base of operations—there. Only later did state officials become aware that Windsor was just as hard hit as Windsor Locks. By then, Windsor's organized response was well under way. State resources, however, remained based in Windsor Locks.

Furthermore, the governor had been personally involved in previous local emergencies, although not to the extent described here. Whether this was a matter of personal leadership style or because it was just plain good politics to do so, we cannot say. In addition, we should point out that Windsor Locks was the governor's hometown, though the evidence suggests that this alone was not sufficient to explain state intervention.

Finally, there is the matter of the type of damage. Damage to residential structures, public buildings, and infrastructure was more extensive in Windsor whereas greater destruction fell upon business and industry in Windsor Locks. In a sense, the physical effects of the storm in Windsor were more "typical" of natural disasters. In Windsor Locks the needs generated by the tornado were more clearly within the domain of state and federal agencies (as well as private sector organizations), as with loans and grants to help local employers recover and unemployment benefits to assist workers. Such aid could begin much sooner in Windsor Locks.

CONCLUSION

In conclusion, we would like to underscore two points that seem to us to be the most important lessons from this comparative case study. First, both the "typical" local disaster response exemplified in Windsor and the unique state-directed response in Windsor Locks provide additional evidence supporting the continuity hypothesis about the relationship between preemergency and emergency social patterns.[17] In Windsor, the daily operation of local government placed the delivery of public services in the hands of specially chosen administrators under the central direction of a full-time, professional chief administrative officer (i.e., city manager). The managerial philosophy was that of providing the best level of service possible for local residents within the fiscal constraints and policy guidelines laid down by the elected city council. The response to disaster by local government was the same, to carry out the necessary tasks in response to demands of the emergency with responsibility firmly in the hands of department heads who in turn were coordinated and directed by the city manager. State and federal assistance during the emergency period was supplemental and was coordinated with the assistance provided by local officials.

In Windsor Locks, the daily method of operation of local government was very different. A variety of voluntary boards and commissions, meeting infrequently, provided supervision over a handful of small municipal departments. The chief executive officer, the mayor, actually had quite limited administrative duties and authority. Those services not undertaken by local government were provided by the state under contractual arrangements. The state staffed, executed, and delivered services almost autonomously with local participation defined by the terms of contracts agreed to beforehand. When disaster struck, this practice reemerged in disaster response and recovery. Unprepared and unaccustomed to performing disaster response activities, Windsor Locks responded by "contracting" to meet these demands as well. For a variety of reasons the governor and state offices moved in to run the show. The mayor and other local officials were accustomed to this kind of working relationship with the state and they did not believe they were being compromised. The Governor made sure that the mayor of Windsor Locks was present for certain public occasions, but no effort was made to make it appear that the mayor was actually in charge. In the United States this is often done when extra-legal organizations, the military for example, direct post-disaster activities.[18]

Not only did the day-to-day operating philosophies of the two local governments carry over into the emergency period, but also the predisaster tensions and squabbles within the network of intergovernmental relations continued as before. These conflicts involved disagreements over exact administrative responsibility among various governmental actors and over financial arrangements. Both during and after the tornado, intergovernmental relations continued to follow their predisaster pattern. Each local government battled with the state; the state in turn fought with the federal government. Much of this had to do with the nature and extent of disaster aid, especially financial assistance, that each level of government would provide. The atypical presence of state agencies in Windsor Locks did not create these intergovernmental conflicts. It only aggravated hostilities that existed before the disaster.

We are not implying that one of these two disaster responses is better than the other. We are not suggesting that because Windsor had a so-called "good government" type structure, it therefore had a better disaster response than neighboring Windsor Locks. Recall, the "good government" term in public administration refers to changes in American municipal government that took place in the early part of this century, a time when many cities moved away from domination by political machines and party bosses to more politically neutral, efficient, and professional management. What we are saying is that Windsor's response was typical of American local government disaster response while Windsor Lock's response was not. A second major assertion of this comparative study is that determining relative benefits and costs of actions taken in disaster situations is more complicated than the literature suggests.

The personal involvement of the governor in the Windsor Locks disaster response filled a vacuum in the pattern of overall coordination not only by orchestrating various local resources but also by integrating local and state activities. By most estimates this would be counted a benefit, but there were some serious costs incurred under this arrangement. State officials, believing federal disaster assistance agencies were too slow, set up a one-stop disaster assistance center. This is normally a federal agency action. As it turned out, the one-stop center was set up in the wrong city. Most of the disaster victims needing some form of aid were in Windsor rather than in Windsor Locks, a fact that was not obvious at the time state officials arrived at the scene. In the process of setting up the one-stop center, the state also established the hours of service for the center and began attempting to determine what types of disaster assistance victims were going to need. Federal officials were very unhappy because their "turf" had been invaded. They also felt that the state had made commitments to victims that the federal government would later be forced to honor, regardless of whether or not federal policy provided for such aid. Disputes such as these in the postimpact period further exacerbated predisaster intergovernmental hostilities.

Much more serious were the postdisaster administrative problems created by the governor's direct involvement in disaster response activities. While regulations, delays in decision making, and other forms of "red tape" were reduced or eliminated by the governor's on-the-spot problem-solving, this also resulted in a reduction in the usual bureaucratic "paper trail." As the crisis passed and the state presence in the two communities was reduced, local officials experienced serious problems regarding noncertification of expenditures and the suspension of normal rules and regulations, such as those requiring that purchases be based upon lowest bid. Events had to be recounted verbally so that unwritten, spoken agreements and decisions made in the immediate aftermath of the event could at last be set down on paper.

In Windsor, a city that had formulated its own local disaster response, there were serious fiscal consequences. When Windsor applied for state reimbursement for $374,209 in tornado damage expenses under a state law, on the advice of the Connecticut Attorney General, the state rejected the claim. Rejection stemmed from a disagreement over the legal interpretation of who can be defined as "local emergency personnel." Because the state took the initiative in area-wide disaster response and had not sought funds from the federal government, Windsor could not be reimbursed by a pass-through of federal funds either. At this writing, Windsor's claim is still being adjudicated. The municipality stands to lose $14.85 per resident as a result of its disaster involvement.

In Windsor Locks, the story was similar but had a different ending. Because the municipality's involvement in disaster activities was less extensive, its direct costs were proportionately much less than Windsor's. These totaled an estimated $42,465. Even though its request for reimbursement was also denied by the state, Windsor Locks stood to lose only $3.48 per resident. A stretch of Windsor Locks' most heavily damaged highway was, after repair and reconstruction, renamed in honor of Ella Grasso, the governor that had so dominated the city's disaster response and recovery.

Notes

[1] Russell R. Dynes, *Organized Behavior in Disaster* (Lexington, Mass.: D.C. Heath, 1970). Compare with Benjamin McLuckie, "Centralization and Natural Disaster Response: A Preliminary Hypothesis and Interpretation," *Mass Emergencies* 1 (1975), pp. 1–9.

[2] Dennis E. Wenger and Arnold R. Parr, *Community Functions Under Disaster Conditions* (Columbus: Disaster Research Center, Ohio State University, 1969), pp. 49–102.

[3] Dennis S. Mileti, Thomas E. Drabek, and J. Eugene Haas, *Human Systems in*

Extreme Environments: A Sociological Perspective (Boulder: Institute of Behavioral Science, University of Colorado, 1975), pp. 90–95.

[4]Dennie S. Mileti, *Disaster Relief and Rehabilitation in the United States: A Research Assessment* (Boulder: Institute of Behavioral Science, University of Colorado, 1975).

[5]Office of Emergency Preparedness, *Report to the Congress: Disaster Preparedness* (Washington, D.C.: U.S. Government Printing Office, 1972).

[6]Robert A. Stallings, "Federal Disaster Aid in Intergovernmental Perspective: Is There Evidence of Abuse by the States?," Paper presented at the Research Conference of the Association for Public Policy Analysis and Management, Austin, Texas, 1986.

[7]The junior author was a resident of one of the communities at the time and was working as a public official in a nearby city where he had personal contact with representatives of federal and state agencies through the "one-stop" disaster assistance center.

[8]See: Lewis M. Killian, *An Introduction to Methodological Problems of Field Studies in Disasters* (Washington, D.C.: National Research Council/National Academy of Sciences, 1956); Russell R. Dynes, Eugene Haas, and E.L. Quarantelli, "Administrative, Methodological and Theoretical Problems in Disaster Research," *Indian Sociological Bulletin* 4 (1967), pp. 215–227; and, Thomas E. Drabek, "Methodology of Studying Disasters: Past Patterns and Future Possibilities," *American Behavioral Scientist* 13 (1970), pp. 331–343. A deeper discussion of the methods used in this analysis may be found in: Charles B. Schepart, "Tornado Disaster in Two Communities: A Public Administration Perspective," Unpublished Doctoral Dissertation, University of Southern California, Los Angeles, California, 1984.

[9]Although there was scattered damage in other communities, including some suburbs of the state capital, Windsor and Windsor Locks were the hardest hit.

[10]In organizational terms, this task force more closely fits what Quarantelli and Dynes refer to as an "extending" organization, not an emergent group. However, it is far from being a pure type of "extending" organization. See: Quarantelli, "Organizations Under Stress," pp. 3–19 in *Symposium on Emergency Operations*, edited by R. C. Brictson (Santa Monica, Calif.: System Development Corporation, 1966); and, Russell R. Dynes, *Organized Behavior in Disaster* (Lexington, Mass.: D.C. Heath, 1970).

[11]Long-term financial, mental health, and other services, as usual, were the responsibility of a variety of state and federal agencies operating out of the "one-stop" center.

[12]See: J. Eugene Haas and Thomas E. Drabek, *Complex Organizations: A Sociological Perspective* (New York: Macmillan, 1973), p. 251. Also see earlier conceptualizations in: Drabek, *Disaster in Aisle 13: A Case Study of the Coliseum Explosion at the Indiana State Fairgrounds, October 31, 1963* (Columbus: College of Administrative Science, Ohio State University, 1968); and, Drabek, *Laboratory Simulation of a Police Communication System Under Stress* (Columbus: College of Administrative Science, Ohio State University, 1970).

[13]See: Haas and Drabek, *Complex Organizations*, pp. 252–259; and, Mileti, Drabek, and Haas, *Human Systems in Extreme Environments*, pp. 78–82.

[14]See: Robert E. Foreman, "Resignation as a Collective Behavior Response," *American Journal of Sociology* 69 (1963), pp. 385–390.

[15]See reviews such as: Charles E. Fritz, "Disasters," pp. 651–694 in *Contemporary Social Problems,* edited by R.K. Merton and R.A. Nisbet (New York: Harcourt, Brace and World, 1961); Fritz, "Disasters," pp. 202–207 in *International Encyclopedia of the Social Sciences,* Volume 3, edited by D.L. Sills (New York: Macmillan, 1968); and, Quarantelli and Dynes, "When Disaster Strikes," *Psychology Today* 5 (1972), pp. 66–71.

[16]Robert P. Wolensky, "How Do Municipal Officials Respond to Major Catastrophes?," *Disasters* 1 (1977), pp. 272–274; and, Robert P. Wolensky and Edward J. Miller, "The Emergency Versus the Disaster Role of Local Officials: Citizen and Official Definitions," *Urban Affairs Quarterly* 16 (1981), pp. 483–504.

[17]E.L. Quarantelli and Russell R. Dynes, "Response to Social Crises and Disaster," in *Annual Review of Sociology,* Volume 3, edited by Alex Inkeles, et al. (Palo Alto, Calif.: Annual Reviews, Inc., 1977), pp. 34–35.

[18]See: William A. Anderson, "Social Structure and the Role of the Military in Natural Disaster," *Sociology and Social Research* 53 (1969), pp. 242–253; and, Wilbert E. Moore, *Tornadoes Over Texas: A Study of Waco and San Angelo in Disaster* (Austin: University of Texas Press, 1958).

Chapter V

ACID RAIN AS DISASTER AGENT

M. ELLIOT VITTES

INTRODUCTION

Most disaster planning involves only local and limited geographic areas, yet the problem of acid rain affects not only local areas but a large portion of North America. This study will examine the Canadian-United States acid rain disaster threat. It will show how regional, national, and cross-national policy making has emerged to address both existing damage and the continuing destructive threat acid rain poses.

One characteristic of North American acid rain policy is governmental layering. At the same time that negotiations have been conducted between the two national governments, separate agreements have been made between U.S. states and Canadian provinces. Also, officials of one U.S. region have argued with officials of another U.S. region over the need for acid rain emissions controls. This is surprising because acid rain policy making authority appears to reside with the national government. As acid rain damage becomes more severe and more widespread, it moves toward disaster status and it exacerbates conflict among policy makers at every level. Yet, in the matter of acid rain different sets of national officials have responded at different times, with different intensities, and with different policy actions and outcomes.

A policy that calls for control of sulfur emissions is emerging at both the cross-national and subnational level.[1] These cross-national relations are a form of trans-border regionalism or subnational microdiplomacy. In U.S. subnational acid rain politics, interests in the upper-Midwest Great Lakes region contradict interests of the Northeast region. U.S. acid rain environmental policy is developing through a subnational and transborder network of United States and Canadian officials. For a long time, acid rain's effects have been ignored, discounted, or debated by the Reagan administration. In negotiating acid rain policy questions, the administration and Congress have sought to alleviate sulfur emissions only through long-term funding of new technology. To date, there has been no national legislative or regulatory rule imposing sulfur emissions limits that specifically address acid rain. Beyond the promise of promoting research and technology, there has been little U.S. national action on the problem of acid rain. The policy void created by this inaction has encouraged a devolution of acid rain policy making to subnational policy makers.

Continental wind currents mixed with human polluting activities have dispersed acid rain over regions of the United States and Canada. The physical devastation caused by acid rain has many ramifications. Differences have arisen about how the problem of acid rain has been conceptualized, how risk of future acid rain damage can be assessed, and how to plan a program that would abate acid rain itself.

This has led to the creation of networks of U.S. subnational, and U.S.-Canadian extra-federal, relations. These relations have spun a surprising web of subsystem politics. As agreements are reached, longstanding ties are being established. These subsystems have influenced policy making. Policy analysts have shown that policy subsystems are most effective when they function out of the view of the public, the media, and top executive and legislative leaders. Consequently, the obscurity surrounding extra-federal interchanges may work to the benefit of subnational, acid rain policy makers.

Acid rain yields two sets of regional problems. Some regions must deal with the damaging effects of acid rain and so are "receptor regions." Other regions are alleged to be causing or contributing to acid rain precipitation and so are "emitting regions." There are limits in intergovernmental relations that make it difficult, if not impossible, for one subnational region to direct the affairs of another subnational region. But, there are some political pressures that governments can apply to one another. Some instruments of pressure may involve physical actions of some type, but symbolic political pressures can sometimes be even more effective. This study will show that subnational political officials can respond to an environmental disaster threat, even one that straddles national borders and even one that does not elicit responsiveness from a national government involved.

THE ACID RAIN ISSUE

The acid rain issue involves interest group members, government agency officials, researchers from a variety of fields, elected officials, businessmen, laborers, and others. The scientific dimensions of acid rain have been described in many other works and therefore will not be pursued here.[2] What is important in this analysis is the political complexity the acid rain problem has produced. New types of intergovernmental arrangements and new interest group dynamics have emerged in both nations.

Acid rain has never been a purely national or international issue. Early studies related acidified rain to nearby smokestacks or other regional sources. Eville Gorham detected and measured acidification at Kentville, Nova Scotia and Sudbury, Ontario in the 1950s. One observer commented that while Gorham's work was truly pioneering, it "was more speculative than empirical" regarding "atmospheric and meteorological questions." For example, Gorham did not address formation and transport of acid rain. Gorham was said to have focused on the short-term, site-specific effects of acid rain, not on long-term or regional issues.[3]

It was Svante Oden's work in Sweden that linked the increasing acidity of rainfall and lakes to transboundary air pollution emanating from Britain and continental Europe.[4] Later, studies by Beamish and Harvey in Canada and by Schofield in the United States turned up acidified lakes and documented the disappearance of fish from these lakes. The lakes in question were located in the La Cloche Mountains of Ontario and the Adirondack Mountains of New York state.[5] Further studies confirmed these findings and found acid rain damage in the upper Midwest, in wider areas of the Northeast and New England, in the Appalachian mountains of the South, and in additional areas of southern Ontario and Quebec provinces.[6] Studies of acid rain's effects on lakes and soils continue to report evidence of damage, some of it potentially disastrous to natural systems.

Lake damage was attributed to the long-range transport of pollution from industrial enterprises often located hundreds of miles away from the lakes in question. Because of the great distances between emitter and receptor areas, conflicts began to emerge between regions of Canada and between regions of the United States. Conflict between the national governments of Canada and the United States also intensified over the problem of acid rain. Transport of sulfur pollution over long distances became a political issue as scientific research into emissions, transport, and effects continued to progress.[7] Some extraordinary coordinated response was needed to alleviate the problem. Acid rain generated conflict between states, between provinces, and between Canada and the United States.

After President Reagan assumed office in January 1981, his "New Federalism" approach to intergovernmental relations brought about a devolution of regulatory responsibility that encouraged subnational action. Also, the lack of U.S. national regulatory action on acid rain and continuing U.S. air pollution emissions created a stalemate in U.S.-Canadian negotiations. U.S. national direction on acid rain policy making has been characterized as weak, divided, halting, and confused.

Acid rain politics became more complex when each nation tried to develop a distinct policy. Bilateral negotiations between Canada and the United States produced a Memorandum of Intent on August 5, 1980 that began a series of discussions that did not resolve the issue. A Special Envoy process that began in 1985 yielded a joint report in January 1986. In all this, Canadian national officials pursued extensive discussions in which promises were made and complaints were voiced. Prime Minister Brian Mulroney and President Ronald Reagan agreed to the recommendations of the *Joint Report of the Special Envoys on Acid Rain* in January 1986. The agreement has two major limitations. First, it has no provisions mandating reduction of U.S. sulfur emissions other than a promise of future reductions when new coal-burning technologies become available. Second, Canadian officials have charged that the agreement does not commit the United States to execute an acid rain abatement program.[8] These exchanges involve international, bilateral relations. They do not disclose the exchanges that have been going on at the subnational level.

In Canada, air pollution control policy has traditionally been the domain of the provincial governments, not the federal government. Canada's federal and provincial governments have enacted a comprehensive plan to decrease sulfur emissions 50 percent by 1994. This cooperative program called for sulfur emission cutbacks to no more than 2.3 tons east of the Manitoba/Saskatchewan border; stricter automobile nitrogen oxide emission limits; $150 million in spending to control nonferrous smelter emissions; $25 million in spending for development of abatement technology; additional spending to monitor sulfur emissions, to research the effects of acid rain, and to study more efficient uses of coal; and, establishment of a national Acid Rain Office and the reactivation of the Parliamentary Subcommittee on Acid Rain.[9] Table V-1 lists target figures for 1994 emission levels.

TABLE V-1

TARGET FIGURES FOR 1994 SULFUR EMISSIONS LEVELS IN THE CANADA COMPREHENSIVE PLAN

Province Objectives	1980 Base (Tons)	Reduction (Tons)	1994 Limit (Tons)
Manitoba	738,000	188,000	550,000
Ontario	2,194,000	1,164,000	1,030,000
Quebec	1,085,000	485,000	600,000
New Brunswick	215,000	30,000	185,000
Prince Edward Isl.	6,000	1,000	5,000
Nova Scotia	219,000	15,000	204,000
Newfoundland	59,000	14,000	45,000
Total	4,516,000	1,897,000	2,619,000

Table developed from Environment Canada's newsletter, Acid Rain: Statistics.

This agreement between the provinces and the Canadian federal government spurred individual provinces to develop plans that would achieve provincial goals. Thanks to this federal-provincial cooperation, Environment Ontario officials were able to introduce their provincial program, "Countdown on Acid Rain Cleanup," as early as December 1985.

In 1985 several American state governments began to control sulfur emissions. New York state was among the first. One report called the state, "the biggest acid-rain emitter in the Northeast, [and] state legislators . . . overcame [the] heavyweight opposition of the big utilities and passed a model bill to reduce the sulfur dioxide being pumped into the atmosphere 30 percent by 1991."[10] In the summer of 1985, New Hampshire mandated a 25 percent reduction in sulfur emissions by 1990.[11] Outside the Northeast several other states also took action. Wisconsin placed a cap on industrial sulfur dioxide emissions and considered imposing a 50 percent emissions reduction.[12] Minnesota acted to reduce emissions, and both Illinois and Ohio officials investigated coal cleaning technologies.[13]

Despite selected state initiatives, the U.S. government was reluctant to set up a national emissions reduction program. The federal government funded acid rain research and coordinated various investigations of acid rain, but no federal funds were earmarked to pay for immediate emissions reductions. In May 1986, the House Subcommittee on Health and the Environment approved an acid rain bill by a vote of 16 to 9. But the measure, H.R. 4567, moved no further through the legislative process. In March 1988, the same subcommittee completed action "on the acid rain title of a multi-part, clean-air bill that [included] provisions on urban smog and auto . . . standards."[14] But even though urban air quality standards had to be approved before August 31, 1988, the measure died in the 1988 session.

President Reagan expressed qualified support for acid rain legislation in general but he opposed any measure that called for controlling current emissions through existing technology. He opposed forcing utilities to use low-sulfur coal burning and he balked at setting out stack scrubbing requirements.[15] The president did support "a program to develop and demonstrate innovative control technologies."[16] His proposal called for funding clean coal technologies that allow burning of high- and low-sulfur coals in an environmentally acceptable manner. Yet, this fell far short of being an emissions reduction agreement because it only promised eventual reduction of sulfur emissions.

The tentativeness of President Reagan's approach has been obvious from the start. Even though Reagan accepted the recommendations of the *Joint Report of the Special Envoys on Acid Rain,* he has been reluctant to take action.[17] The Report called for $5 billion in spending for new technologies and research, half coming from government and half coming from private industry. True emissions controls have clearly been unacceptable to the Reagan administration. In testimony before a House committee in 1986, EPA Administrator Lee M. Thomas and Secretary of Energy John S. Herrington advocated the administration's stand. They claimed that the subcommittee legislation called for too much spending, considering the "continuing uncertainties about the causes and effects of acid rain and of any program to control it."[18] In 1985 one Reagan official claimed that the administration would never support any type of emissions controls, since such controls would inevitably result in "cost maximization" by Congress. The fear was that even limited controls would open the door to dramatic increases in spending requirements by the Congress. To the administration, mandated spending on emissions controls by government and private industry would result in waste and inefficiency.

More evidence that the Reagan administration did not intend to comply with the Joint Report recommendations came in late 1986 and early 1987. On December 3, 1986 Energy Secretary Herrington said, "We cannot apply for a $5 billion acid rain program. We cannot afford it. Our deficits are too large." He later qualified this when he said he did not mean the United States would fail to fulfill its commitments under the Joint Report.[19] Reagan's FY 1988 budget request called for $287 million in research, a sum far less than the one-half billion promised. Vice President George Bush, during a January 1987 visit to Ottawa, said that the White House would wait to see how Congress responds to this spending proposal.[20] Canadian Prime Minister Mulroney expressed skepticism and said "he thought the Administration could do a lot more. I'm from Missouri, I'm going to believe this when I see cash. It's an old Irish habit."[21]

In early February, U.S. Interior Secretary Donald Hodel claimed that Canada's attempts to force the United States to adopt an acid rain program were merely a way of increasing Canada's electricity exports to the United States. He maintained that Canadians are "advocating stringent acid rain controls in the United States, even though they spend less money on air quality by far than the U.S., the effect of which would be to increase the market for excess Canadian electricity. But I hope the U.S. isn't so naive or foolish that we fall for that kind of double-speak."[22]

Allan Gotlieb, Canada's Ambassador to the United States shot back,

> I strongly object to your reference to "double-speak" when commenting on the environmental and energy policies of the Canadian government. While such "conspiracy theories" make attractive headlines in newspapers and are used by special interest groups who are unwilling to accept responsibility for acid-rain emissions from their factories, I am amazed that these views could be espoused by a Cabinet secretary in President Reagan's Administration.[23]

The Reagan Administration later increased the acid-rain spending request to the full $2.5 billion called for in the agreed plan, but given the problems of the high federal deficit and congressional pressures, the motives behind this move were unclear.[24] The U.S. Department of Energy

(DOE) asked for and received $575 million to be spent over two years on clean coal efforts.[25] In the past, clean coal efforts have been directed to developing technologies for new plants, not for existing operating plants. Moreover, this DOE budget authority represents the minimum level of funding needed to comply with the Joint Envoy Report.

Shortly before his April 27, 1988 summit meeting with President Reagan in Washington, Prime Minister Mulroney promised to "renew his call for an 'absolutely indispensable' acid rain treaty." His government also framed a far-reaching air pollution treaty that would cover more than acid rain.[26]

American's promised acid rain actions have differed from actions both advocated and implemented in Canada. Since Canada's provinces have the prime responsibility for regulating sources of air pollution, Canada's approach rests on "cooperative federalism." Based on agreements negotiated from 1982 to 1985, Canada's federal government and provinces have set out a conference system of intergovernmental relations on acid rain. This system markedly differs from the way the United States has arranged its own system of acid rain abatement intergovernmental relations.

U.S. AND CANADA POLICY CHARACTERISTICS

Conflictual relations in the United States and cooperative relations in Canada, seem to characterize each nation's respective acid rain policy. Conflict in the United States is rooted in regional differences attributable to matters of geography, industrial base, mining, utility operations and ownership, ecological sensitivity, public perception of the scope and degree of damage, and other factors. Canada's cooperative approach has been politically feasible, sound public policy because the acid rain issue presents no great differences between the provinces, no clear winners or losers, and no major threats to either employment or business investments. Moreover, most Canadians believe that action on acid rain is needed because they think of it as an agent of disaster.

In the United States, people of the Northeast have recognized and experienced the ecological effects of acid rain. Yet, representatives of emitter regions of the industrial Midwest, for the most part, have opposed acid rain abatement action. Southerners and Westerners have been slower to perceive the relevance of acid rain to regional or national interests.

Midwest industrialists have vehemently opposed retrofit of older plants or purchase of low-sulfur fuels because each approach would increase the cost of business. Utility executives, most from investor-owned companies, perceive federal acid rain legislation as an economic threat. Coal producers are divided on the issue. Low-sulfur coal mining firms stand to gain from a mandated fuel-switching program and are therefore led by executives who favor federal acid rain controls. High-sulfur coal mining business people understandably oppose federal acid rain controls because switching from high- to low-sulfur coal would devastate their market.[27] It would also result in the loss of thousands of mining jobs.

Low-sulfur coals are found predominantly in the plains and western mountain states while high-sulfur coals are concentrated in midwestern and Appalachian areas. Consequently, politicians from the Midwest and Appalachian regions have lobbied against fuel-switching.

Canada's circumstances are different.[28] There, major population centers in Ontario and Quebec provinces are the main acid rain receptor areas. Heavily used vacation and recreation areas north of Toronto suffer acid rain damage as do the forests of Quebec's sugar maplers.[29]

Sources of acid rain emission are located in the Great Lakes area of the United States and in a few remote areas of central Canada. Therefore, control efforts in Canada have targeted nonferrous metal smelters of INCO, Falconbridge, and Noranda, as well as some pulp and paper mills. Sulfur emissions from provincial utilities are small by comparison with U.S. utilities. Quebec generates most of its power from hydroelectricity. Ontario Hydro uses fossil fuels to produce only 28 percent of its power, a percentage that is expected to drop to 25 percent by 1993.[30] Ontario Hydro, a provincially-owned utility, follows Ontario's environmental policy in its operations. Uranium mining is important in Ontario and so the push toward nuclear power as an alternative to fossil fuel burning is something uranium mining interests favor.

LINKAGES OF SUBNATIONAL GOVERNMENTS

The reluctance of the United States to control its acid rain generation has led indirectly to cooperative interchanges between certain U.S. state governments and Canada's federal and provincial governments. Some subnational governments have acted alone or in concert with other subnational governments. Certain American states have created their own programs to reduce acid rain and to pressure other states to act on the problem. Because there are few multistate or national acid rain producing companies, there are few firms arguing for relief from regulation that varies from state-to-state.[31]

Moreover, President Reagan's "New Federalism" called for states to take more initiative and to protect their interests. Touted as a means of greater state self-sufficiency, this approach sometimes leads to state versus state political competition and antagonistic intergovernmental relations. At least two negatives result from disparities in state-level acid rain abatement. First, since clean-up actions of single states cannot alone solve transboundary pollution problems, inefficiencies result. Some ameliorative actions undertaken by states may cost large sums of money and yield little in the way of acid rain reduction. Furthermore, states that produce sulfur emissions do not pay for the negative externalities yielded in other jurisdictions. Consequently, states acting to abate acid rain damage bear the twin costs of paying to curtail their own in-state emissions while they suffer the effects of acid rain emitted by states that oppose acid rain emissions controls.

Second, disagreements frequently emerge between officials of different states over acid rain policy that should logically be resolved by national government. State conflict dates back to the pre-Constitution era of the Articles of Confederation, a time when the sovereignty of states spawned animosities over commerce, currency, and other matters. The U.S. Constitution addressed the need for allowing a federal presence where state sovereignty could not achieve policy coherence. National action was deemed justified in matters of foreign affairs, national defense, postal service, and interstate commerce. In Federalist No. 22, Alexander Hamilton showed that he appreciated the problems caused by the lack of common sovereignty under the Articles of Confederation. He wrote, "No nation acquainted with the nature of our political association would be unwise enough to enter into stipulations with the United States."[32]

Technologies of the 20th century produce transboundary pollution that can cause significant environmental damage. The absence or inadequacy of a national pollution control program can cause distrust and hostility between competing subnational governments, as it has among American states over the problem of acid rain pollution.[33]

Thus far, on each side, state government officials have tried to address the interests of their citizenry. Certain states have allied with one another, and with certain Canadian provincial governments, to apply increased political pressure on emitter states. Cross-national and subnational agreements on acid rain confirm that this strategy is being used. These agreements are policy tools that try to resolve domestic U.S. intergovernmental conflict with the help of Canada and some of its provincial governments. In some respects, U.S. national governmental indifference toward acid rain has helped forge better extra-federal relations but has tolerated an escalating level of U.S. intergovernmental and interregional discord.

Extra-federal Agreements

Acid rain politics have helped create agreements between Canadian provinces and U.S. states. Quebec and New York, as well as the New England Governors and Eastern Canadian Premiers, have made agreements. In the former, an *Agreement on Acid Rain Precipitation* was signed July 26, 1982.[34] The measure includes five agenda items:

1. to ensure compatibility of data from acid deposition networks and jointly publish an annual report of the data;
2. to prepare and carry out joint studies;
3. to exchange the information collected;
4. to establish a documentation center;
5. to embark on an action program to reduce acid precipitation.

The program has not only exchanged information through the Clearinghouse on Acid Rain, but has been a policy tool used to advance acid rain programs inside each respective jurisdiction. Consider this 1984 statement by Adrien Ouellette, Canada's Minister of the Environment:

> The signing of this formal agreement with New York state was initially intended to insure coordination of acid deposition research and data gathering. But as awareness increased, commitments developed both in Quebec and New York state towards controls on acid rain causing pollutants.
>
> Thus, as Quebec was unveiling its acid rain control program this summer [1984], the New York state legislature passed a landmark state acid deposition program. To me, it is very significant that the first two governments to sign a bilateral agreement on acid precipitation back in 1982 are also today the first two governments to enact legislation and propose regulations to achieve significant reductions in sulfur dioxide emissions.[35]

A second agreement, the New England/Eastern Canada Sulfur Dioxide Emissions Reduction Plan of June 1985, was negotiated by the Conference of New England Governors and Eastern Canadian Premiers. It attempted regional control of acid rain in the absence of a bilateral

U.S.-Canadian agreement. Under the agreement subnational and national programs "have complemented the actions of the Conference."[36] For example, emissions caps were adopted by the Canadian federal and provincial governments in March 1984 and three months later by the New England Governor's Conference, Inc.

This type of agreement is regional, federal, and extra-federal but does not preclude more comprehensive national or international agreements that might address the broad scope of the problem. Participants acknowledged in their introductory statement the limitations of the agreement. But they also believed that it could produce measurable progress both in controlling regional sulfur emissions and in getting the issue on midwest state and U.S. government policy agendas. Leon Lindsay reported that Conference participants knew that if they began to control sulfur emission in their own region, "their admonitions to states that 'export' pollution" would more likely be heeded.[37]

Similar agreements now exist or are being negotiated. Ontario developed a Memorandum of Understanding (MOU) with the state of Minnesota on acidification of the environment to improve collaboration in dealing with the effects of acid rain and to work toward integrated national action plans that would abate "emissions of the pollutants that are its cause."[38] Ontario and New York have a similar understanding.[39] Other states and provinces have concluded such agreements. Ontario province has separate MOUs regarding general transboundary pollution with New York and Michigan.[40] Negotiations on the problem of toxic substances in the Niagara basin have also been conducted.

On May 21, 1986 *The Great Lakes Toxic Substances Control Agreement* was signed by governors of Great Lakes states. It declares the Great Lakes to be an integrated ecosystem and a water resource that transcends political boundaries. A similar agreement has been approved between Ontario and Quebec on the Canadian side of the Great Lakes. These two sets of agreements flow from the Great Lakes Charter agreement of February 11, 1985 transacted between representatives of Ontario, Quebec, Illinois, Indiana, Michigan, Minnesota, New York, Ohio, Pennsylvania, and Wisconsin.[41]

Environmental issues have spawned extra-federal relationships in the past and may continue to do so in the future. This may be attributed to either weak or obstructionist national governments. National inaction can elicit extra-federal responses. In acid rain control politics extensive extra-federal relationships suggest national political inaction or ineffectiveness.[42]

CONCLUSION

Acid rain policy making is driven forward by acid rain's disaster potential. U.S. government inaction and, or, obstructionism has impelled a cross-section of American states and Canadian provinces to form subnational policy networks and extra-federal relationships. Extra-federal agreements are becoming commonplace in the Great Lakes basin, not only to address acid rain but to control toxic and hazardous wastes. The regional nature of some environmental problems combined with the absence of a sound national attack on the problems, stimulates subnational interchange.

How the danger of acid rain emission is perceived varies by region and political jurisdiction. Location of physical damage, industrial economic health, level of employment, population density of emitter or receptor areas, and other factors influence the way acid rain is understood as a political and environmental problem. Disagreement among scientists over the threat acid rain poses is exploited by each side in the controversy. In his assessment of damage to North Carolinian forests, plant pathologist Robert Bruck wrote,

> Many factors, both natural and man made may be responsible for the recent forest decline syndromes. The key policy and scientific question that remains to be answered is whether or not the impaction of clouds, gasses; and subsequent deposition of pollutants through high altitude spruce and fir forests in through flow, stem flow, and inputs into the forest soil; are assimilated and cycled benignly by forest ecosystems or whether the doses are sufficient to alter one or more processes enough to promote tree decline leading to mortality. *We believe that gathering concrete, reproducible, experimental results addressing the key question in situ, is difficult to impossible. The lack of unimpacted (control) ecosystems to compare with atmospheric deposition sites makes the above task even more difficult. It is our contention that the scientific and policy making communities will have to reach common ground in dealing with "imperfect knowledge" for the ultimate purposes of making important assessments as to whether or not to control or mitigate anthropogenic pollutant deposition to elevation ecosystems.*[43]

Policy makers have resorted to cross-national and subnational agreements because they are useful, albeit limited, tools. The regional policy problems attendant to shared resource use, as in the Great Lakes area, promote a dialogue among state and provincial officials over how best to preserve threatened resources. Forging agreement may be difficult owing to the variety of interests involved, but shared dependence on a common resource can be a unifying force.

Interregional disputes manifesting conflictual domestic relations can complicate the task of policy making. Extra-federal agreements aimed at abating acid rain are limited by the inability to include governments that tolerate pollution emissions that contribute to acid rain. Parties to these extra-federal agreements do address a portion of the problem, that being the increment of pollution abated through their own programs. They also can pressure or cajole officials of other governments to do something about emissions that add to acid rain. If the U.S. government continues to delay action and if the Canadian federal government does not have the authority to act more directly on the problem, certain U.S. states and Canadian provinces will continue to take the initiative. But the absence of concerted national and international action represents an incomplete policy solution to an insidious disaster threat.

The overall lesson to be learned from this study of a transborder environmental problem is that subnational officials have found new avenues for action and have developed practical and yet novel policy networks and relationships. Frustration, impatience, a sense of emergency, interregional conflict, insufficient national representation, industry vs. environment, the unidirectional flow of acid rain damage, presidential policy, and other forces helped promote formation of these subnational, extra-federal relations. While it is generally true that most disasters are "local" disasters, acid rain's continental effects have elicited the attention of local, state, provincial, national, and international leaders.[44]

Notes

[1]This type of relationship is referred to as "extra-federal." It has been characterized as "transborder regionalism" or "subnational microdiplomacy." See: I.D. Duchacek, *The Territorial Dimensions of Politics: Within, Among, and Across Nations* (Boulder, Col.: Westview Press, 1986); I.D. Duchacek, "The International Dimensions of Sub-national Self-Government," *Publius*, Vol. 14, No. 4 (Fall 1984), pp. 8–9; J. Kincaid, "Constituent Diplomacy: U.S. State Roles in Foreign Affairs," paper presented at the World Congress of the International Political Science Association, Paris, France, July 15–20, 1985; and B. Sadler, "The Management of Canada-U.S. Boundary Waters: Retrospect and Prospect," *Natural Resources Journal,* Vol. 26, No. 2 (Spring 1986), p. 369.

[2]For example, see: Comptroller General's Report to the Congress, *An Analysis of the Issues Concerning Acid Rain* (December 11, 1984); Congressional Budget Office, *Curbing Acid Rain: Cost, Budget, and Coal Market Effects* (Washington, D.C.: U.S. Government Printing Office, June 1986); R.W. Crandall, "An Acid Test for Congress?" *Regulation* (September/December 1984); R. Gould, *Going Sour: Science and Politics of Acid Rain* (Boston: Birkhauser Boston, 1985); P. Huber, "The I–Ching of Acid Rain," *Regulation* (September/December 1984); Interagency Task Force on Acid Precipitation, *Annual Report 1983* (Washington, D.C.: National Acid Precipitation Assessment Program); A.H. Johnson, "Acid Deposition Trends, Relationships, and Effects," *Environment*, Vol. 28, No. 4 (May 1986); J.L. Regens, "Environmental Regulation and the Congress: The Politics of Acid Rain Policy," paper presented at the Southern Political Science Association convention, Charlotte, N.C., November 1987; J.L. Regens, "The Political Economy of Acid Rain," *Publius*, Vol. 15, No. 3 (Summer 1985); J. Schmandt and H. Roderick, *Acid Rain and Friendly Neighbors* (Durham, N.C.: Duke University Press, 1985); E.J. Yanarella and R.H. Ihara, eds. *The Acid Rain Debate: Scientific, Economic, and Political Dimensions* (Boulder, Col.: Westview Press, 1985).

[3]D. Munton, "Acid Rain and Basic Politics," *Alternatives*, Vol. 10, No. 1 (Spring-Summer 1981), p. 23.

[4]Gould, 1985, p. 15.

[5]Ibid., p. 17 and Comptroller General's Report, 1984.

[6]Comptroller General's Report, 1984, p. 2.

[7]One aspect of the long-range acid rain problem involved U.S. air pollution control laws. U.S. law required states to set forth Air Quality Control Regions (AQCRs). To meet emissions limits within AQCRs state officials found it convenient to allow industry to use "tall stacks." This helped transport air pollution much greater distances, even to other regions.

[8]See, M. Weisskopf, "Twenty Months Later, the Acid Rain Issue Hasn't Been Cleared Up One Bit," *The Washington Post National Weekly Edition* (December 14, 1987), p. 31.

[9]See *Release from the Minister*, "Federal Acid Rain Control Program Unveiled—Landmark Decision in Environmental Protection," Environment Canada (PR–HQ-085-16), March 6, 1985.

[10]Neil Peirce, "Breaking the Acid Rain Stalemate," *Public Administration Times*, Vol. 8, No. 19 (October 1, 1985).

[11]R.L. Stanfield, "Environmentalists Try Backdoor Approach to Tackling Acid Rain," *National Journal*, 42 (October 19, 1985), pp. 2365–68 and Peirce, 1985.

[12]L. Lindsay, "Attack on Acid Rain: American States and Canada Take the Initiative," *The Christian Science Monitor* (May 10, 1985), pp. 20–21 and Stanfield, 1985.

[13]Lindsay, 1985.

[14]The subcommittee was chaired by Representative Henry Waxman (D–Calif.). See "Waxman Scores Early Victory in Battle Over Clean-Air Bill," *Congressional Quarterly Weekly Report* (March 5, 1988), pp. 579–80.

[15]P. Shabecoff, "Reagan Aides Say He Will Back Envoys' Plan to Curb Acid Rain," *The New York Times* (April 30, 1986), p. A-11.

[16]Statement by the Principal Press Secretary, March 19, 1986.

[17]D. Lewis and W. Davis, *Joint Report of the Special Envoys on Acid Rain,* January, 1986.

[18]P. Shabecoff, "Reagan Aides Oppose Bill to Curb Acid Rain," *The New York Times* (April 30, 1986), p. 15.

[19]J. Lewington and M. Keating, "U.S. Will Be Pressed on Acid-Rain Battle, Minister Says," *Globe and Mail* (*Toronto*) (December 6, 1986), p. A6.

[20]J. Sallot, "Bush Gets 'An Earful' Over Acid Rain," *Globe and Mail* (*Toronto*) (January 22, 1987), pp. A1–A2.

[21]Ibid.

[22]J. Lewington, "Acid-Rain Complaints Handy Export Device, Top U.S. Official Says," *Globe and Mail* (*Toronto*) (February 12, 1987), p. A7.

[23]J. Lewington, "Canada Issues Stern Rebuke Over U.S. Suggestion of Ploy," *Globe and Mail (Toronto*) (February 14, 1987), p. A7.

[24]Weisskopf, 1987, p. 31.

[25]The figure $575 million was derived from a phone interview of a U.S. Environmental Protection Agency official on April 5, 1988.

[26]*Newscan,* Canadian Embassy, Public Affairs Division, Week Ending March 31, 1988.

[27]R. Stanfield, "The Acid Rainmakers," *National Journal,* No. 24 (June 14, 1986), pp. 1500–3. Stanfield reports that the politically powerful United Mine Workers of America labor union is a "fervent opponent of acid rain control legislation."

[28]This section is based on extensive interviews with government officials, industry representatives, researchers, and others, conducted in Canada during the summer of 1985. Follow-up interviews in Quebec Province over the summer and fall of 1987 also furnished information for this section.

[29]For more about acid rain damage to maple sugar bushes see, L. Robitaille, G. Roy, and R. Pincher, "Sugar Maple Dieback," Summary Conference at the Annual Assembly of the Federation des Producteurs Acericoles du Quebec, Sainte-Foy, Quebec, 5/3/84; "Sugar Bush Mortality," Government of Quebec Internal Report No. 227, Quebec Ministry of Energy and Resources, Land and Forest Research Service; G. Gagnon, L. Robitaille, G. Rie, and C. Gravel, "Dieback in Maple Stands: The Behavior of Some Ecological Variables," Quebec Ministry of Energy and Resources, Land and Forest Research Service; *Maple Decline,* Maple Producers Information Session, 5/8/86; and, L. Carrier, *Decline of Quebec's Forests: Assessment of the Situation,* Quebec Ministry of Energy and Resources, 9/3/86.

[30]Originally this was to have fallen further. See: R. Taborek, *Nuclear and Coal Electric Power Generation Strategies for Control of Acid Rain at Ontario Hydro* (May 1985). Yet, concerns about nuclear power and other problems have kept the fossil fuel power generation percentage at a higher level.

[31]This is unlike the regulatory areas of automobile production or cigarette packing. See, A. Fritschler, *Smoking and Politics,* 3rd. Ed. (Englewood Cliffs, N.J.: Prentice-Hall, 1983).

[32]C. Rossiter, ed., "Federalist No. 22," *The Federalist Papers* (New York: The New American Library, 1961), p. 144.

[33]Acid rain policy is by no means the only such area of conflict. Adjacent states have been in conflict over nuclear power, automobile safety, drunk driving laws, and other matters. But the vacuum of national action with respect to acid rain has opened the door to pronounced conflict among state governments. Shrinking federal funding and perceived vulnerability to acid rain's long-term disaster potential, have aggravated relations between officials of different states.

[34]See *Annual Report: Quebec-New York Agreement on Acid Rain Precipitation* (Quebec: Quebec Ministry of the Environment, 1984).

[35]Remarks by Adrien Ouellette, Ministre de l'Environment, on Quebec's Policy on Acid Precipitation, September 6, 1984. For information about the laws passed by New York and Quebec, see: *The Sulfur Deposition Control Program,* published by the New York State Department of Environmental Conservation, June, 1985 and *Atmospheric Quality [Acid Rain] [Amendment] Regulation* and *Pulp and Paper Mills [Amendment] Regulation,* Excerpt from the Gazatte officielle du Quebec, 9 April 1985.

[36]See the *New England/Eastern Canada Sulfur Dioxide Emissions Reductions Plan,* June 1985. Prepared by the Committee on the Environment, Conference of the New England Governors and Eastern Canadian Premiers; and Resolution 12-2 of the Committee on the Environment, Twelfth Annual Conference of the New England Governors and Eastern Canadian Premiers, Newport, R.I., June 17–19, 1984.

[37]L. Lindsay, 1985, pp. 20–21.

[38]*Memorandum of Understanding on Cooperation in Combating Acidification of the Environment Between the Province of Ontario and the State of Minnesota.* August 5, 1983.

[39]Memorandum of Understanding on Cooperation in Combating Acidification of the Environment between the Province of Ontario and the State of New York). August 28, 1983.

[40]See *Memorandum of Understanding on Transboundary Air Pollution Control Between the State of Michigan and the Province of Ontario.* December 5, 1985.

[41]*The Great Lakes Charter for the Management of Great Lakes Water Resources.* For a concise history see, L.B. Dworsky, "The Great Lakes 1955–1985," *Natural Resources Journal,* Vol. 26, No. 2 (Spring 1986), pp. 291–336.

[42]Duchacek, 1986, pp. 17–18. He claims that physical proximity, trade relations, and investments sometimes foster subnational and cross-national relationships.

[43]R.I. Bruck, et al., *Observations of Forest Decline in the Boreal Montane Ecosystem of Mt. Mitchell, North Carolina — An Integrated Forest Response Approach,* Proceedings of the U.S.-F.R.G. Symposium on Forest Decline, Burlington, Vt., October 19–24, 1987. U.S. Forest Service Technical Publication, Broomall, Pa., p. 2.

[44]This chapter was based in part on grant-support from the University of Central Florida Division of Sponsored Research Starter grant program (1985), the Canadian Embassy's Canadian Studies Faculty Enrichment grant (1985), and the Quebec Ministry of International Relations' Quebec Professional Development Research Program grant (1987) for which I would like to express my appreciation.

Chapter VI

CONFLICT AND COORDINATION IN RESPONDING TO AVIATION DISASTER: THE SAN DIEGO AND GANDER EXPERIENCES COMPARED

JOSEPH SCANLON AND RICHARD T. SYLVES

INTRODUCTION

Two fatal air crashes seem in retrospect to be quite different. One occurred in a residential area of a major American city, San Diego. It killed not only those on the plane but caused death and destruction on the ground. The other happened in a wooded area beside a lake outside a small town in Newfoundland, Canada. Those on the plane died as well but ground damage was confined to a fire and some pollution problems.

On September 25, 1978 a midair collision occurred between a light plane and a commercial 727 jet airliner over San Diego, California. Each plane plummeted to the ground and 151 people were killed. Crash fatalities from the jetliner's impact included seven lives on the ground. The jet also destroyed seven homes, and set 22 more on fire. More than seven years later, on December 12, 1985, a charter jet transporting American military people home for the holidays lost power and crashed near Gander, Newfoundland. As the plane descended it missed cottages and a navigation beacon, but in the end harmed no people or structures on the ground.

Some differences are immediately apparent. San Diego has a huge police and fire department, dozens of hospitals, and the resources of a major naval base. Gander, in contrast, has only the resources of its airport, a three-person municipal police force handling mainly parking and traffic duties, a volunteer fire department, a single hospital, a small military base, and a detachment of Royal Canadian Mounted Police (RCMP) who patrol the town, the province, and the airport.

Even the weather on the day of each crash was different. San Diego had clear September skies and stiflingly hot temperatures. It was so hot that many schools were closed early. In Gander, mid-December temperatures hovered around the freezing mark. Some planes taking off that morning were deiced because of freezing drizzle. Emergency personnel responding to the crash had to scrape ice from their windshields.

But there were similarities between each disaster. Both crashes killed all pilots, crews, and passengers.[1] Both occurred in jurisdictional settings in which only one government had exclusive emergency response obligations. Since the crash scene was totally confined within city limits, San Diego took charge in its incident. In Newfoundland, the plane came down on an expansive tract of Canadian federal government property, and so national authorities directed the response. In each crash, police, ambulance, fire, and hospital response was very fast.[2]

Yet the conditions and competence of emergency response and recovery operations in each case were different. Gander responders did a much better job on the whole than did their San Diego counterparts. There appears to be two general reasons for this. First, Gander had conducted better predisaster preparedness planning than had San Diego. Second, it will be shown that, odd as it may seem, *San Diego was disadvantaged by its large size and population relative to Gander.*

As stated previously, each crash was a nonsurvival type and in San Diego, seven more people on the ground perished when the jetliner came down in their neighborhood. Yet, all died so quickly that no response, no matter how swift or competent, could have saved a single life. Therefore, this study is not about saving lives but is about other aspects of postcrash emergency response and recovery operations. Each incident is first described separately and later, dimensions of each are compared and contrasted paying special attention to the differences jurisdictional size and resources may have made in each case.

THE SAN DIEGO MIDAIR COLLISION

As a Pacific Southwest Airlines (PSA) 727 jet prepared for its descent into San Diego airport, it collided with a Cessna 172 propeller craft that was moving to a higher altitude. The small twin engine plane came down on a street killing both pilots but caused no injuries or significant damage on the ground, but the 727 hit a street, a sidewalk, and then smashed into private homes. The airliner cut power lines, broke a water main, sheered off gas lines, and ignited jet fuel causing a major fire.

Emergency response was almost immediate. A few police officers and firefighters witnessed the collision and raced to the scene. An ambulance that had been only a few blocks away also arrived quickly at the crash area. First responders were slightly confused by a police dispatcher who gave an incorrect street name, but the pillar of smoke rising from the crash made it impossible for anyone to miss it.

Before long almost every on-duty San Diego police officer, and many who were off duty, were at the scene. Police radio traffic was so heavy, police dispatchers had almost no idea who was on-site and who was not. An investigation later showed that there were just nine uniformed officers left to cover the rest of the city during the incident. The first city police officer to reach the 727 crash location knew immediately that there were no survivors, but he never got through to report this. Moreover, peace officers from the state Fish and Game department, the state Forestry department, and the Highway Patrol materialized at the scene, as did officers of the U.S. Border Patrol.[3] Even police from other municipalities started arriving. Over-convergence of police at the site was excessive, unnecessary, uncoordinated, and probably counter productive to recovery operations and crash scene management.

Fire response was better controlled. Three engine companies originally went out to the scene but others were held in reserve and were only to respond if requested; even those sent to the site were directed to specific locations from a staging area near the point of impact. An off-duty firefighter, who lived near the crash site, responded without being specifically dispatched but other San Diego firefighters did not travel to the site unless officially dispatched. There were some firefighters from outside the city who responded without being asked. One unit came because they were passing through San Diego after having fought a wildfire. Another drove to the scene from San Clemente.

Emergency medical services proved to be extremely confused. A communications foul-up flooded the 727 crash site with ambulances, almost none of which were actually needed. At that time, San Diego's public ambulance service was part of the Police Department. Ambulances were driven by specially trained police officers, they were dispatched by police radio operators, and when they were not on duty the vehicles were used to perform normal police functions. Each ambulance had two radios, one for police calls and another operated by the county that was used for emergency medical calls. The emergency medical radios were referred to as station X. These radios were switched off when vehicles did not have a message for the county. If police operating ambulances wanted to transmit to station X, they switched that radio on. If station X wanted to radio the police ambulance, county dispatchers had to first notify police communications people who in turn would contact the ambulance through the police radio system.

When the first ambulance arrived where the 727 had gone in, its crew discovered a mother and her child who were slightly injured and badly shaken. Both had been cut by flying glass when a body part came through the windshield of their car. The unit turned on station X and radioed county emergency medical dispatch that there had been an air disaster and that they were bringing in two injured persons. They then turned that radio off.

The county immediately notified area hospitals that there had been a disaster. They also alerted the city's private ambulance firms. The hospitals promptly went on emergency status and sent medical teams to the site. Private ambulances began to arrive one after another at the site. This continued unabated for as long as three hours after the crash. One official remarked,

> . . . various hospitals called repeatedly all morning, asking what was happening, station X could only tell them to stand by. It was not possible to make any contact with an incident commander [on-site] and it was not possible to tell whether any medical support was required.[4]

The response was so great that the ambulances eventually parked in long lines on both sides of the site, their presence unnecessary except to treat or transport exhausted officials and onlookers.[5] It was a classic, textbook example of convergence in postdisaster settings, the overload of people and material at a disaster site.[6]

Station X could not reach police at the site because the police ambulance station X radios were turned off. It could not reach the police or the private ambulance system by telephone because local phones were jammed.[7] Pacific Southwest headquarters is in San Diego and callers deluged that office with demands to know identities of victims in the crash. Station X dispatchers could not reach private ambulances in the field because none carried county radios. Police supervisors did not have station X radios; other police ambulances that responded failed to turn their station X radios on and, therefore, never even heard the first message called in from the field.

Despite the ambulance debacle, three main activities continued at the site in the hours after the crash. Police and firefighters combed through the wreckage hoping to find survivors. Firefighters extinguished the blazes that had been started by the burning aviation fuel, a task that took two hours. Finally, utility crews labored to restore electricity to the 10,000 homes left without power after the crash. Unfortunately, power crews neglected to inform firefighters from the outset that electric power was out.[8]

Once the fire was completely out, firefighters made one final but fruitless search for survivors. They then left standby crews at the site and departed the area. Most returning firefighters sat around the station house talking about the ghastly sights they had seen, dismembered bodies, bugs, blood, and so on. This type of discussion is called "grossing out" and is an accepted way they attempt to cope psychologically with such horror.

Police stayed on after the firefighters left. They used a nearby school as a casualty clearing post. They established a site perimeter. They brought in a mobile van that served as an on-site command post and they maintained an off-site support command post at police headquarters. They got the Sheriff to assign a helicopter crew the task of overflying the site. The copter was intended to serve as an aerial spotter and was to control media helicopters that converged over the site. Police also had San Diego's Lindbergh field restrict air traffic over the crash site through the airport's issuance of a NOTAM (Notice to Airmen). Police officers also assisted the coroner in recovering body parts.

Police also worked through their off-site command post and through the County Emergency Preparedness Office to locate and secure refrigerated trucks which could be used to protect corpses from the hot weather. They obtained body bags for the coroner, they supplied ice and iced drinks for disaster workers, and they even furnished hats for their many hatless officers.[9]

Some postdisaster decisions were made and carried out on-site. Others were made by officials at the headquarters command post and relayed out to the field. As will be shown, some decisions were correct and appropriate, others were not.

For example, responders used a school as a casualty station. This was sensible, but the school selected was not in the county emergency medical plan. It did prove to be appropriate for use as a temporary morgue. The police perimeter was set out too far from the center of the crash site and it did not provide for adequate routes of access or egress. Adding to perimeter problems, there was no communication from site command to those patrolling the perimeter. Emergency vehicles drove onto and off the site unimpeded. This also meant area residents or spectators could slip past perimeter police.

Communications also proved to be a headache. Telephone circuits were saturated. Radio channels were flooded. The police site commander actually turned his radio off because the constant chatter of radio squawk was too distracting. Somehow media people got hold of the number of the radio phone located in the police command van. They tied up that line with calls.

Furthermore, the Sheriff's helicopter did manage to restrict overhead air traffic but it also drowned out the fire radios used on the ground. This forced firefighters to use runners to communicate. The copter also was not much value as an aerial spotter because its Sheriff's radio was incompatible with that used by the San Diego police. Investigations proved that, "It was not until noon when [San Diego] police observed the area by helicopter, [and] realized [that] cars were being rerouted in circles, and that the area of impact involved only two blocks."[10]

The media posed problems as well. When the mid-air collision took place several reporters and correspondents were at a demonstration in the area. When they heard the collision they looked up, photographers snapped pictures, and all of them ran to the crash site. One photo of the fiery jet, pointing nose first toward the ground, won a photo journalism award. From this original point of disaster onward, media people pervaded the crash scene. Reporters strode in and out of the police command area. They walked all over the impact area before it had been secured and investigated. They persisted in shooting pictures and video tape of the carnage, some insisting that they had a right to do so.[11] The conflict continued until police roped off the immediate crash area, ordered the media to stay out, and arrested and charged those who refused to obey. Police were so irritated by media incursions that they later took those arrested to court and won convictions.

Yet, one tormenting media problem stemmed from a police error. Some officers, who were previously on a drug detail and therefore dressed in old clothes, went about collecting valuables at the site using green garbage bags because they were worried about the possibility of looting. What they failed to realize was that those items, once moved, were no longer useful in trying to piece together what happened to the plane and its occupants at impact. What was perhaps worse was that reporters who observed these plain clothes people picking up valuables thought they were thieves. When reporters asked a police spokesman if there had been any looting at the crash scene, the officer answered yes and mentioned seven arrests. Actually, there had been no looting. The spokesman had been misled by an erroneous entry in an arrest book. It had listed seven arrests for looting under the standard police code 459. What he did not know was that the arresting officer had meant to register the arrests as code 409, which is failure to disperse on request. Consequently, reporters concluded that the people collecting valuables must have been some of those arrested on the looting charges. The San Diego Chief of Police wrote a national magazine to set the record straight. He insisted, "There is absolutely no evidence any looting occurred on the crash site or in the immediate vicinity."[12] The looting story, myth that it is, nevertheless persists years after the crash.

As if media annoyances were not enough, there were also intrusive politically influential gapers at the site who had no business being there. One municipal councillor and his child wandered across the crash site.

The San Diego crash itself was never treated as a disaster. The mayor assessed the incident and decided not to open the city's Emergency Operations Center. The crash, though tragic, affected just one part of the city, had a limited area of impact, and posed no continuing threat. The mayor's decision meant that various emergency response organizations never fully acted together in a coordinated fashion either on-site or in other locations. For example, police and fire mobile vans both arrived at the site but parked some distance apart. These units did not get around to exchanging liaison officers until more than an hour after they set up.

Field interviews for this study were conducted seven years after the San Diego air disaster, but even then, emergency responders retained vivid memories of the scene. Many police officers recalled spending seemingly endless hours helping the coroner recover body parts. Many expressed frustration that they were helpless and unable to render medical aid to the victims. There were mental "flashbacks" of numerous disaster images. For one it was two hands clasped together, one with a wedding band, one without. For another it was a priest offering last rites over the remnants of a body. And for yet another it was the pervasive bugs crawling over pieces of human flesh.[13]

For a few police officers the experience was too much. Some resigned from the department not long after the crash. The resignations encouraged the San Diego Police Department to offer special counseling services to help officers cope with stress and traumatic experiences. In 1984, one of these counselors rendered aid to officers at the scene of a mass murder at a McDonald's Restaurant in nearby San Ysidro. Some patrolmen sought help after that incident but no one who responded to that tragedy resigned as a result of the incident.

San Diego's response to the crash could have been better. The decision not to invoke the emergency plan was logical because the crash was not a continuing threat and not a city-wide disaster, but if the city emergency plan had been put into effect it probably would have improved coordination. In the absence of a declared city emergency it was, perhaps, inevitable that poor on-site coordination and communications breakdowns would result. Also, although the response was strictly a matter for city emergency authorities, area hospitals were responding as part of the *county* medical emergency plan. City police were not familiar with the elements of that plan. For example, they did not know which schools were designated and provisioned as medical centers. The biggest problem, of course, was convergence by police, ambulance personnel, and onlookers. The lack of adequate perimeter control and the inability of police on the ground to communicate with the sheriff's helicopter overhead, were serious deficiencies. If there had been survivors, there might well have been major problems moving them from the site to hospitals in the area.

THE GANDER AIR DISASTER

On the morning of December 12, 1985 a military chartered stretch DC-8 raced down a Gander, Newfoundland runway and became airborne. But it failed to gain altitude, began to clip treetops, and then bore into a wooded area beside Gander Lake a short distance from the Trans-Canada Highway. A few motorists saw the plane pass over head at very low altitude and witnessed the fiery explosion of the jetliner as it hit the ground. The fireball was also observed by the lone airport tower operator on duty at the time.

First response began when drivers on the Highway stopped and ran down an icy side-road to the crash site. It also began when the tower operator activated the airport's emergency notification plan. He called the field's Crash, Fire Rescue (CFR) using a direct phone.[14] He told fire personnel that a plane had crashed within a five mile radius of Gander Lake. The large, heavily wooded areas around Gander do not make downed-plane searches easy tasks. When a Belgian plane crashed near Gander in 1946, it took searchers two days to find it.

The CFR did not roll immediately because the crash was off airport grounds and firefighters had to first plot the general location of the downed craft. This took 13 minutes. Nevertheless, CFR people were the first official emergency responders to arrive at the site of the crash. As they prepared to depart the station, a crew member phoned the airport fire chief who was at home at that hour. The chief rushed immediately to the airport then, after picking up his emergency vehicle, drove to the site.

The call from the tower to the CFR was monitored by members of the Royal Canadian Mounted Police (RCMP) because both the CFR and the RCMP were on the same "hot line." The RCMP detachment alerted their people and contacted the airport duty manager. He, in turn, phoned the airport manager and staff, and opened the Emergency Coordination Centre (ECC). The RCMP unit also notified their regional office. That subdivision called in more police employing a prearranged call-out plan that drew additional officers from neighboring areas. RCMP officers were the second official group to reach the crash scene.

The tower operator succeeded in alerting a wide variety of essential organizations besides police and fire units. He called Canadian Forces Base (CFB) at Gander and they sent in medics and Military Police (MPs). Other base personnel were warned to be on standby if they too were needed. The tower official also reached the Gander Aviation Area Control Centre, a key point of North Atlantic air traffic control. The aviation centre warned other aircraft of the crash and began storing air traffic control data and tapes that would undoubtedly be needed for the crash investigation. The tower operator contacted Gander's hospital, as did the RCMP. Hospital officials then activated their own disaster plan. Normal procedures were suspended, medical staff were called in through a planned fan-out system, a medical command post was set up, and a nearby community college was asked to clear a cafeteria for use as a casualty clearing post.

The tower controller called the local telephone office and, by previous agreement, operators there relayed word to selected municipal officials, including the volunteer fire department chief. During all these calls the tower operator managed to radio an inbound commercial flight and got the pilot to circle the suspected crash area in order to pinpoint the site.

His telephone calls triggered other actions. Air controllers at the aviation centre told maintenance staff to inspect navigation aids to check whether faulty equipment on the ground may have caused the crash.

Other maintenance crews were put on standby and asked to monitor
their radios. This was because maintenance station wagons could be
converted into ambulances. The centre checked back with the tower to
make sure that the operator was emotionally able to carry on.

Telephone company people were unable to find their call-out plan so,
instead of informing the volunteer fire chief that he *might* be needed, an
operator dialed the fire phone that automatically mobilizes the local fire
department. Fortunately, just as the fire phone issued an alert, the
airport manager phoned from the off-site command post and asked for
fire-fighting help. The manager's call was monitored by municipal police,
who immediately sent one officer to join the search under way and
another to establish a check point on the Trans Canada Highway near
the crash.

The call alerting the hospital drew a medical team to the site. The
group decided to go to the crash site even though they were not the
designated first response triage [medical sorting] team and even though,
at that point, no triage team had been requested. The medical team did
gain access to the site but since there were no survivors they were not
needed. Soon after they left, the hospital did receive a request for a
medical team and so the official triage team proceeded to the site. When
they reached the crash area an RCMP officer told them that they were
not needed and therefore would not be allowed access to the site. This
second team resented that the uninvited and "unofficial" first group had
been allowed to enter the site, while they, having been officially invited,
were denied entry to the site.

The tower radio transmission to the inbound flight indirectly led to
notification of the news media. As soon as the inbound plane landed, a
flight steward rushed to a phone and called a local radio station.

Only minutes after these tower calls an all-out emergency response
had begun. Within half-an-hour site command had been smoothly transferred from the CFR crews, to the airport fire chief, and finally to an
RCMP inspector who would be the paramount on-scene national governmental authority. The airport fire chief and crew stayed on to fight the
fire. In the same 30-minute period an off-site command post was put into
operation at the airport. Here the airport manager, the head of the
RCMP detachment, the commander of the military base, airport staff,
and a representative of the charter airline, all went to work.

Police established site control and also managed security duties at
locations outside the crash zone. A uniformed constable, posted at the

intersection of the highway and the only road to the site, managed to screen out unwanted vehicles. Responders to the crash immediately recognized that the RCMP held jurisdiction and so these officers were consulted about almost every action. For example, when volunteer fire-fighters wanted to move some wreckage that blocked the road to the lake, they first sought permission from an RCMP sergeant.

The RCMP force was augmented by unarmed but uniformed Canadian military personnel posted along the highway. They stopped people from slipping through the bush and into the crash site. A few tried to do so but were unsuccessful. A military on-site commander brought a command van to the site, parked it next to the RCMP command van, and took direction from the RCMP inspector.

Two main activities were conducted at the crash scene. First, there was a search for possible survivors. It was first carried out on an impromptu basis by a few motorists who stopped to help. Soon after, firefighters, the RCMP, the town police officer at the scene, and the Military Police launched a more organized search. The most precise search took place after town fire fighting volunteers arrived. They furnished enough workers to conduct a thorough search.[15] The memory of survivors in two earlier crashes near Gander years before made some responders confident that someone might have lived through the crash. It was not until the search was concluded that the Royal Canadian police reassigned a patrol car unit from its position near the edge of the town. It had stood ready to clear a direct corridor from the site east of town to the hospital on the town's west side by temporarily closing a portion of the Trans Canada Highway.

The second main activity was that of fire fighting. Even as the searches progressed, airport fire crews used sophisticated chemical foaming equipment to suppress the raging blaze. They were not too successful. The burning wreckage was difficult to approach. Some unignited jet fuel streamed over portions of the site or collected in pools. The area was strewn with bodies, many of them engulfed in flames. The fire burned on for 20 hours.

Other things also did not go smoothly. When CFR vehicles drove over the brow of a hill near the site, they lost radio contact with the airport. There were several times when the ECC at the airport did not know what was going on at the crash site. This problem was remedied when it was discovered that the two-way radio in the fire chief's vehicle, as well as one being used by the RCMP, had enough range to reach the airport despite the hill. A phone company truck with a radio telephone arrived on the scene and provided a third link between the two command areas.

When it was learned that there were no survivors, the response settled into methodical patterns. Firefighters continued to attack the blaze on the crash site. Police went about marking the area into a grid and then recorded and photographed everything within each grid square, one square at a time. This done, bodies and other human remains were removed. At the airport ECC officials dealt with outside agencies and prepared for an invasion of investigators, officials, and victim relatives from the United States. Air crash investigations are conducted by the country in which the crash occurs, but with help from the country of the aircraft's owners.

Here again there were some complications. A technical problem with the Canadian government phone system disrupted communication between Ottawa, the federal capital, and Washington, D.C., the U.S. capital. Consequently, for a time Ottawa-Washington communication was maintained via amateur radio operators. There was also a mix up over body bags because both the RCMP and the airport placed an order for additional bags, but each canceled their orders when each learned that the other had placed an order. As a result, body bags had to be reused.

There was a problem of too many phone calls from the media, just as in the San Diego crash. CKCM, a radio station in nearby Grand Falls, obtained the ECC phone number, called and managed to get a live interview with Gander's airport manager. The airport number was initially made available so that local media could obtain quick, reliable information. But because the number was passed around so widely, the ECC ended up being overwhelmed by calls from the media.[16]

An unanticipated disaster recovery problem turned out to be one of water pollution. Water sprayed on portions of the site washed unignited jet fuel down a hill and into Gander Lake, the town's water supply. Teams of specialists had to be called in to control the problem. This was complicated further because Gander's deputy mayor had neither been informed about the threat nor invited to the airport ECC. When she learned of the pollution threat at a news conference, she was understandably angered. The oversight was later corrected when she was invited to the airport command post and told what was being done.[17]

Another delicate problem involved military ordnance. The victims were armed U.S. soldiers en route from the Middle East to their home base in Kentucky. The crash littered a wide area with weapons. MPs convinced the site commander that some might accidentally discharge or might be stolen. The RCMP commander agreed and had all the weapons carefully collected. An MP cordoned off an area that ended up encompassing stacks of M16 rifles, automatic and 38 calibre pistols, grenade launchers, and other military hardware. Unfortunately, because the weapons had been moved before grid-square photo records were made of their original location, they could no longer be of help in body identification at the scene. Even if the weapons had been tagged and then moved, this would have helped in documentation of remains.[18] All 256 bodies were eventually recovered and identified. Serial numbers on each weapon were later traced back to each individual soldier on the plane.

Many postdisaster functions at Gander went well. Site control was extremely tight. Anyone seeking access had to clear approval of an RCMP officer posted at the highway. Before he allowed entry, he first secured the approval of the site commander by radio. Records were kept of visitors to the site and the site itself was patrolled for trespassers. Later, entry had to be approved by an official at the airport ECC, relayed to the on-scene commander, and then radioed to perimeter officers.[19]

Despite some early radio problems, communications between on-site and off-site emergency officials were satisfactory. Fire, police, military, and ambulance service people all had radio links between the scene and their home base offices. The first three could also communicate from the site to the airport ECC.

The airport ECC itself did extraordinary work. When police needed a way to ship recovered weapons, airport staff designed and built suitable boxes and crates, all overnight. ECC staff even took precise orders and made deliveries of soft drinks and other items to workers at the temporary morgue. The airport and its ECC had to accommodate the people and requests of 65 different agencies, all of whom sent representatives to the site. As might be expected, most were from U.S. organizations: an army general examined the area, a Coast Guard officer helped in clean-up of the lake, a navy chaplain led a collective worker prayer at the crash site. Agents of the Federal Aviation Administration, the National Transportation Safety Board, and Federal Bureau of Investigation collected information in the impact zone. The Canadian Aviation Safety Board (CASB) played a lead role in collection of aircraft debris, analysis of events before the crash, and investigation of the cause of the disaster.

Other workers at the site included road maintenance crews, heavy equipment operators who helped move wreckage and trees, telephone and power field crews, and Salvation Army volunteers, to name a few. Among other things that went well, the Gander hospital stand-down went as planned. When it was clear there were no crash survivors, the hospital returned to normal operations.

Just as in the San Diego crash, there was an incredible amount of media convergence. An estimated 325 electronic and print media organizations from throughout eastern Canada and much of the United States traveled to Gander. NBC network news even imported a satellite ground station from England. Media people were first greeted by the airport staff and then briefed by a succession of officials from the RCMP and the CASB.

The CASB chief investigator proved deft in handling reporters. He divulged an immense number of details about the events leading up to the crash but was careful not to put forward yet unproven reasons why the craft went down. For example, his briefings included statements like, "The plane took off at 0645. It was one minute and forty seconds from take-off to the crash. The black box has been found. The pilot did not deice the plane, etc."[20] He declined to explain whether any of this information was significant in determining why the jetliner crashed. He also instructed American media people about Canadian law and customs. He told news people that Canadian law prohibited the release of what was said on voice recorders unless the material was relevant to the cause of the crash and then only a summary of what was said could be released to the public.

The CASB's image did suffer when a draft copy of the investigation report was leaked in 1988, 18 months after the crash. The Board was divided over findings and there were allegations that key evidence was missing from the draft. The chairman of the CASB resigned in the ensuing controversy.[21] The final crash report was issued in late December 1988 but was still surrounded with controversy owing to allegations of incomplete information.

Media relations were well managed both in terms of public relations and in terms of site security. A media bus was allowed to visit the site, but only after bodies were removed from view. A minor snafu occurred when the airport manager sent local media to the site in an airport vehicle during the early stages of response operations. The manager neglected to inform the RCMP road guard who, when he saw the vehicle had airport markings, waved it through the perimeter checkpoint. Several correspondents in the car managed to film some of the scene, but they were soon discovered and asked to leave the area. This was the only known instance of people entering the site without officially being cleared by site command. It was also perhaps the only misunderstanding between officials on-site and officials off-site.

In Gander, just as in the San Diego tragedy, many emergency responders had psychological difficulty dealing with the carnage. "A physician became distraught after tagging body after body. He threw down a set of tags beside a pile of bodies and left. Another went back to the hospital, took off her bloodstained and dirty outer clothing, and [insisted] that it be destroyed."[22] Cold weather at Gander helped suppress odors which San Diego responders could not escape. Yet, Gander firefighters spent two days extinguishing fires, many of which engulfed dead bodies. Several RCMP officers spent several days virtually up to their waists in burned bodies.[23] Many fire and police responders had nightmares in the weeks following the crash. Some police officers reported serious family problems in the wake of the disaster. Community mental health workers attempted to monitor these difficulties and rendered aid when they were able to identify problems.

To sum up, the Gander crash episode yields some important findings. The area's low habitation and relative isolation may have been more of a help than a hindrance in post-disaster emergency response and recovery operations. Clearly, the remote location of the crash site and the single route of entry helped maintain perimeter security. Moreover, the Gander airport was a key trans-Atlantic refueling point for many aircraft. It had experienced a few airplane crashes in the years before this incident and so several responders there had familiarity and experience with both downed-plane searches and crash site management. It is also notable that alert notification was handled initially by the airport and not by other authorities. The crash notification plan followed by the tower operator produced a somewhat systematic emergency response. Moreover, convergence of emergency personnel on the site was limited both by sound police management and because Gander is not surrounded by populous municipalities, and is not layered with numerous governmental organizations.

THE SAN DIEGO AND GANDER CRASHES COMPARED

San Diego and Gander both confronted nonsurvival jetliner crashes, but each responded very differently. From the moment after impact, San Diego's response seemed out of control. Many police officers and several firefighter crews converged on the site when they were clearly not needed and not asked. Private ambulance units flooded the scene in the hours after the crash even though there were no injured to transport. Media people freely roamed the crash site because of the over-large and porous site perimeter set up by police. Worse yet, many area residents, sightseers, and unneeded officials were not screened away from the impact zone.

By comparison, Gander's response was more controlled. Almost all fire, police, and military personnel were there either as first responders or because their presence had been officially approved by the on-scene commander. For the most part, media were kept away until conditions at the site permitted an official managed tour. No spectators were known to have invaded the site.

Differences in communications between each crash are stark. On-site to off-site communications in San Diego were bad to nonexistent. Incompatible radios and radio frequencies, radio and telephone transmission saturation, plus confused and uncoordinated radio communications procedures, all complicated or impeded San Diego's postdisaster activities. By comparison Gander's communications appear excellent, even though they too experienced human and technical problems.

The Role Of Size

In offering closing observations about each crash, the matter of area size and population will be given emphasis. Much of the difference between San Diego and Gander postcrash activities can be attributed to size-related factors. Clearly, the San Diego crash area was more difficult to manage than the Gander crash area. The first was a neighborhood of single family homes, the second a sparsely populated, little developed wooded area accessible only from a single dirt road.

Moreover, Gander had a crash plan. It involved all key agencies, including the military. That plan was understood by people in the organizations that were expected to respond to air disasters. Moreover, responders were cognizant of their duties and tasks because the plan was regularly tested through drills, exercises, and simulations. The last full simulation had been conducted only 27 days before the crash. The airport manager activated the ECC every time a plane reported a problem. This proved useful because the airport plan was used at the location of the crash even though the crash area was not on airport grounds. In San Diego there also was an airport crash plan and municipal police are part of that plan. There is, among other things, a hot line that connects the airport to police dispatch. But the San Diego crash was not at that airport and it was not reported by that airport. At first, air traffic controllers were not aware immediately that the crash had occurred. Airport accident planning therefore played no part in the response.

While San Diego has had some emergency experience since the PSA air crash, the San Ysidro mass murder at a McDonald's, flooding, and canyon fires for example, the crash was the first major San Diego city emergency in recent times. In Gander emergency authorities had some experience with plane crashes, but San Diego's emergency responders were dealing not only with their first major air disaster but also with their first major emergency.[24] Consequently, the Gander response benefited both from preparedness planning and previous aviation accident experience.

Nevertheless, there are enough parallels between each crash to suggest that Gander could have experienced the same problems as San Diego, to the same degree, were it not for Gander's small population and remote location. Consider this,

1. In both communities spectators converged on the crash site. In San Diego this meant a great many people would show up, but in Gander it meant only a small number would come out.

2. In both communities unrequested police turned up at the site. In San Diego all but nine of the city's on-duty officers showed up, as well as numerous off-duty San Diego police and a plethora of federal and state peace officers. At Gander only a single city police officer came to the scene without first securing permission.

3. In both communities medical staff traveled to the site when they were neither needed nor wanted at the scene. In San Diego a procession of private ambulances and scores of medical personnel flowed in. But in Gander the same phenomenon could attract only a carload of physicians and a nurse, all from a single hospital.[25]

4. In both communities outside firefighters set off without being officially dispatched. This proved to be something of a headache for San Diego crash scene officials, particularly since many fire

units were from outside the city and therefore not accountable in a direct sense to city authority. When Gander volunteer firefighters began unilaterally to go out to the crash behind the CFR crew, they proved to be both needed and welcomed. Recall, that the airport manager had asked for their help as they were departing.

5. In both communities police picked up material from the crash site that, if left in place, might have helped in postcrash investigations. In each case there was a fear of looting. San Diego police worried about valuables scattered over the site. Gander CFB MPs worried about the twin problems of stolen weapons and accidental weapon discharges. However, the San Diego valuables recovery operation was conducted on an impromptu basis by plain clothes officers. Gander's was conducted more methodically, and with on-scene commander permission, by Canadian MPs. Again, San Diego's site was flooded with so many police personnel, management was extraordinarily difficult. Gander's RCMP and MP contingent was smaller and therefore much more responsive to a chain of command on-site.

Whether it be unauthorized police, undispatched firefighters, overzealous medical staff, or intrusive sightseers, numbers make the difference. In Gander the numbers of these people were so small that they did not pose serious problems for official emergency responders; in San Diego these numbers were large enough to pose very serious emergency response problems.

San Diego was disadvantaged by an overload of telephone calls, many to PSA offices in the city. Saturated lines confounded on-site/off-site communications, particularly when radio communications were impossible. In the Gander crash most inquiries about victims went to Fort Campbell, Kentucky (the soldiers' home base), or to other locations in the United States. Gander only experienced phone problems during the night following the crash, as media people phoned in stories or established telecommunications links to their home offices.

Gander's crash site, more than San Diego's, permitted better control of the media. Convergence of media at both locations was immense, but distance from major population centers gave Gander officials a bit more lead time to prepare for an avalanche of media people. San Diego was less fortunate in that some media people observed the collision and arrived at the site with first responders. Moreover, the metropolitan area's many news organizations, both print and electronic, were drawn within minutes to the site. Things were so bad in the San Diego case that media people had to be arrested so authorities could establish site control.[26]

Gander's small population meant that most responding officials knew each other before the crash. The RCMP superintendent, the RCMP inspector, the airport manager, the airport fire chief, the base commander, and the ambulance driver all knew each other from previous work activities. Many officials at the San Diego site were strangers to each other before the accident. Site commanders never really got together. This compounded problems of communication and site control.[27]

If Gander had as an asset its small population and geographic remoteness, it was helped even more by its degree of predisaster emergency preparedness and because an off-site emergency operations center was used. Thomas Drabek maintains that time and again a key factor in emergency response coordination is the presence or absence of an emergency operations center of some kind.[28] An airport Emergency Coordination Centre was put into operation in the wake of the Gander crash. Authorities in San Diego, most particularly the mayor, decided that an emergency operations center was unnecessary in dealing with postcrash activities.

CONCLUSION

In closing, there appear to be three general distinctions between each crash. First, Gander had been well prepared, had done better predisaster planning for an aviation accident, and had some local emergency responders that had crash recovery experience. San Diego was more unprepared, emergency planning for an aviation disaster may have been conducted at Lindbergh field but was not well integrated with San Diego city emergency organizations, and San Diego had not suffered a major airliner crash, off airport grounds, in the memory of most responders.

Second, Gander's small population and geographic remoteness from large population centers worked to its advantage. San Diego is, and was at the time of the crash, one of America's fastest growing cities. It is not only densely populated and heavily developed, but is surrounded by a mammoth metropolitan area. Demographics added an immense degree of complexity to San Diego's response.

Finally, something not mentioned to this point, is the matter of "luck" in a perverse sense of the word. If there had been many injured and burned survivors in each crash, it is conceivable that San Diego would be judged to have done a better job in emergency response than did Gander.

This is because Gander's single hospital would have been overwhelmed. Injured survivors, especially burn victims, would have been evacuated by air to Halifax or Montreal, a life-threatening and time-consuming ordeal for those transported. The specter of transporting possibly a hundred or more victims from the Gander site would have been daunting for emergency responders. On the other hand, San Diego would have enjoyed the advantages of innumerable police-medics on-site, a surplus of public and private ambulance transport, and a host of alerted hospitals to which victims could be conveyed and treated, all in a short time. In each of these crash response and recovery incidents, had there been survivors or had there been injuries to numerous people on the ground, the demographic advantage might have swung in favor of San Diego. Notwithstanding, there are important lessons to be learned from these two aviation tragedies under the conditions in which each actually occurred.

Notes

[1]Note that in the San Diego collision two pilots in a second plane were killed. Their small aircraft carried no other occupants.

[2]In the Gander crash military emergency personnel also responded speedily.

[3]San Diego's southern city limit is Mexico and border patrol operations in and around the city are commonplace.

[4]Joseph Scanlon and Angela Prawzick, *The 1978 San Diego Air Crash Emergency Response to an Urban Disaster* (Ottawa: Emergency Preparedness Canada, 1985), p. 11.

[5]Ibid., p. 8.

[6]Charles E. Fritz and J. H. Mathewson, "Convergence Behavior in Disaster," National Research Council Disaster Study #9 (Washington, D.C.: National Academy of Sciences, 1957).

[7]Even if they had made intermittent contact with the police, recall that police radio traffic was overwhelmingly heavy as well.

[8]A danger of fire and electrocution is posed whenever power is restored to damaged homes.

[9]Summer regulations do not require San Diego police to wear a hat.

[10]Scanlon and Prawzick, 1985, p. 19.

[11]Ibid., p. 24.

[12]Kendrick Frazier, *The Violent Face of Nature* (New York: William Morrow and Company, Inc., 1979), p. 351.

[13]Scanlon and Prawzick, 1985, p. 31.

[14]He could have simply pressed a crash alarm button instead, given that he had many other crash-related duties. However, by using the phone he was able to give them a better idea of the location of the crash. This act saved time.

[15]There were two other checks, one by RCMP officers using specially trained dogs and another by an RCMP helicopter crew from the air.

[16]Emergency Communications Research Unit, *The Gander Air Crash December 1985* (Ottawa: Emergency Preparedness Canada, 1987), p. 62.

[17]The mayor of Gander was out of town at the time of the crash. Had the plane come down in Gander itself, the deputy mayor would have been in charge of the ECC.

[18]Emergency Communications Research Unit, 1987, p. 24.

[19]Ibid., p. 40.

[20]Ibid., p. 66.

[21]John J. Burns, "Canada Safety Panel Split Over '85 Gander Air Crash," *The New York Times* (May 1, 1988), p. 6.

[22]Emergency Communications Research Unit, 1987, p. 67.

[23]A task made even more trying because there were no wash basins or sanitary facilities on-site.

[24]Many of those involved in Gander's crash response had also been involved 18 years earlier in response to the crash of a Czech aircraft at the airport. There were 38 killed and 36 survivors in that crash.

[25]E. L. Quarantelli, in reviewing many aviation accidents, reports that convergence of unneeded medical units and ambulances is commonplace. See his, "Community Impact of Airport Disasters: Similarities and Differences When Compared with Other Types of Disasters," Article #133 (Columbus, Oh.: Ohio State University Disaster Research Center, 1980), p. 7.

[26]Media convergence after aviation disasters is a virtual certainty because such accidents tend to get disproportionate attention and sensationalized treatment by the media. See Quarantelli, 1980 and Scanlon et al., "Coping With the Media in Disasters: Some Predictable Problems," *Public Administration Review* (January 1985), pp. 123–133.

[27]Nevertheless, living in a small community where people know one another does not in and of itself prevent communication problems. A study of response to an ice jam with threatened flooding in the small town of Princeton, British Columbia, turned up enormous interagency communications problems. See, Joseph Scanlon, Angela Prawzick, and Dan Conlin, *The Princeton Ice Jams of 1984: The Case for an EOC* (Ottawa: Emergency Preparedness Canada, 1984).

[28]Thomas E. Drabek, *Human System Response to Disaster: An Inventory of Sociological Findings* (New York: Springer-Verlag New York Inc., 1986), p. 186.

PART 3

Chapter VII

ISSUE SALIENCE AND PREPAREDNESS AS PERCEIVED BY CITY MANAGERS

Sandra Sutphen and Virginia Bott

INTRODUCTION

During 1985–86, under the auspices of the Center for Governmental Studies at California State University, Fullerton, a survey of nearly 400 California city managers was conducted.[1] The purpose of the survey was to solicit city managers' opinions about the major changes that they have experienced in California local government, their roles as city managers in the past ten years, and their assessment of the future. A wide variety of opinions was gathered, including responses to items about emergency management. These items included two questions about the salience of emergency management and one additional question about their estimate of city preparedness. The first two questions asked city managers to rate the importance of the issue and to assess perceptions of public concern. The third general question defined preparedness as the need to develop emergency management planning skills in the future. Responses were analyzed along standard demographic variables. Emergency management responses were also analyzed with other attitudinal variables using regression analysis.

Methodology

The survey procedure was a conventional "Delphi" process in which the population of California city managers (approximately 400) was mailed a two stage questionnaire.[2] The purpose of a Delphi is to achieve consensus on an issue or issues and it is especially effective when the participants are experts asked to speculate about some future state of affairs. In the usual Delphi, participants respond to an open-ended set of questions initially, and then a second round asks for consensual (agreement) responses in light of the group's first set of answers. The

133

first questionnaire in our Delphi consisted of five open-ended questions inviting city managers to comment on changes they perceived in California local government, their roles during the past ten years, and prospects for future change.[3] One hundred and fifty-five city managers (39%, about normal for such mailed questionnaires) returned the first survey, usually writing in great detail. From this initial pool of responses, the second questionnaire was constructed by using content analysis. Responses were analyzed according to certain themes and 129 specific themes covering the five questions were identified. These were modified for clarity and consistency and several themes were further elaborated by adding specific response items. The final list of themes was organized for the second round of questionnaires so that the most frequently mentioned responses were the leading responses on the new questionnaire. The final questionnaire, with topics listed in order of descending frequency of mention, consisted of eight legal-size pages with 178 individual items plus 22 demographic questions. Respondents were asked to rate each of the items on a seven-point scale, ranging from "very significant" to "inapplicable" (questions were phrased so that "inapplicable" represented the seventh point of the scale).

For the second Delphi round, 233 of 398 California city managers responded. This represents a 59 percent response rate. Respondents were assured anonymity, although their questionnaires were to be returned in coded envelopes that allowed their location to be differentiated between northern and southern California, with the Tehachapi Mountains as the dividing line. The first set of questionnaires were mailed and returned completed over the spring and summer of 1985. The second questionnaire went out and came back during the winter of 1985–86.

The Sample

The sample is similar to that of the International City Management Association (ICMA) survey of city managers in 1980.[4] There are some differences between our sample and the national sample, but this is largely attributable to common differences between California and the nation as a whole. Demographically, the California sample is similar to the national sample with respect to age and sex of respondents. However, fewer California respondents are married and more California city managers have divorced and remarried than have managers in the national sample.

The sample is evenly divided between northern and southern cities in

California (117 from south, 109 from the north, 7 undetermined) and well distributed across city size. It is dissimilar from the national sample on several key variables. It is more ethnically diverse (though still not representative of the ethnic diversity of the state as a whole), more politically partisan, or at least, more willing to identify with a political party, better educated in terms of graduate degrees, and more likely to identify a religious affiliation.

Table VII-1 shows the average ages of city manager respondents through the categories of sex, race, and size of the city in which they work. According to the table, female city managers tend to be younger than male city managers. Also, racial minority city managers tend to be considerably younger than their white (Caucasion) counterparts. Age differences of city managers across categories of city size show no significant differences other than that cities larger than 100,000 people tend to have slightly older city managers.

The first questionnaire divided income of city managers into categories. Median and mean city manager income for the sample was between $50 thousand and $60 thousand a year. Table VII-2 shows the distribution of income across four general categories marked in $10 thousand units. Of the eight female city managers, average income was $50 thousand, while the 219 male respondents averaged $54.8 thousand. Except for two black city manager respondents, hispanic and other ethnic minority nonwhite city managers average lower pay than white city managers. Moreover, southern California city managers average higher annual incomes than do northern California city managers. This may be because there are more large cities in southern California where incomes do tend to be higher.

California is noted for its north-south political division, with northern California historically more liberal and Democratic and southern California more Republican and conservative. Of the total 222 city managers responding to the question of party affiliation, 41 percent of the Democrats were in the south, 59 percent were in the north and 55 percent of the Republicans were in the south while 45 percent were in the north. "Other" affiliations ("none," and "decline to state" or independent) were more likely to be found in the south (18%) than the north (10%). Looking at the data another way, Republicans dominated in the south. About 54 percent of southern California city managers indicated a Republican affiliation and only 28 percent indicated Democratic. The sample clearly reflects the historic California political split.

TABLE VII-1

AGE OF RESPONDENT TABULATED
WITH SEX, RACE, AND CITY SIZE

	Cases	Mean of Age
SEX		
Male	221	45.04
Female	8	41.38
Race		
Black	2	39.50
Hispanic	13	40.62
White	211	45.25
Other	2	38.50
City Size		
<5,000	27	44.93
>5,000 and <10,000	40	42.08
>10,000 and <25,000	50	44.08
>25,000 and <50,000	57	46.51
>50,000 and <100,000	38	44.76
>100,000	17	48.94

In summary, the California sample parallels the national sample in most respects. However, California city managers tend to have had more graduate education than city managers nationally, plus California city managers as a collectivity exhibit more ethnic diversity than the national sample. Remember, the national sample was compiled in 1980 while the California surveys were conducted in 1985–86. It may well be that if a national study were undertaken in 1986, it too may show that respondents are better educated and more ethnically diverse than they were in 1980. Our results show that women and nonblack minorities are generally paid less than white males. The California sample is more politically

TABLE VII-2

DEMOGRAPHICS ANALYZED BY LEVEL OF INCOME

	Cases	Mean of Income*
California region		
Southern	117	5.82 ($50,000-60,000 category)
Northern	108	5.10 ($50,000-60,000 category)
Sex		
Male	219	5.48 ($50,000-60,000 category)
Female	8	5.00 ($50,000-60,000 category)
Race		
Black	2	7.50 ($70,000-80,000 category)
Hispanic	13	5.08 ($50,000-60,000 category)
White	210	5.49 ($50,000-60,000 category)
Other	2	4.00 ($40,000-50,000 category)
Age		
<35	26	4.62 ($40,000-50,000 category)
>34 but <45	105	5.32 ($50,000-60,000 category)
>44 but <55	72	5.81 ($50,000-60,000 category)
>55	24	6.00 ($60,000-70,000 category)

*For example, a 5.82 mean score for southern California city managers represents an annual gross personal income of about $58.000.

partisan than the national sample. Like the state as a whole, there are proportionally more Republicans in the south and proportionally more Democrats in the north. As we examine their attitudes toward emergency management, we will find that some of these differences are quite relevant.[5]

CITY MANAGERS AND EMERGENCY MANAGEMENT

It will come as no surprise to students of emergency management that city managers in California place a fairly low priority on planning for disasters.[6] The Delphi survey is instructive in displaying the scope of the problem. California is a particularly emergency-prone state that often suffers natural and man-made disasters. According to the *National Journal*,[7] California, West Virginia, and Puerto Rico absorbed 40.5 percent of $1.1 billion in federal disaster assistance allocated to the states from 1982 through 1986. In 1980 alone, California experienced three declared disasters and 362 of its 400 or so jurisdictions received federal assistance. California had six federally declared emergencies over the period 1982–83 that included floods and an earthquake. In 1985, major forest fires that often imperiled homes and communities generated disaster aid requests from 58 local governments. Table VII-3 is a summary of California disasters since 1980.

TABLE VII-3

DISASTER AID REQUESTS FROM CALIFORNIA

Date	Type of Disaster	State Agencies	Private Non-profit Agencies	Localities: Counties Cities & Districts
02/21/80	Storms/flooding	8	12	315
10/02/80	Levee break with flooding	4		1
11/27/80	Brush & timber fires	3		18
01/07/82	Storms, flooding with high tides	44	10	167
09/24/82	Levee break	1		1
02/09/83	Rain flooding with mudslides	18	17	488
05/05/83	Earthquake	2		11
07/01/83	Flooding	1		15
09/22/83	Flashflooding	1		25
07/18/85	Fires	2	1	58

Data provided by the U.S. Federal Emergency Management Agency. Region 9, San Francisco.

In the five years preceding our city manager survey, California experienced losses from flooding, high winds, high tides, fires, earthquakes, and mudslides. In one disaster alone, 488 local jurisdictions, among them cities, road departments, water-, flood-, and sanitation-districts, all requested U.S. Federal Emergency Management Agency (FEMA) aid. Californians and their city managers have extensive and frequent experience with emergencies and local disaster.

California contains about 400 municipalities. From 1980 to 1985, 245 of them received direct federal assistance following an emergency or disaster.[8] One hundred and seven of these jurisdictions were in the north and 138 were in the south. Managers of 144 cities that had received federal disaster aid, responded to our survey; 66 of them were in the northern half of the state and 78 were in the southern half. Of the total 245 cities that received federal disaster aid in the period 1980–85, 111 did so more than once. Our sample contained 63 managers of cities that had received disaster aid at least twice in the 1980–85 interval. Of these 63, six requested and received FEMA aid three or more times in the interval. Table VII-5 depicts a frequency distribution for aid requests from 1980 to 1985. Our sample of cities is quite representative of the universe of all California cities as data in Table VII-4 shows.

TABLE VII-4

DIRECT DISASTER ASSISTANCE TO
CALIFORNIA CITIES, 1980-1985

	Population		Sample	
	N*	(%)	N**	(%)
Direct Assistance	245	61.3	144	61.8
Northern cities	107	26.8	66	28.3
Southern cities	138	34.5	78	33.4
Aided More Than Once	111	27.8	63	27.0
Northern cities	44	11.0	25	10.7
Southern cities	67	16.8	38	16.3

*Population was 400 cities.   **City managers from 233 different cities comprised the survey sample.

TABLE VII-5

DISASTER ASSISTANCE REQUESTS
FROM CITIES IN SAMPLE

Number of Disaster Requests 1980-85	City Cases	(%)
0=No request by city	89	38.20
1 Request by city	81	34.76
2 Requests by city	57	24.46
3 Requests by city	4	1.72
4 Requests by city	2	.86

In the first Delphi round there were open-ended questions that asked respondents to identify major areas of concern. Surprisingly, despite relatively frequent experience with emergency and disaster, not one city manager identified emergency management as a major concern. In fact, with the exception of a few references to disposal of hazardous materials, city managers reported few priorities that involved emergency management. Though it was not raised explicitly by respondents in the first round, the second round of questions added the topic of emergency management in three places. Emergency management was added as a "salience" item in an umbrella question encompassing seven other topics. It was added as a "preparedness" item in a question that asked respondents to consider specific skills they thought practitioners would need to have in the next ten years. Emergency management was one of four specialties listed under "planning skills." The arithmetic mean of responses was in close agreement with median and mode scores in the survey and arithmetic mean proved to be a good indicator of the collective sentiments of respondents.

The first "salience" question asked city managers whether they thought California local government would have to give more attention to emergency management in the next ten years. A seven point scale was used in which "1" indicated greatest likelihood and "6" least likelihood. Recall that "7" was used as an inapplicable category. The mean response score on this was 3.17, suggesting only moderate likelihood. The second "salience" question asked whether there would be a decreased emphasis on emergency management because of a lack of public concern. Again a seven-point scale was used so that strongest agreement with the assertion was a "1" and strongest disagreement was a "6." The mean response score was 4.41, suggesting moderate disagreement with the assertion. In other words, most managers did not think there would be a decreased emphasis on emergency management because of lack of public concern, but they expressed only moderate disagreement with the assertion.

The third question pertained to "preparedness" and asked respondents to think about the specific skills city administrators would need to have during the next ten years. Emergency management was one of four items listed under planning skills. Again, a seven-point scale was used and "1" meant most needed while "6" meant least needed. The mean response score was 3.29, suggesting, albeit weakly, that emergency management would be a necessary planning skill required in the next ten years. For the entire survey there was a slight tendency for managers to judge other skills as more important than emergency management.

Several independent variables were recategorized as dichotomies to measure differences using a difference of means test and the "t" statistic. Sex of the respondent, respondent north/south location in California, and respondent political party affiliation are natural dichotomies. The 31 respondents who listed their party affiliation as "other" were omitted from the difference of means test. Several other dichotomies were constructed from the data. For example, respondents who reported earning a Master of Public Administration (MPA) degree and those who did not hold the MPA comprised two categories in our analysis. Also, a dichotomy was made between respondents who had previously served as a city manager before assuming their present post and those who had not been city managers before. Respondents were asked if they had worked as an "assistant city manager" or its equivalent in their last job, and again two sets of responses resulted. Respondents were also asked if their last job had been with the public sector or with the private sector, again yielding dichotomous answers. In our analysis, race was divided into white and nonwhite. Also, undergraduate major was split into political science or public administration *versus* all other types of undergraduate majors. City manager annual income was divided at the median range of $50,000 to $60,000 and city population was divided at the median of 25,000.

Number of years respondents had been city managers was also divided into two categories: those who worked seven or fewer years and those who worked more than seven years. The results of this division appear in Table VII-6. It presents the number of original observations, the mean dependent variable score on each independent variable, and the probability of "t" which represents the chance in 1000 that the difference of means score could have occurred at random.

Table VII-6 contains few demographic variables that show significance at the .05 level of confidence. That is, few of the difference of means of each dependent variable are statistically meaningful. Among those few that are significant is the "attention" variable for the independent variables "previous position," "sector," and "years as city manager." The data show that city managers who have not been assistant city managers previously and who came out of the private sector, are more likely to view emergency management as demanding more attention in the future than city managers who came from the public sector or who worked as assistant city managers before. Very close to .05 confidence level was "years as city manager." Our findings suggest that those respondents who have been city managers for seven years or less are more likely to think emergency management is important than respondents who have worked as city managers for more than seven years. Thus, people newer to the job and newer to public sector employment tend to see emergency management as more important than longer-serving city managers and long-time public sector workers.

Our second dependent variable listed across the top of Table VII-6 is that of "public concern." City managers were asked if emergency management will be less important in the future because of a lack of public concern. A score of "1" on this question means that the respondent believed a lack of public support would indeed mean a decline in the importance of emergency management in their work. At the other extreme, a score of "6" infers that respondents thought there would not be a lack of public concern in emergency management or that if public concern about emergency management was low, it would not effect the importance of emergency management for city managers. We prefer the interpretation that respondents thought that a lack of public concern would not diminish attention to emergency management.

TABLE VII-6

DIFFERENCE OF MEANS CALCULATIONS FOR EMERGENCY MANAGEMENT VARIABLES

Independent Variable	Group Label	Number** of Obs.	"Attention" Mean Value	T	Prob. of T	"Public Concern" Mean Value	T	Prob. of T.	"E.M.Skills" Mean Value	T	Prob. of T.
Sex	Male	220	1.73	.33	.376	1.93	4.01	.001*	1.72	.80	.227
	Female	6	1.67			2.00			1.57		
Geography	South	118	1.70	.95	.172	1.91	1.74	.042*	1.71	.38	.351
	North	108	1.76			1.96			1.73		
Party	Democrat	77	1.70	.36	.358	1.94	.16	.437	1.67	.85	.198
	Republican	113	1.73			1.93			1.73		
Graduate Degree	MPA	128	1.73	.63	.265	1.95	1.13	.133	1.72	.22	.413
	Other	37	1.78			1.89			1.74		
Other City	Yes	118	1.74	.30	.383	1.93	.07	.472	1.75	.96	.168
	No	107	1.72			1.93			1.69		
Previous Position	Asst.CM	125	1.79	2.08	.019*	1.94	.78	.217	1.73	.05	.481
	Other	96	1.67			1.92			1.72		
Sector	Public	208	1.75	2.18	.022*	1.94	.79	.220	1.74	1.56	.069
	Private	15	1.47			1.87			1.53		
Race	Nonwhite	15	1.73	.06	.476	2.00	4.02	.001*	1.47	2.04	.029*
	White	208	1.73			1.93			1.74		
Major	Pol.Sci.	113	1.75	.10	.458	1.92	1.41	.081	1.78	1.19	.118
	Other	87	1.76			1.97			1.71		
Income	$60 K	109	1.75	.81	.210	1.92	.91	.183	1.73	.42	.337
	$60 K	115	1.70			1.95			1.70		
City Population	25 K	114	1.74	.08	.468	1.93	.23	.408	1.73	.21	.419
	25 K	112	1.73			1.94			1.71		
Years as City Mgr	7 yrs	115	1.69	1.50	.068	1.91	1.28	.102	1.71	.38	.351
	7 yrs	111	1.77			1.95			1.73		
Recvd. Disaster Aid	No	86	3.37	1.93	.028*	4.10	2.96	.002*	3.41	1.05	.148
	Yes	142	3.08			4.61			3.23		

*Statistically significant at .05 level or above.

**Totals may vary due to answers that are left blank.

Table VII-6 shows that on "public concern" four independent variables prove significant at the .05 level. Female, more than male, respondents think that a lack of public attention will *not* reduce city manager concern about emergency management. Similarly, nonwhite respondents more than white respondents maintain that minimal public concern about emergency management will *not* reduce the salience of emergency management for city managers. Caution must be exercised in examining the variables of sex and race because the number of women and non-whites in the survey is so small, 6 women and 15 non-whites respectively. However, the "t" test is sensitive to as few as three cases. Our findings also show that northern California city manager respondents, more than their southern California counterparts, believe a lack of public concern for emergency management will *not* diminish the importance of emergency management for city managers. While not quite significant at the .05 level, there is an indication that public administration or political science undergraduate majors, more so than those who majored in other fields, think low public concern for emergency management will *not* reduce the significance of emergency management for city managers.

The third dependent variable, "Emergency Management skills," yielded a significant difference of means only in the category of race. With a probability of "t" score of .029, there is evidence that nonwhite city managers think emergency management planning skills are more important, while white city managers attach less importance to such skills. Very nearly significant was the "sector" variable. City managers who last worked in the private sector are somewhat more likely to judge emergency management skills as necessary than are managers who last worked in the public sector. However, the nonwhite category of race and the private sector category of sector both contain only 15 cases, but repeating, the difference of means test is sensitive and valid for categories as small as three cases.

Because the race variable shows significance on the "public concern" variable as well as on the "E. M. skills" variable, this may affirm a general claim made about disasters. Major emergencies frequently devastate less affluent communities, and have lead some to label disaster as "instant urban renewal."[9] Poorly built homes in locations made less desirable by higher disaster risk, such as in a floodplain that is regularly inundated, are often occupied by people of low income, just as older unreinforced buildings in central city areas are usually occupied by the poor. Poverty in the United States is a burden carried disproportionately by ethnic minorities. Consequently, it may be that nonwhite city managers working in municipalities with large concentrations of low income people who live in high disaster vulnerability circumstances are more aware of the importance of emergency management than are white city managers.[10]

The final difference of means test involved city experience with disaster. If a respondent reported that his or her city had requested and received FEMA disaster aid in the period 1980–85, those respondents were placed in a category we labeled "disaster." Those respondents who neither requested nor received FEMA disaster aid over the period were labeled "none." Table VII-6 shows that the "attention" and the "public concern" dependent variables are significant in the difference of means for "Received Disaster Aid." City managers who report receiving FEMA disaster aid in their cities are more likely to believe that emergency management should get more attention in the next ten years, when compared with city managers who had not requested or received FEMA aid. Moreover "disaster" category managers are more likely to believe that emergency management will remain important even if the general public does not think so.

To summarize the key findings of Table VII-6, there is some indication that managers "new" to the public sector tend to rate emergency management as more important than other managers. Managers who majored in political science or public administration as undergraduates, more so than others, tend to judge emergency management as important. Women, as well as ethnic and racial minority, managers also seem to be more interested in emergency management. Yet, the most responsive group of city managers proved to be those whose city requested and received FEMA aid after a disaster. Oddly, this same group is not apparently persuaded that the acquisition of emergency management skills is vitally important for city managers.

Regression Analysis

A regression analysis was run to determine the cumulative effect of the independent variables as a force that may account for city manager attitudes toward emergency management. In multiple regression one attempts to predict a single dependent variable from a number of independent variables. "Attention," "public concern," and "E.M. skills" were our dependent variables. In separate tests for each, using the independent variables of Table VII-6, multiple correlation (or R^2) scores were very low, about 2 to 4 percent of the variance. So the ability of the independent variables to explain the responses of city managers on emergency management-related questions was negligible.[11]

More definitive results were obtained by examining other attitudinal questions put to the city managers. To do this, 175 of the remaining attitude question scores were correlated with emergency management question scores. Those questions yielding response scores that correlated with emergency management question response scores, were entered into a regression equation. The cut-off point (above which correlations were judged significant) varied for each of the three emergency management questions. "Attention" correlations were used that ranged from .28 (cut-off) to .59 (highest). "Public concern" correlations between .25 (cut-off) and .40 (highest) were used. Finally, "E.M. skills" correlations were significant if they measured .40 (cut-off) to .52 (highest). The higher "E.M. skills" cut-off point of .40 was chosen because this question was highly correlated with other questions about skill acquisition.

A second regression analysis was then run that included those variables showing a "t" significance of .05 or less. The results of this analysis are shown in Table VII-7. In all three cases those variables that were individually correlated with each emergency management variable proved also to be collectively correlated with each emergency management dependent variable. As V.O. Key's "10 percent rule" states, if you can account for 10 percent or more of the variance, you've made a finding. In Table VII-7, each multiple correlation (R-squared) much exceeds 10 percent (or .10).

This means that city managers responded in a similar way on items that were statistically associated and that the chance this could have happened at random is less than one in a thousand. Admittedly, the beta weights or standardized coefficients are modest, but the amount of variance explained in each multiple correlation is high: 30 percent for "public concern," 40 percent for "E.M. skills," and 46 percent for "Attention." In the analysis below we will explain reasons why certain attitudinal variables are strongly statistically associated with each emergency management dependent variable.

TABLE VII-7

REGRESSION ANALYSIS
EMERGENCY MANAGEMENT VARIABLES
AND OTHER ATTITUDINAL VARIABLES

DEPENDENT VARIABLE "ATTENTION"

Attitudinal Variable	Coefficient	T Ratio	Prob of T	Beta	R2
City managers will spend more time using the City Council as advocates at the State level	.2073	4.2939	.0001	.2202	.46
In the next ten years:					
city managers will pay more attention to energy conservation	.2415	4.2347	.0001	.2430	
city managers will pay more attention to hazardous materials	.4205	7.1725	.0001	.4137	

"Attention" dependent variable	.6784	3.4866	.0003		

DEPENDENT VARIABLE: "PUBLIC CONCERN"

Attitudinal Variable	Coefficient	T Ratio	Prob of T	Beta	R2
In the last decade California local governments experienced a decline in the quality of City Councils because of increased partisanship	.1340	2.5886	.0051	.1505	.30
In the next ten years:					
California local governments will devote less attention to social service needs because of less revenue	.1520	2.6881	.0039	.1633	

DEPENDENT VARIABLE: "PUBLIC CONCERN" CONTINUED

Attitudinal Variable	Coefficient	T Ratio	Prob. of T	Beta	R2
governments will experience less conflict in their workforces	.2587	3.9159	.0001	.2432	
governments will experience a declining work ethic and a decline in productivity	.2564	5.0343	.0001	.2960	

"public concern" dependent variable	.9992	2.7474	.0033		

DEPENDENT VARIABLE: "E.M. SKILLS"

In the next ten years:

practitioners will need political skills in intergovernmental relations	.3126	4.1365	.0001	.2766	.40
practitioners will need planning skills	.3782	4.3194	.0001	.2842	
practitioners will need personal skills dealing with stress management	.2549	3.9750	.0001	.2425	
"E.M. skills" dependent variable	.9968	4.9507	.0001		

Regression Analysis Findings

The dependent variable "Attention" in Table VII-7 refers to a question that asked city managers whether they thought California local government would have to give more attention to emergency management in the next ten years. Table VII-7 shows that three attitudinal variables collectively account for 46 percent of the variance in the dependent variable response set called "Attention."

Emergency management has long been part of the intergovernmental policy process. This is especially true in California, where the state Office of Emergency Services works closely with the U.S. Federal Emergency Management Agency and with county emergency offices. Few cities have emergency services offices but most local officials know that when disaster strikes, cooperation with higher levels of government is necessary in securing needed assistance. Managers who indicated that city managers must spend more time using the City Council as advocates at the state level also believed that emergency management would have to receive more attention from California local government in the future. Agreement with the "advocates at the State level" question implies that these respondents see city relations with state agencies as very important. Since so much city postdisaster aid flows through state agencies, the link between responses to the two questions becomes apparent.

The second attitudinal variable in the "Attention" set of Table VII-7 asks if city managers will have to pay more attention to energy conservation in the next ten years. This was associated with the question of more attention to emergency management probably because California has several nuclear power plants producing electrical energy, and these facilities must maintain emergency warning and evacuation capabilities that often involve city governments and city resources.

The third attitudinal variable in the "Attention" set of Table VII-7 asks if city managers will have to pay more attention to hazardous materials problems in the next ten years. It is reasonable to expect that managers anticipating future problems with hazardous materials would also be concerned about emergency management. Hazardous materials production and transport accidents, as well as the severe problems posed by improper hazardous waste disposal, sometimes cause local emergencies or disasters. Many respondents may have experienced one or more hazardous materials emergencies.

Note that an "environmental awareness" question proved not to be statistically associated with the emergency management attention variable. One explanation may be that "energy conservation" and "hazardous materials" are more concrete phenomena than "environment," which is perceived as softer and more ambiguous.

The dependent variable "Public concern" in Table VII-7 refers to a question that asked city managers whether there would be a decreased emphasis on emergency management because of a lack of public concern. Here four attitudinal variables were individually and collectively associated with the dependent variable.

Here the substance of each variable is less important than the direction each implies. Attitudinal variables in this set all reflect the concept of decline or reduction. Respondents who expect a decline in the quality of city councils, a decline in attention to social service needs owing to less city revenue, and a decline in city government work ethic and productivity, also expect a decline in concern for emergency management. The question regarding conflict in government workforces also should be interpreted to connote decline because we phrased the question so that "less conflict" meant diminished vitality, not increased harmony.

We believe we have tapped a vein of pessimism among respondents. We interpret these expressions about decline to be a combination of pessimistic attitude and a reluctance to accept the increasing politicization of city manager work. Our previous analysis suggested that experienced city managers are not likely to see emergency management as important. They may feel this way in part because they see emergency management and other elements of city administration as an encroachment of political forces into their profession.

The dependent variable "E.M. skills" in Table VII-7 refers to the question that asked city managers to think about specific skills city administrators would need to have in the next ten years. Emergency management was listed as one of four items under planning skills. Here three attitudinal variables proved to be individually and collectively associated with the dependent variable.

Much like what was discovered in the "public concern" regression analysis above, managers who believed political skills in intergovernmental relations would be important over the next ten years were also likely to think that emergency management planning skills would be necessary in the future. Respondents who said practitioners will need more planning skills in the future also tended to hold that emergency management planning skills would be needed in the next ten years. It was particularly notable that city managers who indicated that practitioners will need more personal skills dealing with stress management were also likely to be those who said emergency management planning skills would be needed in the future. Obviously, coping with disaster imposes extraordinary management stress, particularly for the city manager.

CONCLUSION

The most important general finding of this study confirms what is already known about emergency management: city managers do not place a high priority on emergency management. Emergency management was not a topic raised by respondents in the original Delphi questionnaire. When it was included in the second and final evaluative questionnaire, few city managers judged it to be highly significant. Fear of an impending great earthquake and frequent experience with lesser disasters does not seem to have inspired city managers to place greater emphasis on emergency management.

Of course, not all city managers surveyed are unconcerned about emergency management. The data indicate that the attitudes of city managers toward emergency management vary widely. Most of the demographic variables do not help to explain this variation. However, city managers whose cities have requested and received FEMA disaster aid are more likely to consider emergency management essential than managers whose cities have not asked for or received FEMA aid. Also, women, as well as racial and ethnic minorities, tend to place more emphasis upon emergency management than do men and whites respectively. Those relatively new to the job of city manager also place more emphasis on emergency management than do those with more than seven years experience in city management. Northern California city managers, and those whose last job was in the private sector, tend to express more interest in emergency management than southern California city managers and long-term public sector employees respectively. Caution should be taken in interpreting some of the findings regarding demographics because some categories contained few cases and because the amount of variance explained in statistical analysis of the variables was small.

Stronger associations were evident in analysis of attitudinal, more than demographic, questions. As a group, city managers who are concerned about hazardous materials and energy conservation are also likely to think that emergency management deserves more local attention. Those who think the City Council should be used as an advocate in city relations with state agencies also tend to believe emergency management warrants more attention. This should be heartening for those who work in some domain of emergency management because it means there is a cohort of city managers willing and ready to engage in intergovernmental relations, a cohort that appreciates disaster potential and the need for preparedness. Yet, among city manager respondents there is also a pessimistic attitude stemming from an expected decline in city services, city revenue, and city worker productivity. This pessimism is associated with the belief that a lack of public concern will diminish the importance of local emergency management.

City managers may acknowledge the political risks that disasters hold for them. A recent study of a flood disaster in Wilkes-Barre, Pennsylvania, reported that the disaster mobilized the citizenry and forced a replacement of the city manager system itself in that local government. The disaster helped bring about a major shift in the community power structure.[12] This suggests that if city managers continue to ignore disaster threat, and emergency management that would help cope with this threat, they may be putting their jobs in jeopardy.

In California, unless a FEMA-declared emergency or disaster has struck the city manager's community, most city managers will not devote much attention to emergency management. Those city managers who think intergovernmental relations are important, those who believe hazardous materials pose threats to their jurisdictions, and those managers who are women or minority people, are likely to be those who plan for local emergencies and disasters. We fear, however, that most city managers will not be compelled to undertake emergency management until after disaster has struck their cities.

Notes

[1]We wish to thank the Faculty Small Grant Research Program, California State University, Fullerton, for funding this project. This article is a revision of a paper originally presented at the national meeting of the American Society for Public Administration, Boston, Massachusetts, March 1987. We also wish to thank our colleague, Alana Northrop, for her help and advice.

[2]For a discussion of the Delphi method, see Harold A. Linstone and Murray Turoff, eds., *The Delphi Method* (Reading, Mass.: The Addison-Wesley Publishing Company, Inc., 1975).

[3]The questions were as follows:

1. Over the course of the last decade, what have been the major changes you have experienced in your role as a city manager in California?

2. Over the course of the last decade, what have been the major changes you have witnessed in city government in California?

3. What do you think will be the major changes in the role of the California city manager in the next ten years?

4. What do you think will be the major changes in California city government in the next ten years?

5. What skills should public administration programs teach their students to enable them to cope with changes in the next ten years?

[4]As reported by Richard J. Stillman II in "Local Public Management in Transition," *Public Management* (May 1982): 2–9.

[5]For a more complete analysis of the city manager profile, see Bott and Sutphen, "A Profile of California's City Managers," *Western City* LXIII (June 1987): 13, 18–20.

[6]For a general discussion of attitudes toward the policy issues of emergency management, see particularly James D. Wright and Peter H. Rossi, "The Politics of Natural Disaster: State and Local Elites," pp. 45–67 in *Social Science and Natural Hazards* (Cambridge, Mass.: Abt Books, 1981. See also, Wright et al., *The Social and Psychological Consequences of a Natural Disaster: A Longitudinal Study of Hurricane Audrey* (Washington, DC: National Academy of Sciences/National Research Council, Disaster Study No. 18, 1963), and J. Eugene Haas, ed., *Reconstruction Following Disaster* (Cambridge, Mass.: The MIT Press, 1977).

[7]W. John Moore, "After the Deluge," *National Journal* (April 18, 1987), p. 933.

[8]Data supplied by Region 9, Federal Emergency Management Agency, San Francisco.

[9]C. Dacy and H. Kunreuther, *The Economics of Natural Disasters: Implications for Federal Policy* (New York: The Free Press, 1969).

[10]For a further elaboration of the economic effects of a disaster upon a poor community, see Sutphen, "Lake Elsinore Disaster: The Slings and Arrows of Outrageous Fortune," *Disasters* (March 1983): 194–201.

[11]For an explanation of regression analysis, see Norman H. Nie, et al., *SPSS*, 2nd edition (New York: McGraw Hill, Inc., 1975), Chapter 20.

[12]Robert P. Wolensky, *Power, Policy, and Disaster: The Political-Organizational Impact of a Major Flood* (National Science Foundation Grant #CEE 8113529; 1985). But compare Joseph G. Marone and Edward J. Woodhouse, *Averting Catastrophe* (Berkeley: University of California Press, 1986) which argues that low public concern is understandable in light of political and scientific systems which have operated relatively effectively to prevent disasters.

Chapter VIII

THE ROLE OF THE
EMERGENCY SERVICES COORDINATOR
IT STARTS WHEN THE EMERGENCY ENDS

FRANCES E. WINSLOW

INTRODUCTION

"Emergency services coordinator" is not a career choice that is promoted in graduate school. Most people have no idea what it even means. It conjures up images of ambulances and emergency rooms, but then most people have never heard of it. As the emergency services coordinator in a medium size American city, my role has been a mixture of administration, legislative action, liaison, legal writing, and public information resource. Is this a career choice?

I often ask myself that question when I think about one emergency incident in particular. After accepting this position and its carefully defined set of goals, I soon discovered that there was a whole area of responsibility after an emergency that no one had ever mentioned. Beyond the duties of this position in time of earthquake or major public safety emergency, I am not sure anyone has given much thought to the many other responsibilities of this post. Since confronting one of the largest hazardous materials clean-up operations ever, and seeing it through to its complete resolution, I think I have learned some lessons that might be profitably shared with others in this "profession."

THE PIPELINE BURST

On November 22, 1986, a major southern California underground gasoline pipeline ruptured and disgorged 500,000 gallons of unleaded supreme into the adjacent flood control channel. The break occurred in Tustin, 100 yards from the border of my city, Irvine. The gasoline gushed down Peters Canyon Wash toward a tributary of Upper Newport Bay, a major wildlife refuge area six miles from the accident site.

155

Orange County Fire Department (OCFD), the first agency responder, and the Orange County Environmental Management Agency (EMA), owners of the channel system, quickly constructed two dams that halted the huge gasoline flow. The first dam confined a portion of the spill to the flood channel thereby preventing pollution of Upper Newport Bay's delicate salt marsh ecology. The second impoundment, situated in Peters Canyon Wash, protected the Alton dam and helped to check the flow of freshwater into the gasoline contaminated pool.

In the first 18 hours after the gasoline discharge the OCFD and the Irvine Police Department handled key emergency duties. An Incident Command Post was set up near the scene. Fire officials used the petroleum industry's emergency notification system to identify and contact the pipeline owner, to determine the exact characteristics of the leaking substance, and to locate the nearest shut-off valve along the pipeline. Fire department personnel attempted to carefully restrict and control the flow, fully aware of the danger of fire and explosion.

The San Diego Pipeline Company, owner of the pipeline, was notified about the incident 40 minutes after the initial fire department response had begun. The firm went about immediate mitigation, remediation, and clean-up. According to federal officials, this was the first time that a private corporation attempted to restore a damaged ecology to its original state. The company called in IT, a business that specializes in hazardous waste removal. Within 24 hours 98 percent of the spilled gas had been vacuumed up. The gas and water mixture was hauled off in tanker trucks to a facility that reclaimed much of the gasoline. During the early phases of the clean-up special cellulose fiber was floated on the surface of the channel in order to absorb hydrocarbons. Booms composed of this fiber trapped the gas as it moved downstream. Pumps at the Alton dam also helped skim some of the gasoline from the surface water.

MY INITIAL DUTIES

At first it seemed that there was no need for my services. I was not even initially called, but on the first work day after the spill (November 24), I arrived to find a request from the mayor for information on the pipeline rupture. He needed to make a public statement at the next day's city council meeting. This began my odyssey. For ten successive weeks my professional life revolved around the pipeline accident. Every morning I walked along the banks of the channel to monitor odor, aesthetics, and the progress of the clean-up crews. I became concerned about the many residents who crossed police lines and braved pungent gasoline smells in order to ride bicycles on the trail next to the channel. On Thanksgiving Day I biked a trail that enabled me to trace the path of a pipeline constructed to divert fresh water around the spill site. On Christmas Day my daily pilgrimage to the channel was made between opening gifts and serving turkey. On New Year's Eve I led a team of three pipeline company engineers through three city departments in search of paperwork and permissions needed to remove tainted dirt that had formed the dam during clean-up and containment. I even ran down to the clean-up site following the first rainstorm after the spill.

For someone who wasn't called out to the initial emergency, I got pretty involved. How did my role develop? To be honest, I improvised as I went along and I learned in the process that there is no simple job description for the emergency services coordinator.

When I first investigated the scene I realized that the pressure of responding to the emergency had prevented any one agency from collecting all of the facts about the incident. My discussion with OCFD's public information officer and my calls to people at the county Environmental Management Agency, at the Irvine Police Department, and at the San Diego Pipeline Company all proved to be invaluable as the clean-up progressed. I also phoned the Office of the State Fire Marshall, an agency empowered to oversee hazardous liquid transmission in California.

The Problem Of Tainted Soil

By December 1, the Regional Water Quality Board determined that the greatest threat to water quality was from the tainted dirt in the dam used to block the channel. That dirt had been exposed to gasoline for a period of nine days and had absorbed a quantity of gasoline and related hydrocarbons. About 100 cubic yards of dirt had to be excavated from the channel. Moreover, the earthen dam built above the spill was strained by increased irrigation water run-off from farming operations during this unseasonal dry period. Furthermore, a rainstorm could have washed the tainted dirt down the flood control channel and into Upper Newport Bay. San Diego Pipeline company was ordered to remove it. The firm retained Intellus, a Fluor Corporation subsidiary, to advise on how to go about the job.

Several questions arose concerning the best method for treating the tainted dirt. While the dirt could have been simply shipped to a landfill, the technology exists to return the soil almost to its original state. In the first method, the tainted soil is containerized, transported, and buried at a certified hazardous materials storage site. In the second method, referred to as land farming, techniques are used that aerate the soil enabling the gasoline to vaporize. Once vaporization is complete, the soil can then be safely used as fill or for agricultural purposes. The pipeline company and its contractor opted for the land farming aeration alternative.

The pipeline company and its contractor began a search for an appropriate site on which to recycle the contaminated earth. When they contacted the Irvine city manager's office, I was asked to serve as city liaison during all phases of the dirt removal operation. An Intellus representative called me about the question of land farming on a city-owned site, but no city-owned property proved to be appropriate for soil aeration.

The first land farming site selected by San Diego Pipeline was located in Tustin but was owned by Sante Fe Railroad Company, a firm with business ties to the pipeline company. The dirt was first piled on a shoulder of the flood control channel. There it was allowed to aerate and the trapped gasoline began to evaporate. Once the flashpoint rose to a relatively safe 140 degrees (Fahrenheit), the dirt was trucked to its treatment site in Tustin. There the soil was spread over a wide area, again allowed to aerate, but with daily discing. This allowed the remaining gasoline to evaporate rendering the dirt safe for farming or clean fill. Because the dirt had to be conveyed over Irvine city streets, I assisted San Diego Pipeline in securing advice from the Irvine Police Department.

Later, testing by Water Quality experts revealed that residual gasoline was still in portions of the flood channel and its embankments. San Diego Pipeline was asked to remove more soil. The site had been approved for this type of use by the Orange County Health Department, but not yet by Irvine's city departments. I assisted the pipeline executives in obtaining approvals from the city manager, the Police Department traffic section, and the soil removal control section of the Department of Public Works. On January 2 earth moving operations began in the channel and continued for several weeks. By the end of the month the dirt that had been shipped to Tustin was ready for use as fill. I helped to promote interaction between company officials and city staff over what to do with the cleansed soil at the Irvine location. Public, private, and interagency cooperation, both during the clean-up (response phase) and the soil treatment (recovery phase), was exceptional.

Legal Agreements, Permit Approvals And Public Information

I investigated legal matters with the city staff and city attorney. I then drafted a 16-point legal agreement protecting the city from lawsuits that could arise from soil relocation or the aeration operation. It included a hold-harmless clause, a performance bond for the soil aeration project, and the addition of the city as a coinsured party to the pipeline company's insurance policy. It also required San Diego Pipeline to reach proper agreements with other government agencies exercising oversight in the clean-up. For example, the county Environmental Health Agency had to approve the soil aeration site, the city Department of Public Works had to approve the soil removal and grading operations, and the Irvine Police Department traffic section had to approve the route to be followed by the trucks conveying the contaminated dirt. It was part of my job to make sure that San Diego Pipeline complied with all aspects of the agreement.

To oversee the implementation of the agreement I had to deal with many public agencies and many departments of city government. To speed municipal action, I spent New Year's Eve leading pipeline company representatives through a variety of city departments. Because the State Fire Marshall has enforcement powers over liquid transmission pipelines in California and is an agent of the federal government, I was in regular contact with engineers of this office who oversaw the entire pipeline repair and clean-up process. The California Department of Fish and Game played an official role in clean-up supervision and its people evaluated the wildlife loss caused by the spill. Technical monitoring of clean-up activities was carried out by state water quality personnel and county EMA inspectors. The OCFD hazardous materials team frequently visited the accident site to check for vapors. At first, I was in daily contact with these authorities. Later, contact was weekly, but at times I was forced to become an arbiter among contending authorities and between those with differing viewpoints.

With an issue as politically sensitive as a hazardous materials spill, it was crucial to keep the city manager and elected officials fully informed about all activities related to the clean-up. I handled resident inquiries and I supplied the assistant city manager with up-to-date information he needed to effectively deal with the press. I provided timely memos when any change in the project looked eminent. These were intended to help city leaders confidently discuss the recovery operations with residents, the broader public, and the press. They also needed to understand the nature of the activities under way so that they could act in the best interest of Irvine's citizenry.

PUBLIC SERVICE COMMISSION REVIEWS THE SPILL

In mid-December, the Irvine City Council asked its Public Safety Commission to review the entire spill incident. Because I am on the staff of this commission, I invited representatives of the pipeline company, the State Fire Marshall's Office, the EMA, and the OCFD to publicly discuss the event at a commission meeting. Company officials came and outlined their response plan, clean-up effort, and plans for installation of extra shut-off valves along the line.[1] The State Fire Marshall representative stated that extensive metallurgical studies of the ruptured pipe section were being performed by his agency. He remarked that the failure of an electric resistance weld seems to have been a manufacturing defect. County agency people then reviewed their responses to the accident. This was the only public forum in which both the company and emergency responders explained their actions. This open sharing of information facilitated development of recommendations to mitigate future similar problems.

I drafted the commission report. It recommended: (1) that the State Fire Marshall's office ask the pipeline company to install an additional check-valve in the pipe between the county high point at Mission Viejo and at Irvine, a local low point along the line, (2) that this same office petition the company to install an automated flow monitoring system that would pinpoint the location of future problems more quickly, (3) that this office get the company to report back on a quarterly basis its progress in implementing requested changes, (4) that the Orange County Fire Department explore with the pipeline company ways to more quickly respond when valves must be shut-off,[2] (5) that the city staff request funds from the council to pay for incorporation of storm drain data into the city's computerized map-making system, thereby better tracking hazardous materials flows that enter city storm drains.

Lawsuits And Insurance Claims

Several weeks after the incident began legal issues started to crop up. The few companies and businesses which had to close as a result of the pipeline rupture, sustained financial losses. I became an information center for businessmen who filed insurance claims or who made claims against the pipeline company. As is common in emergency situations, a great deal of misinformation circulated through the affected community. Clarifying facts, dates, times, and the nature of the emergency was an important part of my work. Alleviating public concern helped to reduce unwarranted claims against the city and, indirectly, the company.

Filming The Incident

Finally, visual documentation of the event unexpectedly became a part of my job as well. Soon after the mayor first asked me for information about the spill, Irvine Police Sergeant Phil Povey and I traveled along the path of the spill with a video camera. We filmed a hole where the outflow of gasoline was still visible, a trench where repaired pipe would soon go, and the path of the gasoline down the channel. Our shots included the two dams, clean-up work then underway, and spill remnants. We thought our video might be useful for training purposes. However, this footage became a key visual record of the spill for the Public Safety Commission, particularly when clean-up had progressed to the point that there was little remaining visible evidence of the spill or its effects. The film went out to public agencies and to the pipeline company. It has become a video archive of the event. Aerial photos of the site taken by an Irvine police officer have also been duplicated for various public agencies and for the company. In addition, my 35mm photographs of the phases of clean-up, including soil removal, land farming operations, and channel bank restoration, furnish a visual progress report. My Minolta has recorded, or will soon record, valve and monitoring equipment installation, hydroseeding, and other continuing activities at the site.[3]

Interorganization Cooperation

From the outset, the OCFD, the EMA, the State Fire Marshall, and people from the state Fish and Game office worked together to contain the spill and to protect the environment. The U.S. Coast Guard was on stand-by in the event any gasoline flowed into the bay. Police officers from Irvine and Tustin, as well as the Tustin Air Base Provost Marshall[4], rerouted traffic around the spill site and evacuated occupants of military housing that bordered the flood control channel. Workers at an industrial site adjacent to the breached pipeline were also evacuated. As soon as San Diego Pipeline workers arrived at the scene they took responsibility for the clean-up. IT people worked around the clock to limit the area of spill and to protect sensitive environmental areas. To continue restoration work, San Diego Pipeline maintained an on-site professional staff presence through all phases of the clean-up. The firm has cooperated with the U.S. Environmental Protection Agency, county environmental and health agencies, and other units called in.

CONCLUSION

I found that my tasks fell into five general areas of responsibility: (1) legal protection of the city, (2) coordination with various levels of government, (3) information conduit to the city manager and to elected officials, (4) information source for other concerned parties, and (5) developer of visual documentation.

First, legal protection of the city through all phases of the incident was paramount. The drafting and monitoring of compliance with the legal agreement approved by the city and the pipeline company was a significant contribution. It helped shield the city from liability, most particularly the section that moved the city under the company's insurance umbrella.

Second, maintaining coordination among and between county and state agencies in their dealings with Irvine departments was crucial to the success of the endeavor. At times I helped direct the flow of interagency communications. I compiled and shared information resources that helped to document all phases of the operation.

Third, it was important to keep the Irvine city manager, mayor, and city council apprised of new developments as the clean-up progressed. My first-hand knowledge gathered from frequent visits to the site made me a key source of information. Each time the operation moved to a new stage, or when any activity began that would be noted by local people, I directed a memo to the assistant city manager. This helped him take questions from the media or the public and it enabled Irvine's elected officials to be more responsive to inquiring constituents.

Fourth, owners and tenants of effected buildings used me as a resource when they gathered evidence for claims they wanted to make against San Diego Pipeline, or for claims they wanted to file with their own insurance companies. Several businesses lost production time because of the spill and others experienced minor disruptions in the days following the spill. It was essential that Irvine city government be an information resource that was perceived as accurate and unbiased. No less important was to provide public warning about the nature of the spill and, later, to allay unwarranted public fears about aftereffects.

Fifth and finally, the collection of written data and visual documentation was critical. Once a clean-up operation is completed, judgments of its effects become a matter of opinion or conjecture. Good logged and dated photographic records depicting effected areas can provide unbiased information which can be used in court, in public hearings, or in insurance investigations. This visual documentation assists the city if lawsuits are later made against it.

Emergency response operations lasted 18 hours, but coordination of recovery and mitigation activities have lasted three months and will continue for most of the year. At this writing, the gasoline has been removed and water quality in the channel has returned to its prespill condition. The healthy salt marsh and pristine Upper Newport Bay show no effects from the gasoline spill. Hydroseeding and animal replacement will complete the restoration process. Later tests by Water Quality officials will determine whether or not the clean-up is designated complete. The Office of the State Fire Marshall will soon decide when new valves and a monitoring system should be installed by San Diego Pipeline.[5]

It seems that the emergency services coordinator's job really begins when the immediate emergency ends! Can a job description incorporate all the duties and tasks that emerged for me in the aftermath of this event? I doubt it. Can a job description anticipate what emergency service coordinators need to know for other types of disaster agents and hazard incidents? Probably not. Nevertheless, I can set forth a skills and activity list that might be a good guide in hiring someone for this position. The ideal candidate should be an administrative generalist familiar with civil law and intergovernmental agency relations, an excellent writer, a knowledgeable negotiator, someone with "connections" in virtually every city operating department, and an individual possessing outstanding interpersonal skills. But, obviously, some of this can only be learned or acquired from on-the-job experience. My experience leads me to conclude that one should add "flexible" and "willing to learn" to the list of emergency service coordinator job qualifications.

Notes

[1]The line that ruptured was 23 years old and 10 inches in diameter. The company's new 16-inch line was implanted across Irvine one year before the Tustin break, but was not completed in the area of the spill.

[2]This may enable firefighters to assume more immediate control of emergency shut-off valves.

[3]So, when looking for an emergency service coordinator, remember that photography and video taping should be on the skills list.

[4]The spill happened across from a Marine Corps Air Station located in Tustin.

[5]All recovery and mitigation efforts were completed by June 30, 1988.

Chapter IX

POLITICAL LEADERSHIP AND CANADIAN EMERGENCY PLANNING: THE ROLE OF THE MAYOR

JOSEPH SCANLON

INTRODUCTION

Many scholarly studies suggest that a key to effective local emergency planning is the active support of the mayor or chief executive officer. But this assertion is seldom tested empirically. This study compiles evidence to test the validity of this claim. Nineteen Canadian emergency or disaster incidents were examined. For each it was determined whether the mayor or local chief executive was actively involved in, or measurably in support of, emergency activity *before* the incident occurred in their locality. Leaders who were, were labeled "active," and leaders who were not, were labeled "inactive."[1]

Then, the 19 incidents were grouped by "active" and "inactive" mayor categories. Within each group an investigation was made to find out if an emergency plan existed and was used when the emergency occurred. For example, was a call-out system used to initiate emergency response, was a community Emergency Operations Centre set in operation, were interagency communications carried out in some form, and was some clearly recognized authority structure apparent during the emergency?

The central premise of this investigation was to determine whether "active" mayor communities had a more effective emergency response than did "inactive" mayor communities. A related premise was to learn whether "active" mayor communities evidenced effective emergency response in general.

Sources Of Information

Data for this study were collected by the Emergency Communications Research Unit (ECRU) at Carleton University in Ottawa, Canada. ECRU has conducted quick-response field research on emergency communications since 1970. This research is funded mainly by the federal crisis agency, Emergency Preparedness Canada. Among the types of incidents studied have been tornadoes, snow emergencies, floods, hazardous materials accidents, a plane crash, a hostage taking, windstorm, mudslide, building explosion, and major fire.

Information was gathered by observation, by interview, and by use of written records. Observation was possible because the ECRU is often able to get researchers to the site during an emergency. ECRU people were in Sydney, Nova Scotia, the day of a devastating windstorm. The unit had people in Port Alice, British Columbia, while it was being evacuated under threat of mudslide. There researchers traveled in by boat. ECRU was present in Oak Lake during a hostage taking. Unit researchers were at the Medicine Hat and Petawawa emergency operations centres while these centres were still attempting to deal with the hazardous materials problems posed by their respective train derailments. ECRU had investigators in Pemberton during flooding, in Gander the day of Canada's worst aviation disaster, and in Edmonton the morning after it had experienced major tornado damage.

Interviews were done while memories were fresh. Observations and interviews were corroborated by examination of records, stored either on paper or on audio tape.

Literature On Disaster And Local Government

The scholarly literature about disaster includes little on local government or on the role of the mayor in emergencies. This applies to the disciplines of sociology[2] and political science.[3] Petak states, "Public administration, as a discipline, has generally neglected to consider emergency management within the mainstream of its activities.[4]

In his classic work, *Canadian Municipal Government,* K. Grant Crawford claimed, "in an emergency the mayor has to make final decisions," but he says nothing else about the mayor's role.[5] Some suggest that the mayor's role is often overlooked: "Not all municipal agencies were seen to play important disaster roles . . . even the roles of the city manager and mayor were not clearly defined."[6]

Others see the problem differently:

[I]nvestigators have concluded that the major barrier to improved preparedness is simply the apathy of political and administrative officials.[7]

Managers were more interested by far in discussing the general climate for disaster planning . . . rather than specific demands. . . . To many the salient issue was whether disaster planning has any priority at all.[8]

In 1976, Scanlon, Jefferson, and Sproat observed that local emergency planning requires outside pressure because local authorities, "are too involved in day-to-day responsibilities to worry about planning for emergencies that may never happen." They concluded that the pressure needed to stimulate local emergency planning had to come from a higher authority.[9] Cigler said much the same thing from the American context: " . . . the governments least likely to perceive emergency management as a key priority—local governments—are at centerstage in terms of responsibility for emergency management. . . . One means of increasing local . . . emergency management is state involvement."[10]

CANADIAN MAYORS

Canadian local government varies from community to community and from province to province. Often there is an elected council and mayor. Sometimes, instead of the title "mayor" there is some other name for the head of council: reeve, warden, chairperson, etc. In Prince Edward County, for example, the senior elected official holds the office of warden. "Mayor," is used here as a generic term encompassing all these titles. Moreover, the cases included in this study involve cities, towns, counties, and some special governmental entities. For example, the case study of Courtenay actually investigates the Regional Municipality of Comox-Strathcona.

Mayors have one vote on council like everyone else. But, while most council members are elected from specific geographic sublocal areas, usually called "wards," the mayor is elected by the entire local electorate [at-large] or by council. Because the mayor represents the entire electorate, and for additional reasons, the mayor is undoubtedly *primus inter pares* or "first among equals." Whether in a general election or in important council votes, the mayor is often the only person who can mobilize broad support.

As chairperson the mayor controls many council procedures. Even more important, the mayor is often the municipality's chief administrator.[11]

The mayor also represents the council on bodies such as the semi-independent police commission.

Finally, Canadian mayors are treated as "very important people." The mayor speaks for the municipality on formal occasions, welcomes visitors, hosts civic receptions, and represents the municipality at functions held in other places. The mayor "personifies the whole government in the minds of the electorate." The social status that the mayor holds as first citizen and the mayor's appearances on special occasions "as the ceremonial head of the municipality, all serve to emphasize his [or her] position."[12]

The mayor is able to set local priorities, though sometimes he or she may have to work through some form of an executive committee.[13]

Features Of Emergency Planning

The following five elements are commonly considered essential components of emergency response.

First, an emergency plan is necessary. While this may seem obvious, many municipalities have no emergency plan. Sometimes municipal officials say they have an emergency plan but when they are asked to produce one, they cannot.

Second, a call-out system is needed. Plans work only if those mentioned in the plan are notified when an emergency occurs. There must be a call-out procedure that works if an emergency response is to be effective.

Third, an emergency operations centre (EOC) should be part of emergency response. In a crisis various political officials and agency representatives must meet and share information. Drabek reported that "no other structural element contributed as much to the degree of coordination attained," as did an EOC.[14]

Fourth, a communications system is essential. Key agency personnel must be able to communicate with one another. "There needs to be an established," or rapidly assembled communications system, "so various disaster agencies can work together."[15]

Fifth and finally, there must be effective leadership in emergencies. There should be a recognized authority structure for emergency response.

THE EMERGENCY INCIDENTS

The 19 incidents analyzed here were scattered across six of Canada's ten provinces: Alberta, British Columbia, Newfoundland, Nova Scotia,

Ontario, and Quebec.[16] They extend from Newfoundland on the Atlantic coast to Vancouver Island on the Pacific coast. The range of municipality sizes in this study is equally great. There are hamlets, like Port Alice or Nickabeau, medium-sized cities such as North Bay and Sydney, and major cities like Mississauga and Edmonton. The time span for the 19 incidents begins with the St. John's snowstorm of March 11, 1974 and ends with the Edmonton tornado of July 31, 1987.

Snowstorms

Two snowstorms appear on the incident list. The St. John's, Newfoundland, snowstorm, mentioned above, forced the closing of schools and businesses. Movement overland was possible only by snowmobile. The snow accumulation was so great that people had to dig their way out of their homes. The city proclaimed an emergency.

Another snowstorm partially shut down Prince Edward County, Ontario, in late January 1977. In some areas snowdrifts reached nine metres, or almost 30 feet, in height. Schools and businesses closed in this storm as well. Roads were impassable for days and farmers could neither ship hogs to market nor get their milk picked up for distribution.

Windstorms And Tornadoes

Three tornadoes and a major windstorm were also among the emergencies analyzed. On October 20, 1974, Sydney, Nova Scotia, experienced a windstorm that knocked out electric, telephone, and water utilities. Many homes and businesses were damaged. One residential area had to be evacuated. It took several days to repair and restore services.

On August 7, 1979 Woodstock, Ontario, was hit by a tornado that caused many injuries and widespread devastation. Homes and businesses were destroyed, power was knocked out, the city's water supply was cut off, and roads were blocked by debris. Compounding problems was the loss of ambulance radio, the malfunctioning of police radio, and an intermittently successful fire department call-out system. About 180 people went to the hospital with injuries.

Another tornado struck Nickabeau, Quebec on July 15, 1984. It tore apart a Roman Catholic parish church, damaged other buildings, and injured many people.[17]

Perhaps most destructive was a tornado that devastated the east side of

Canada's largest northern city. On July 31, 1987 Edmonton, Alberta, was smashed by both a tornado and an accompanying rainstorm. Industrial facilities were ripped up, power and phone lines were knocked down, hazardous chemicals were discharged from damaged tanks, and roads were blocked with water and debris. Flooding was extensive. Twenty-seven deaths and between 350 and 400 injuries were attributed to the tornado disaster.

Explosions Or Fires In Buildings

On January 8, 1975 an office building in North Bay, Ontario, exploded as a result of a natural gas leak. Eight died and 23 were injured in the blast. Telephone systems were jammed as thousands tried to call each other and traffic was tied up as many people attempted to travel to the scene.

A nursing home fire in Goulds, Newfoundland, on December 26, 1976 killed all 21 of the facility's residents. The home was 12 kilometres from St. John's, the provincial capital. City police, firefighters, and hospital staff responded to the tragedy. Provincial officials also were involved.

Mudslide

On November 12, 1975 Port Alice, British Columbia, was evacuated after warm weather and heavy rains caused a mudslide. Ensuing floods swept away a bridge on the only road between Port Alice and the closest neighboring town 64 kilometres away.

Hostage Taking

Oak Lake, Manitoba, was virtually forced to a halt after two persons shot three Royal Canadian Mounted Police (RCMP) officers and then took three hostages, one the village's physician. Beginning on January 23, 1978, the incident lasted four days.

Floods

Heavy rain and warm temperatures caused flash flooding in and around Terrace, British Columbia, on October 30, 1978. Flood waters knocked out all bridges of the Trans-Canada Highway in the area, ruptured a natural gas pipeline, and undermined railroad trackage. The incident temporarily isolated Terrace.

Princeton, British Columbia, experienced an unseasonably warm early January thaw that led to ice break-up and flooding along two rivers. The 1984 incident triggered both warnings and evacuations of low lying areas. The nearby Trans-Canada Highway was temporarily closed.

On October 7, 1984 another flood struck Pemberton, British Columbia, when heavy rain caused rivers to wash over their dykes. There were evacuations in the valley and the town. Several campers were isolated when roads were washed out.

Hazardous Substance Incidents

Among the five hazardous substance accidents investigated here, Mississauga's posed a threat to the most people. On November 10, 1979 this Ontario city experienced a train derailment that led to a fire, a series of propane explosions, and the spilling of chlorine, styrene, and toulene, each dangerous to humans. The evacuation that followed was considered to be the largest in peace-time history.

In Courtenay, British Columbia, another railroad tanker leaked propane following a collision just south of the town. The area of the accident was evacuated immediately. A second problem involved diesel fuel from the collision. It flowed toward an ocean-front area where salmon were plentiful, thus threatening an important local resource. The Courtenay incident began on January 7, 1983.

Three days later another railroad tank car leaked a large volume of gasoline in Curling, a suburb of Corner Brook, Newfoundland. The gasoline flowed into sewers and basements, forcing a local evacuation.

On January 7, 1984 a freight train rolling through Medicine Hat, Alberta, broke apart, collided with adjacent trains, and overturned numerous railroad cars. A fire and hazardous substance discharge led to evacuation of several areas of the city.

When a train derailed and caught fire in Petawawa, Ontario, on February 24, 1985, corrosive acids billowed up in the smoke. The incident led to evacuations of areas surrounding the derailment and for a time forced a nearby Canadian Forces Base and Petawawa to prepare for an evacuation.

Aviation Disaster

On December 12, 1985 a U.S. military charter jetliner crashed outside Gander, Newfoundland just after take-off. All 254 people on board were killed, most of them soldiers. A stubborn fire resulted and for a time Gander Lake, the city's main water supply, was threatened with pollution by unignited jet fuel flowing from the crash area.[18]

MAYORS AND EMERGENCY PLANNING

Having furnished an overview of the incidents, the actions each mayor took before each incident will be examined. As stated earlier, the incidents were grouped on the basis of whether the mayor was involved in emergency planning or not, before the emergency incident occurred. In the end, each group will be compared.

Mayors were judged to be involved in emergency planning before the incident in six of the 19 communities. They were Sydney, Corner Brook, Medicine Hat, Pemberton, Gander, and Edmonton. Therefore, these six were classified as "active" mayor communities and the remaining 13 were categorized as "inactive" mayor communities. These designations should not be misinterpreted. "Active" or "Inactive" status was determined by whether mayors engaged in predisaster emergency *planning* activity, or not. In nearly every case, mayors were deeply involved in emergency *response* at the time of the incident itself.

When all the communities were examined with respect to use of the five elements of emergency response, the results were striking. All six "active" communities employed each of the five elements needed for effective emergency response. Of the 13 "inactive" communities, only Mississauga exhibited all five elements. In four of the "active" communities, it was the mayor who was responsible for planning. That is, in Sydney, Corner Brook, Medicine Hat, and Pemberton, it was the mayor who brought emergency planning to the community. These mayors did not necessarily do the planning themselves, but instead provided the leadership and impetus to undertake emergency planning. For example, in Sydney the work was done by a community planner. In Corner Brook, a retired Royal Canadian Mounted Police officer did the work and in Medicine Hat, a social service administrator took on the task.

All six "active" communities had prearranged emergency operations centres (EOC) and all but Pemberton had installed interagency communi-

TABLE IX-1

INVOLVEMENT OF THE MAYOR IN EMERGENCY RESPONSE

Yes = Involved, No = Not Involved

Time Order	Community	Incident Type	Before Incident	During Incident
1.	St. John's	snowstorm	No	Yes
2.	Sydney	windstorm	Yes	Yes
3.	North Bay	bldg. explosion	No	No
4.	Port Alice	mudslide, flood	Yes	Yes
5.	Goulds	fire	No	No
6.	Prince Edward County	snowstorm	No	Yes
7.	Oak Lake	hostage taking	No	No
8.	Terrace	flood	No	Yes
9.	Woodstock	tornado	No	Yes
10.	Mississauga	hazmat derailment	No	Yes
11.	Courtenay	hazmat derailment	No	No
12.	Corner Brook	hazmat tanker leak	Yes	Yes
13.	Princeton	ice jam, flood	No	Yes
14.	Medicine Hat	hazmat derailment	Yes	Yes
15.	Pemberton	flood	Yes	Yes
16.	Petawawa	hazmat derailment	No	Yes
17.	Nickabeau	tornado	No	Yes
18.	Gander	air crash	Yes	Yes
19.	Edmonton	tornado	Yes	Yes

cations equipment before the incident took place. In Pemberton, agency officials brought their own radios to the EOC.[19]

Only two "inactive" mayor communities had anything comparable. Mississauga initially used a mobile police command post but it did not provide enough space for all those involved in the response. It took almost 24 hours to set up an adequate EOC there. Petawawa eventually established an EOC at a nearby Canadian Forces Base. Petawawa's mayor, who was out of town at the time, got involved in the emergency response by telephone.

Community Differences

In "active" mayor communities the prearranged emergency response system not only existed before the incident, but worked effectively during the incident. For example, in Sydney a special communications channel allowed the mayor to put the emergency system into effect before the storm struck. In Corner Brook, the RCMP opened a radio channel to the EOC and to all key agencies operating on-site, just as planned. The base station was at the mayor's office.

In Gander, key agencies had people on-site and at the EOC. When airport radios lost contact with radios on-site, two back-up radio systems were immediately established and used. In Edmonton, when emergency medical people at the disaster scene reported that there were vehicles available for emergency transport but devoid of insurance and appropriate licenses, police and city financial officers at the EOC resolved the problem within minutes. In all six communities the mayor was regularly at the EOC when the emergency was in effect.

All 19 communities experienced emergency response problems, but in those classified as "inactive" mayor, problems seemed more serious. In Port Alice an evacuation began spontaneously. In Prince Edward County, police could not talk with highway crews and the highway department could not locate its snowplows in the field. In Terrace, emergency officials did not know there was a flood crisis until they heard about it in a local radio broadcast. In Woodstock's tornado experience there was no initial coordination of emergency response.

During Princeton's flood each agency used its own operations centre. Things got so confused that an evacuation was conducted without the mayor's knowledge, without police involvement, and with fire department personnel instructing people that there was a warning in effect, not an evacuation. During Oak Lake's hostage taking an ambulance crew picked up one of the abductors, but the police were not informed about it at the time. In the Goulds nursing home fire, the city fire department, which handles 911 emergency calls, failed to inform the RCMP about the incident.

TABLE IX-2

ELEMENTS PRESENT IN EMERGENCY RESPONSE

Yes = Present, No = Not Present, ? = Unknown

Time Order	Community	Plan	Call-Out	Com.-Sys.*	EOC	Leader**
ACTIVE MAYOR COMMUNITIES						
2.	Sydney	Yes	Yes	Yes	Yes	Yes
12.	Corner Brook	Yes	Yes	Yes	Yes	Yes
14.	Medicine Hat	Yes	Yes	Yes	Yes	Yes
15.	Pemberton	Yes	Yes	Yes	Yes	Yes
18.	Gander	Yes	Yes	Yes	Yes	Yes
19.	Edmonton	Yes	Yes	Yes	Yes	Yes
INACTIVE MAYOR COMMUNITIES						
1.	St. John's	No	No	No	No	No
3.	North Bay	No	No	No	No	No
4.	Port Alice	No	No	No	No	No
5.	Goulds	No	No	No	No	No
6.	Prince Edward County	No	No	No	No	No
7.	Oak Lake	No	No	No	No	No
8.	Terrace	No	No	No	No	No
9.	Woodstock	No	No	No	No	Yes
10.	Mississauga	Yes	Yes	Yes	Yes	Yes
11.	Courtenay	No	Yes	No	No	Yes
13.	Princeton	No	Yes	No	No	No
16.	Petawawa	No	No	Yes	No	No
17.	Nickabeau	No	No	No	No	No

*Com.-Sys. = Interagency communications system
**Leader = Emergency leadership structure understood and followed

Community Size And Disaster Experience

Other factors may be at work in explaining why some of the communities did better than others in emergency response. For example, there is the issue of disaster experience. Did communities that had experienced a recent emergency, or that had been through a succession of similar previous emergencies, do better than communities that had not experienced such events before? Also, the size of the community may be important. Do larger, more populated communities do better than small, less-populated communities?

In the first instance, three of the communities classified as "active" mayor had previous emergency experience. In Medicine Hat's hazardous substance accident, emergency planning resulted in part from the mayor's experience years earlier in an emergency incident that he thought was badly handled. Corner Brook's plan for local emergencies began years before that community's hazardous substance accident. The mayor there heard about the problems of the Mississauga incident and wanted his community to be prepared for such an event. About three years after the Mississauga hazardous substance emergency, Corner Brook experienced its own "hazmat" emergency.

Previous community experience with emergency incidents does not guarantee that the community will have an "active" mayor. Seven of 13 communities that were classed "inactive" mayor, had experienced previous, and sometimes similar, emergencies. Port Alice had suffered major mudslide damage before. Prince Edward County had confronted an almost identical snow emergency 30 years earlier, that many area residents remembered. Princeton had been hit by floods before and Courtenay had been through two previous hazardous substance spills. Note, however, experience did enable Courtenay to launch a well coordinated initial response and its emergency leadership structure was understood and followed. Courtenay did unfortunately have problems with social services, problems that had been unanticipated in its emergency exercises.[20] Mississauga also had previous experience with disaster. Its Peel Regional Police Force had an emergency plan in effect because its chief had previously been through an unsatisfactory experience in a hijacking incident and did not want the force to be underprepared again.

Besides previous experience with emergencies, size too is a relevant variable. The smallest communities studied were Port Alice, Oak Lake, Goulds, Pemberton, and Nickabeau. Except for Pemberton, none of these small communities had developed an emergency plan, and none had designed an EOC, before their respective emergency incidents. The Port Alice and Oak Lake predicaments have already been mentioned. During the nursing home fire tragedy outside Goulds, city police, fire, and ambulance teams could not reach their base radio stations from the fire location. Only the RCMP possessed the needed long-distance radio communications capability, and as noted, the RCMP was not alerted about the incident. In Nickabeau, it took one emergency agency an entire day to find the tornado damage area.

The evidence suggests that smaller communities tend to be less prepared for emergencies than larger communities, however, there is considerable variation in levels of emergency preparedness even among larger communities.

Provincial Influence, Time Factors, And Incident Magnitude

There may be three other variables at work in explaining why some communities had emergency plans and response elements in place and others did not.

First, communities may have been influenced by their provincial governments to undertake emergency planning. Correspondingly, communities located in provinces that were indifferent or slow to adopt emergency planning may have been reluctant to engage in this type of activity. Consider, five of the 13 communities classed as "inactive" mayor are in Ontario, a province that has lagged behind others in emergency planning. For several years it was the only province without emergency laws and without a provincial emergency organization.

To contrast, Alberta has a strong provincial emergency organization and local emergency planning there is required by law. Edmonton and Medicine Hat, each in the province of Alberta, had emergency plans and "active" mayors before they confronted their respective incidents. Provincial influence showed up elsewhere as well. Officials of Nova Scotia's provincial government urged the mayor of Sydney to attend a course at the Canadian Emergency Preparedness College (CEPC). The mayor was then challenged by the same people to create and test an emergency plan. Provincial authorities in British Columbia invited the mayor of Pemberton to attend a similar CEPC course and she returned home committed to local emergency planning. Less than a year later Pemberton experienced its floods.

So, while the mayor's involvement is crucial to planning, that involvement is likely to stem from disaster experience, training, and education, and in some instances from outside forces, such as provincial government inducements.

In addition, there are the matters of disaster recency and incident magnitude. Table IX-1 lists incidents in chronological order. The first was the St. John's snow emergency of March 1974, then Sydney's windstorm in October of the same year, and then North Bay's office building explosion of January 1975. One might ask if disasters in some communities encourage emergency planning in others? Consider the last eight incidents listed on Table IX-1. Looking at the period from Corner Brook's gas spill in January 1984 through Edmonton's tornado in July 1987, five of the eight communities shown had "active" mayors. Princeton, Petawawa, and Nickabeau, all small communities, were classified as "inactive" mayor communities before their incidents. It may be that major incidents, such as the November 1979 Mississauga incident, have increased local government awareness of emergency planning, at least for large- or medium-sized communities.[21]

Finally, there is the question of magnitude or seriousness of destruction in each incident. The most serious incidents, in terms of deaths and/or injuries, scale of damage, and number of people immediately affected, were: the Edmonton and Woodstock tornadoes, the Mississauga hazardous materials accident, the Gander plane crash, the Port Alice mudslide and flood, the Sydney windstorm, and the Pemberton flood.[22] This assessment of severity attempted to control for differences in community size and population. For example, Mississauga, a large municipality, involved 217,000 people. When the much smaller community of Port Alice evacuated 1400 people, this constituted most of the residents of the town.

Four of the seven communities considered to have sustained "most serious" incidents had "active" mayors. Among the three that had "inactive" mayors, Port Alice and Woodstock failed to set up an EOC despite the severity of the problems they confronted. Three of the four communities labeled "active" mayor established EOCs before they experienced their emergencies and before the severity of the incident could be determined. It appears, therefore, that the magnitude of disaster effects is unrelated to community preincident emergency planning and preparedness. In other words, the mere fact that a community fell victim to a serious emergency or disaster does not necessarily imply that the community and its leaders were well prepared for the event before it struck. This may be a testament to the randomness of emergency and disaster incidents more than it is an observation about local emergency preparedness.

CONCLUSION

Nineteen community emergency incidents were reviewed to learn whether individual mayors of these localities had been active in local emergency planning *before* the emergency incident occurred. If the mayor did engage in pre-emergency planning, the community was classified as "active" mayor. Where mayors did not engage in such planning, communities were classified "inactive" mayor. From here it was then determined whether each community had the five main elements of emergency planning: a written plan, a call-out procedure or notification system, an emergency operations centre, inter-agency communications, and some form of prearranged authority structure for emergency conditions.

The "active" and "inactive" groups were then compared. Communities with an "active" mayor were far more likely to have an emergency plan and an organized response to an emergency than those classed as "inactive" mayor communities. Communities that had previously experienced emergencies or disasters seemed more likely to have "activistic" emergency-minded mayors and well developed local emergency preparedness. Larger communities were somewhat more likely to have "active" mayors and advanced emergency planning than smaller communities.

An intervening force in gauging preincident mayoral interest in emergency planning was provincial pressure. Communities in provinces that had promoted local emergency preparedness through laws and public agencies dedicated to emergency management were more likely to have "active" mayors and the requisite elements of emergency response. Because "active" mayor communities tended to handle their emergency incidents well, this may spur provincial emergency officials to press for more local emergency preparedness, confident that benefits will result. The ECRU reached this same conclusion following its 1976 Port Alice study. The organization asserted that local authorities, no matter what their roles, are too involved in day-to-day responsibilities to worry about planning for emergencies that may never happen, so "the pressure for emergency planning must come from . . . the province."[23]

Each community with a mayor that did not engage in, or that did not promote, emergency preparedness tended to be less well prepared for the emergency it experienced. This is not a tautology because emergency planning can certainly be conducted without mayoral involvement or promotion. "Inactive" mayor communities encountered many emergency response problems that "active" mayor communities did not. Correspondingly, each mayor that had been actively involved in the preemergency planning process apparently helped insure that his or her community had an emergency response capability before the disaster struck or before the emergency took hold. More than this, if a community fit the "active" mayor category, this seemed almost to guarantee that an organized response to the emergency incident would result.

Notes

[1] Leaders here refer specifically and only to mayors or chief executive officers comparable to mayors.

[2] See Thomas E. Drabek, *Human Systems Responses to Disaster: An Inventory of Sociological Findings* (New York: Springer-Verlag, 1986).

[3] See William J. Petak, "Emergency Management: A Challenge for Public Administration," *Public Administration Review* (January 1985), pp. 3–7.

[4] Ibid., p. 3.

[5] K. Grant Crawford, *Canadian Municipal Government* (Toronto: University of Toronto Press, 1958), p. 90.

[6] Russell R. Dynes and E. L. Quarantelli, "The Nature and Scope of Local Disaster Planning in American Communities," Disaster Research Center Report, Newark, Del., 1978, p. 10.

[7] Beverly A. Cigler, "Contingent Conditions for Research Based Local Emergency Planning—Executive Summary," Program in Environmental Science & Regional Planning, Pullman, Wash., 1986.

[8] Jack D. Kartez and William J. Kelley, "Adaptive Planning for Community Emergency Management," Environmental Research Center, Olympia, Wash., 1987, p. 217 and see Chapter I of this book.

[9] Joseph Scanlon, Jim Jefferson, and Debbie Sproat, *The Port Alice Slide* (Ottawa: Emergency Planning Canada, 1976), p. 58.

[10] Beverly A. Cigler, "Emergency Management and Public Administration," in *Crisis Management: A Casebook*, Michael T. Charles and John Choon K. Kim, eds. (Springfield, Il.: Charles C Thomas Publisher, 1988), pp. 10–11.

[11] Michael J. Strobo and Carolyn P. Strobo, *Head of the Council* (St. Thomas: Municipal World Inc., 1985), pp. 3–4.

[12] Crawford, 1958, p. 90.

[13] C. R. Tindal and S. Nobes Tindal, *Local Government in Canada* (Toronto: McGraw-Hill Ryerson Limited, 1984).

[14]Thomas E. Drabek, "Managing the Emergency Response," *Public Administration Review* (January 1985), p. 90.

[15]Scanlon, Jefferson, and Sproat, 1976, p. 55.

[16]Most of the incidents compiled for this study have been investigated in these publications. See Joseph Scanlon's, *The St. John's/Watt Study* (Ottawa: Emergency Planning Canada, 1974); *The Terrace Floods* (Ottawa, Emergency Preparedness Canada, 1978); *The Woodstock Tornado: An Unplanned Event* (Ottawa: Emergency Communications Research Unit, 1980); *Toxic Spills in Courtenay and Corner Brook: How Two Canadian Communities Handled Similar Chemical Emergencies* (Ottawa: Emergency Communications Research Unit, 1983); with Angela Prawzick, *The Princeton Ice Jams* (Emergency Preparedness Canada, 1988 forthcoming); with Brian Taylor, *The Warning Smell of Gas* (Ottawa: Emergency Preparedness Canada, 1975) and their *Two Tales of a Snowstorm* (Ottawa: Emergency Communications Research Unit, 1977); with Gillian Osborne, *The Petawawa Train Derailment* (Ottawa: Emergency Preparedness Canada, 1988, in press) and their study *The Medicine Hat Train Derailment* (Ottawa: Emergency Preparedness Canada, 1988, in press); with Jim Jefferson, *The Sydney/Big Storm Report* (Ottawa: Emergency Planning Canada, 1974); and et al., *The Pemberton Valley Floods: B.C.'s Tiniest Village Responds to a Major Disaster* (Ottawa: Emergency Communications Research Unit, 1985).

[17]See Gillian Osborne, "The Nickabeau Tornado," a publication of Carleton University, Ottawa, 1985.

[18]See Emergency Communications Research Unit, *The Gander Air Crash* (Ottawa: Emergency Preparedness Canada, 1986).

[19]To reduce radio noise, the Provincial Emergency Program had installed a special radio containing all local emergency channels.

[20]Joseph Scanlon, Angela Prawzick, and Al Farrell, "Experience vs. Planning: Challenges to the DRC Model on Toxic Spill Responses." Paper presented at the American Sociological Association conference, San Antonio, Texas, 27–31 August 1984.

[21]Joseph Scanlon, "The Roller Coaster Story of Civil Defence Planning in Canada," *Emergency Planning Digest* (April-June 1982), pp. 8–9.

[22]None of the six listed here are in any specific order.

[23]Scanlon, Jefferson, and Sproat, 1976, p. 58.

PART 4

Chapter X

THE BIG APPLE AND DISASTER PLANNING: HOW NEW YORK CITY MANAGES MAJOR EMERGENCIES

RICHARD T. SYLVES AND THOMAS J. PAVLAK

INTRODUCTION

New Yorkers like to believe that no other city is like "The Big Apple." While it is true that different cities have different vulnerabilities, many cities share New York's problems. Yet, many problems that would be considered unusual in smaller cities have become almost routine in New York. On a "typical" day the city averages two reported hazardous materials accidents and a hostage-taking incident. Added to this is a nearly predictable rash of transportation mishaps on the roads and in the subways. New York is, like Washington, vulnerable to political protests by dissident exiles and by feuding ethnic, racial, or political groups. The United Nations and a host of foreign missions impose special antiterrorisim planning responsibilities on the city. Architecture, perhaps more than politics, has complicated New York's emergency management. Incidents in multistory buildings that involve fires, hazardous materials spills, structural failures, or construction accidents impose special demands on emergency responders.

But beyond this, the city's huge and heavily unionized city work force holds the potential for serious disruption of essential services during extended strikes or job actions. The loss of services, such as police, fire, emergency medical, transportation, sanitation, etc., can lead to disasters or major emergencies in the city. Sometimes jurisdictional disputes between departments encourage competing unions to exert political leverage. A recent series of confrontations between the city's police and fire departments over who does what in emergency management involved heavy police and fire union wrangling. Therefore, municipal labor strikes can and have created havoc in the city, and unions themselves are an integral force in matters of city emergency management.

185

It would be an understatement to say New York City is huge, complicated, and densely populated. But, at the same time, the city possesses
considerable resources to address mass emergencies and disaster threats.[1]
These include a public work force of more than 400,000 workers, large
but tightly supervised public financial resources, and a vast pool of
private resources, some contractable but much of it volunteer, that can be
brought to bear in major emergencies. The essence of emergency management in New York is interdepartmental and intradepartmental coordination of emergency and disaster preparedness, response, and recovery.
Predisaster mitigation is a lower priority in the city because most city
land areas have already been intensively developed and because zoning,
building ordinance enforcement, and inspection duties are done through
the Department of Inspections, fire inspections by the Bureau of Fire
Prevention in the Fire Department, and related duties sometimes
jurisdictionally reside with federal, state, or special district government
agencies.[2]

In this study we examine a variety of emergencies and disaster threats
that the city has experienced, has planned for, or has classified as too
remote to be given high priority. The study will show that what New
York emergency managers regard as a major emergency or disaster
threat is rooted in the city's unique physical, socioeconomic, and political characteristics.

Municipal Organization

New York City is considered to have a "strong mayor" form of
government. The mayor has considerable budget authority and appoint-
ment power within city government. However, the mayor also faces a
powerful City Council and Board of Estimate.

New York actually is a single municipality encompassing five boroughs.
Each city borough technically is a New York State county, but all boroughs are governed by the central municipal administration such that
they have only limited powers of self-government. Most city departments are organized with a sense of borough geography such that borough-
level officials, managers, directors, or commanders exist within each
department or agency.

In their classic work, *Governing New York City*, Sayre and Kaufman
concluded that the city was governed by ceaseless bargaining and fluctu-
ating alliances among the major participants in each center, and in

which the centers are partially but strikingly isolated from one another." They claim that New York is governed through a process of "decisions as accommodation."[3] Decisions as accommodation is still a good way to characterize how emergency management is addressed in the city.

DEFINING EMERGENCY IN NEW YORK

What does New York define as an emergency? In official terms, an emergency is classified as any circumstances in which multiple city agencies must become involved to deal with a natural, technological, or social hazard of some kind and it is assumed to have widespread life- or health-threatening effects. Normal systems for the delivery of services, such as transportation, communication, public services, and government will be disrupted.[4] At the risk of posing a circular definition, any situation that falls under the jurisdiction of the Mayor's Emergency Control Board (ECB) may be considered an emergency.

An emergency and/or disaster cannot be more precisely defined in this context because city officials cannot understandably predict every conceivable life-, health-, or property-threatening event that the city might face. A routine problem sometimes unexpectedly turns into a disaster. Also, incidents or problems that embarrass the city administration or that carry negative electoral consequences for the mayor and other city officials, can be escalated to emergency status. Moreover, New York's emergency managers, and perhaps most professional emergency managers, prefer to talk in terms of "incidents" or "major incidents," not in terms of "emergencies." One official of the NYPD emergency management unit drily added that some "incidents" are triggered more by federal reporting requirements than by the event itself.

How does an emergency escalate to a disaster in New York? There are at least four general criteria that can propel an incident or emergency to disaster status. First, when a significant loss of life occurs or a significant area of the city is threatened, the scale of emergency can move it into disaster status. A second general criteria applies exclusively to electric power outages. An emergency exists if at least 3,500 people in the city are without electric utility services for more than two hours. The duration and demographic extensiveness of the outage may reach disaster dimensions. A third criterion entails significant loss, or threat of loss, to private property. Here the public and private dollar loss may create disaster conditions. A fourth category is political or ministerial. When the mayor chooses to define a set of circumstances as an emergency, an emergency is in effect until he or she deems the problem corrected. Disaster here is defined in political as much as social terms.

Emergency Planning In New York

Before 1975 the city's emergency management operations were directed by the Office of Civil Defense (OCD). In that year, the OCD's operational functions were transferred to the Police Department. The following March, the Office of Emergency Management (OEM) was created to serve as the administrative arm of the Mayor's Emergency Control Board (ECB). OEM is responsible for:

- Monitoring daily events in the case of potential emergencies
- Creating, maintaining, and updating procedures to ensure the most effective and coordinated response in an emergency
- Notifying appropriate agencies
- Collecting from agencies data that are essential for use in an emergency
- Using information provided by agencies about technical and personnel resources and changes
- Incorporating knowledge gained from events to revise the Emergency Management Plan
- Updating procedural manuals on emergency situations and agency participation
- Encouraging the development of agency training programs
- Providing centralized training when the situation dictates the need.[5]

The police commissioner serves as director of both the ECB and the OEM, with the chief of the department responsible for overseeing OEM operations and its daily management under the direction of a high-ranking inspector. The OEM's staff of fifteen is divided almost evenly between police officers and civilian personnel. Two lieutenants, three sergeants, and three peace officers make up the police staff. There are also seven civilian planners in OEM. Most OEM personnel hold postgraduate degrees and many have completed specialized training programs. Office morale is visibly high and, for police officers assignment to the OEM is considered to be an excellent career step.

OEM's fiscal year 1988 budget was about $1.8 million, with $696,000 coming from the U.S. Federal Emergency Management Agency (FEMA) through the New York State Emergency Management Office.[6] Most of the budget consists of labor costs and it includes support for several external activities that are funded by OEM. The Department of General Services stockpiles emergency provisions and maintains the city's emergency broadcast system, the Fire Department operates an emergency radiological unit, auxiliary police are used in circulating emergency information to city neighborhoods, and the Human Resources Administration subsidizes some American Red Cross functions. Funds for all or portions of these services come from the OEM budget.

In addition to preparing emergency plans, OEM processes a regular flow of required state and federal government paperwork, maintains an inventory of resources that the city might need in emergencies, and promotes emergency management education, training, exercises and drills. Emergencies frequently generate lawsuits, and so OEM people and records are often made available to litigants. The essence of OEM work is notification, mobilization, and coordination of city departments in responding to disasters and emergencies. The unit also has major responsibility for warning the public about emergencies and disaster threats.

Mobilizing For Emergencies

New York government has three phases of emergency mobilization. Phase I activates an in-house monitoring system if the city has enough advance warning of the threat or event. OEM staff are alerted and 24-hour rotating work schedules go into effect. The mayor, the police commissioner, the mayor's director of operations, the mayor's press office, the Emergency Control Board liaison team, and selected city officials are also notified. The ECB liaison team consists of 95 people who serve as OEM links to all city offices or agencies that might need to be consulted or used in various emergency circumstances. The primary purpose of a Phase I mobilization is to provide expert personnel needed to analyze the situation and to determine what further actions may be needed.[7]

Phase II signifies that a serious condition has developed into a citywide emergency. If a Phase II activation is declared from the outset, phase I and II actions occur simultaneously. ECB members assess the magnitude of the event threat and decide what necessary actions or precautions the city should take. The mayor chairs the ECB, the police commissioner directs the ECB, and the board itself has as other members, the mayor's director of operations, city deputy mayors, city agency commissioners, private executives (such as those of major utilities), and leaders of volunteer organizations, such as the Red Cross and the Salvation Army.

After the ECB has evaluated the event and determined appropriate emergency response needs, the OEM staff ask ECB liaison people to report either to a specific site in the field or to the permanent Emergency Coordinating Section (ECS) at city police headquarters. A temporary field-based ECS may be set up in localized emergencies such as floods or major fires. The permanent ECS is used in emergencies that have large-scale or city-wide consequences as in snowstorms, hurricanes, or major labor strikes.[8]

Phase III emergency mobilization can be authorized by the mayor or the police commissioner. If an emergency rapidly escalates to phase III, phase I and II actions may take place concurrently with those of phase III. As the highest state of mobilization, phase III places top priority on direction and control of the entire emergency response. The mayor, policy-making agency heads, and key city officials named by the mayor, meet at an Emergency Management Center (EMC). Policy-making officials of the EMC communicate specific directions and assignments to the ECS, who in turn delegate tasks to operational level people. Phase III involves broad policy decisions that are often outside the purview of mid-level agency officials. This level of mobilization seeks to shorten lines of communication, to bring people from a variety of agencies together, and to share operational personnel.

In phase III, as in lower phases, the ECB's Communications and Resources Network is used to collect information about problems or circumstances in the field, to issue instructions or advice to emergency responders, and to assemble information that can be used for press releases. Included in this network is a web of agency telephone hotlines, a dedicated radio frequency for emergencies, as many as 50 field radios used to supplement or temporarily replace standard police radio communication, a helicopter-borne video camera with live-feed to headquarters, and permanently placed video cameras positioned in noted city "hot spots" which are used by police in crime surveillance.

A key feature of phase III is the compilation of information about the emergency that can be conveyed by the mayor or his aides to the media and the public. The ECS is expected to relay information for media releases or press briefings to the mayor's press information unit. [No city agency official is allowed to speak for himself or herself during city emergencies.] The OEM also can put its public enquiry unit into operation. A large group of people in a secure location man the unit by handling as many as 50 phone calls at a time from the general public. The enquiry unit provides a loop in the information flow. Once the press information unit disseminates information to the media, and the media in turn publicize this information, individuals may call the public enquiry unit to seek clarification or more information. Based on the public questions received, the public enquiry unit can apprise the ECS of what the general public fears or needs more information about. Policy makers at the Emergency Management Center might then release new or revised information to the press unit in response to what callers are asking.[9]

911 Emergency Operations

A critical component of New York's emergency management capability is its 911 emergency telephone operation. The Police Department has responsibility for the 911 system, which has its operations center in lower Manhattan. Citizens dialing 911 are seeking immediate help in police, fire, or medical emergencies. The 911 operations center averages seven million calls each year, a total approximating the New York's resident population. About 3.5 million of these calls trigger a police radio car dispatch. Many 911 calls result in response by fire fighting units, ambulance units, or both. A great many 911 calls prove to be false alarms or pranks.

Police precinct radio dispatchers for the five boroughs are centrally located at the 911 operations center and are linked by telecommunications with 911 dispatchers, making possible a more coordinated police response. This is particularly important when problems overlap police precinct boundaries or involve a multiple precinct police response. In addition, 911 operators are linked by computer and voice phone to Fire Department and emergency medical service dispatchers, as well as to other city emergency response units. OEM staff, whose offices are adjacent to the 911 operations center, are kept informed of emergency calls that may require monitoring and possibly an OEM mobilization.

The calls streaming into the 911 operations center cover the complete spectrum of human distress: domestic disputes, traffic accidents, drug overdoses, accidental poisonings, homicides, shootings, property crimes, heart attacks, work or household injuries, suicide threats, missing persons, fires, explosions, building collapses, boating accidents, water main breaks, and even reports of police or public official corruption. The magnitude of the demands placed on the emergency management system can be seen in just one statistic. While most North American cities may experience a hostage taking incident occasionally, New York averages two to three such incidents each day, most initially reported through 911.[10]

Compounding the stressful work of 911 operators is the problem of language. The city is a mosaic of ethnic and language groups that include many people who know little or no English. Since the city has a large Hispanic population, concerted effort has been made to hire bilingual English-Spanish speakers as 911 operators. Moreover, there is a Spanish-speaking 911 unit available 24 hours a day. For 911 callers who do not speak English or Spanish, operators attempt to identify the language being spoken. Whenever possible, someone in the unit with at least some knowledge of the language will be assigned to speak with the caller.

As of this writing, New York City does not have "enhanced 911" capacity. Enhanced 911 is an automation that prints out on the 911 operator's computer screen the caller's source phone number and phone location. A request has been placed in the city budget for such a system, but it is not yet approved or available. Enhanced 911 would help when the language of the caller is either unidentifiable or when an interpreter is not immediately available at 911 operations. Moreover, there are many calls in which the caller is unable to speak or is so inarticulate that he or she cannot be understood. Fear, panic, infirmity, semiconsciousness, shock, and other factors may account for this. Some callers are young children. Enhanced 911 would be a major benefit to city emergency response.

Adding to the daily stress of the work itself is the public criticism the 911 system receives periodically, particularly when the system fails to provide needed help. A dramatic illustration came during the March 1987 Schaumburg Plaza high-rise fire in which seven died and forty were injured. A contributing factor in this tragedy was the failure of 911 operators to recognize the seriousness of the callers' pleas. The fire began in a basement trash compactor. At first firefighters failed to realize that it had spread through a chute to upper floors of the building. Operators were led to believe that the fire had been extinguished when only the basement fire had been put out. Consequently, when residents of the upper floors of the building frantically begged 911 operators for help, those operators dismissed the pleas and responded insensitively. Burns and smoke inhalation to residents of upper floor apartments produced most of the deaths and injuries in the incident. It is noteworthy that the average emergency operator lasts only two to three years before "burning out," transferring to a new job, or quitting.

Despite the heavy volume of work and occasional criticism for delay or insensitivity, it would be fair to say that the most critical organ of city emergency communication, particularly initial notification, is 911.

THE ROLE OF LABOR UNIONS

Two New York City firefighters were slightly injured in a November 1987 incident involving firefighters and police officers who were responding to separate false alarms in the South Bronx. Ladder Company 33, responding to a report of a fire at 2312 Loring Place, discovered a police radio car in front of a fire hydrant. The 52nd Precinct patrol car had gone out earlier on a report of shots being fired at 2318 Loring Place. When the driver of the police car backed up to move it away from the hydrant he struck and slightly injured the two firemen. According to the official report of the incident, a fire department lieutenant then pounded his flashlight on the police car's rear window, causing it to "accidentally shatter."[11] This incident, and some others, represent more than unrelated misunderstandings between police and firefighters. In recent years a rift has developed between New York's police and fire departments over their respective roles in emergency response. This broader "turf" battle has led to a succession of highly publicized, albeit minor, police-firefighter confrontations.

The clashes stem in part from a charge by the firefighter's union that the police have failed to call the Fire Department to certain emergencies and also on occasion have interfered with fire fighting operations. Police officials have denied these charges. Friction between the departments grew out of the emergency response issue, in part, because Mayor Edward Koch's staff had earlier engaged in a review of the city's decline in fires to see "if the Fire Department could be better used by taking over some emergency functions now handled by the police."[12] When First Deputy Mayor Stanley Brezenoff initially recommended shifting some emergency response duties to the Fire Department, police officials and police union leaders objected angrily. At one point in the dispute the Uniformed Firefighters Association, a firefighter union, "began a campaign with posters in Chinese, Spanish, and English, urging the public to call

fire dispatchers instead of 911 because firefighters have specialized training for rescues and other emergencies." A spokesman for the Patrolmen's
Benevolent Association, a police union, countered by claiming that
firefighters had been monitoring police calls and responding even though
it is not their job, adding "We resent the incursion on our jurisdiction."[13]

On November 12, 1987 Mayor Koch sought to put an end to the
conflict by declaring that the Police Department would remain in charge
of all emergencies except fires. Firefighters won a few concessions, i.e.,
police-operated 911 emergency dispatchers would automatically alert
the Fire Department of all bomb threats, enabling firefighters to be on
standby alert in case of explosion and would dispatch firefighters to all
building collapses. The president of the Uniformed Firefighters Association denounced the Mayor's decision as "ridiculous," however, interdepartmental quarreling has subsided in the months since the mayor's
ruling.[14]

This dispute over emergency response has been a minor territorial
disagreement. What is noteworthy is the effect that labor unions can have
on emergency operations, particularly when union leaders seek to promote or defend the job security interests of their members.

COMMON DISASTER AGENTS

New York has considerable experience dealing with a variety of major
disaster threats, including snowstorms, hazardous materials spills and
releases, major labor strikes, civil disorders, building collapses, major
structural fires, and electric power failures. The city has invested considerable time, effort, and resources in planning for these disaster threats.
The sections that follow provide a brief overview of the city's emergency
planning for each type of threat.

Snowstorms

Although they are seasonal threats, snowstorms and cold weather
emergencies rank near the top of New York's emergency planning
priorities. Snow, strong winds, sleet, freezing rain, and extreme drops in
temperature can cause a variety of serious problems for the city. The city
has many snow days each year and usually suffers at least one major
snowstorm annually. Over the past decade eight major blizzards have hit
New York, each averaging over ten inches of snowfall. On February 12,

1983 the city recorded a 16-inch accumulation, the second highest amount of snow in metropolitan history.[15]

Snow and cold weather can be forecast, sometimes up to a week in advance. However, reliable estimates of snow accumulation are available usually only a day or two before the storm strikes, thus allowing the city to mobilize only hours before the storm arrives. The effects of the initial snowfall are limited but grow as the bulk of the storm is felt.[16] Sometimes storms gradually gather strength as they develop, but most have their greatest impact on the city in the first day or two after they reach the metropolitan area. Recovery time can range from several days to a week.

The effects of a blizzard are city-wide in scope, but a storm may produce different consequences for different areas of the city. For example, flooding is more probable in the waterfront areas of Brooklyn, Queens, and Staten Island, while power outages are more likely to occur in outlying city zones where electrical lines run above, rather than below, ground.

Weather exposure, during periods of heavy snowfall and low temperatures, can cause death and injuries. The unsheltered homeless are particularly vulnerable under such circumstances, but even those with housing may be at risk if heating is inadequate. However, the primary direct effect of heavy snow accumulation is its blockage of New York's 6,000 miles of city streets. Transportation services, such as those at airports, above-ground rail lines, and bus routes may be disrupted if not suspended. Snow conditions require extra municipal services that may be needed for several days. Snow removal by the Streets and Sanitation Department and resettlement operations by the Human Resources Administration are two obvious planned emergency responses.

The secondary problems created by a major snowfall are likely to require extensive effort by emergency responders. For example, the Fire Department expects that inadequate home heating increases the number of residential structural fires as people attempt to heat their homes with stoves, open fires, or other unsafe heating devices. Emergency medical authorities predict that there will be many more heart attack cases and other medical emergencies in the wake of a snowstorm. The Department of Environmental Protection expects melting snow to cause flooding and blocked sewer lines. Utility officials know that power blackouts and phone disruptions may be triggered by damage to overhead lines and downed power lines may cause fire or electrical accidents. Less obvious storm effects include damage to gas and water pipelines or equipment. If the storm's effects are prolonged for days, delivery of food, medical supplies, and heating fuel to the city will be impeded. Moreover, the removal of garbage and waste products may be obstructed so long that health problems or epidemiological emergencies can arise.[17]

Snowstorms, as much as any other disaster agent, force interdepartmental coordination in the city's emergency response. The Office of Emergency Management mobilizes an Emergency Coordination Section before an impending snowstorm. Through this unit, the Streets and Sanitation Department, the Police Department, the Fire Department, other city agencies, and the transit authorities put into effect the emergency snow plan. This plan represents a negotiated agreement that reconciles individual departmental or agency priorities in snow emergencies. According to Table X-1, mobilization for possible snow emergencies occurred on three occasions in 1987. In each case the snowfall rates, accumulations, and transportation problems proved manageable for the city.

Snow emergencies are particularly vulnerable to labor problems. Sometimes during or after snow emergency operations, municipal labor unions contend that contract violations have been committed by the city. Disputes about overtime pay, temporary workers, hazardous duty compensation, vacation schedules, and allegations of overwork may arise. Any type of city-wide emergency mobilization that lasts for a day or more can lead to considerable labor problems because of nonroutine demands, pressures, and risks that certain workers must accommodate.

Hazardous Materials Incidents

Hazardous materials incidents rival snowstorms as one of the city's most perilous disaster agents. Unlike snowstorms, hazardous materials incidents can occur at any time of the year, usually with little or no warning. Most hazardous materials accidents can be confined to a building location, industrial site, or neighborhood. Yet, "hazmat" exposure or contact can sometimes cause death, injury, illness, or incapacitation to the public or to unprotected emergency responders.[18]

Some substances pose biological or toxic hazards to humans and to the environment. Often property damage results from corrosiveness of the materials, from accompanying fires or explosions, or from chemical reactions of other types caused by hazardous substances. Evacuation, site management, spill containment, clean up, plus decontamination of people, vehicles, and equipment, often prove to be difficult for authorities.

TABLE X-1

OFFICE OF EMERGENCY MANAGEMENT
MAJOR INCIDENTS OF 1987

Date	Type	Location	Boro	#Injured	DOA
1/08	Hazardous Materials	208 S. 14 Ave. Mt. Vernon	Bronx	0	0
	[Signo Warehouse declared potential hazard by EPA, cleanup & precautionary evacuation of local area.]				
1/16	Hazardous Materials	Port Authority Bldg Goethals	Staten Island	0	0
	[0645 hrs. OEM responded to spill of 10,000 gals. of methyl isobutyl ketone in Arthur Kill. 1230 DEP & NJ EPA conclude no danger, high dilution.]				
1/22	Snow	Greater New York area	All	0	0
	[ECS convened 1200 hrs. with predicted 6-10" of of snow. Major problem cleaning streets & hghwys prior to rush hour. ECS closed 0800 1/23.]				
1/26	Snow	Greater New York area	All	0	0
	[Snow Center monitored conditions but storm bypassed city. Center closed at 0800 hrs. 1/26.]				
2/10	Bldg Collapse	242 Adelphi St.	Brooklyn	4	0
	[0830 hrs. unoccupied 4 story building collapsed injuring 4 workers, 1 worker trapped & removed to hospital. Adjacent bldgs. evacuated, evacuees sheltered at nearby church.]				
2/12	Hazardous Materials	63 Mott St.	Manhattan South	9	0
	[0845 hrs. high level carbon monoxide from gas burner at Hofat Rest. Six civilians, 1 ems tech., 2 policemen slightly overcome. Brief evacuation. Owner issued violation.]				
2/18	Fire	1070 Bushwick Ave.	Brooklyn	0	0
	[0330 hrs, fire at switching station, service disruption to 41,000 customers. Eight fire houses and 81, 83 pcts respond.]				
2/19	Hazardous Materials	Canal & Wooster Sts.	Manhattan South	0	0
	[1300 hrs. acetic acid from tractor trailer, three 55 gal. drums partially spilled. Fire Dept. over-packed drums & washed down road. Summons issued.]				
3/10	Hazardous Materials	58-35 Granger St.	Queens	0	0
	[Peroxidized ether found in bldg. basement, 40-45 residents evacuated and given temporary shelter. Bomb squad disposed of substances.]				

Date	Type	Location	Borough		
3/22	Fire Highrise	1295 5th Ave.	Manhattan North	40	7

[Two-alarm fire in trash compactor traveled up chute to 23, 24, 29, 33, 34, 35 floors. Temporary shelter set up at church. Four apts. gutted.]

4/04	Rainstorm	Citywide	All	0	0

[Flooded roadways, bldg. debris airborne in Manhattan, Queens minor outages. Sections of Long Isl. Expwy, Belt Pkwy., FDR Dr., & 62nd to 96th Sts. temporarily closed.]

4/08	Bldg Collapse	2634 3rd Ave.	Bronx	29	6

[Apparent gas explosion collapsed 4 story apt. bldg. (apts. vacant) and adjoining bldg (Var. Store & 3 vacant floors).]

4/08	Labor Dispute	Jail (Flushing Ave.)	Brooklyn	0	0

[120 Correction officers elected to accept suspension and picketed jail to protest recent suspensions for alleged brutality. All later returned to duty.]

4/14	Hazardous Materials Leak	Brooklyn Navy Yard	Brooklyn	6	0

[Accidental discharge Red Hook Sewage Plt. causes sludge exposure & hydrogen sulfide fumes to air.]

5/22	Explosion	122 Poillon Ave.	Staten	2	1

[Apparent gas explosion at private house, heavy damage to 3 adjacent homes. Cleanup by private contractor.]

6/09	Hazardous Materials	208 S. 14th Ave. Mt. Vernon(NYC border)	N/A	0	0

[Removal of all remaining potential explosive chemicals from Signo warehouse to remote NY State facility for safe detonation, see item of 1/08.]

6/15	Hazardous Materials Fire	19 West St. Downtown A.C.	Manhattan South	0	0

[Transformer fire with suspected PCB involvement, 54 firefighters, 35 police officers decontaminated as precaution. Negative PCB involvement.]

6/17	Hazardous Materials	49 W. 32nd St. St. Martinique Hotel	Manhattan South	0	0

[Dept. of Sanitation observed asbestos in duct work of fully occupied hotel. Area hosed down by Fire Dept. Cleanup by Crossbay Contracting.]

6/17	Bldg. Collapse	39 Tomkins Ave.	Brooklyn	0	0

[Abandoned 3 story building collapsed. Search conducted for possible victims, negative results. Cleanup performed by Dept. of Sanitation.]

Date	Type	Location	Borough		
6/17	Hazardous Materials Spill	43-30 Court Square LIC	Queens	4	0
	[Forklift accident, 55 gal. container "dry acid" ruptures. Tests on aided cases proved negative.]				
6/30	Hazardous Materials Spill	224 W. Houston St. (Jail)	Manhattan South	2	0
	[Accident spilled 5 gal. container of Biosperse 255 on 11th floor. Fire Dept. hazardous materials team overpacked container. Cleanup by private contractor.]				
7/01	Hazardous Materials	Fort Place & St. Mark's Pl.	Staten Island	0	0
	[Vehicle accident with utility pole causes transformer to fall. DEP tested PCB levels and found them within acceptable limits. Con. Ed. removed transformer.]				
7/07	Pedestrian Overpass Falls	Van Wyck & Jewel Avenue	Queens	3	0
	[Dumpster truck accidentally activated hydraulic lift thereby taking down pedestrian overpass. Two vehicles crushed, massive traffic tie up ensued.]				
7/17	Bldg Collapse	3500-08 White Plains	Bronx	2	0
	[Brick bldg. front facade broke away falling onto sidewalk, 8 storefronts affected.]				
7/21	Explosion	5005 18th Ave.	Brooklyn	32	4
	[Propane tank accident causes explosion in basement of plumbing supply co. collapsing 3 bldgs.]				
7/23	Transformer Fire	E 165th St. & Grand Concourse	Bronx	0	0
	[Transformer fire with PCBs (137 PPM) compels decontamination of 32 firefighters, 28 police officers, plus 6 Fire Dept., 10 Police vehicles.]				
8/05	Hi-Rise Fire	42 South St.	Manhattan South	0	0
	[Bldg. under construction had electrical fire in basement supply cabinet. Heavy smoke condition. PCB test negative.]				
8/25	Hazardous Materials Spill	1300 Morris Park Ave.	Bronx	25	0
	[Accidental rupture of pressurized air line caused containers of sulfuric and nitric acid to spill resulting in caustic fumes and scorched area.]				
8/27	Bldg. Collapse	460 Hart St.	Brooklyn	2	0
	[Condemned 4 story building collapsed due to water accumulation on roof. Two squatters injured.]				

10/07	Hazardous Materials Spill	Chrystie & E. Houston Sts.	Manhattan South	0	0

[Haz. chemicals illegally discarded inside truck. DEP contracted out removal. Dept. of Inspections and Dept. of Sanitation inspections ongoing.]

11/11	Bldg. Collapse	1430 Bedford Ave.	Brooklyn	3	0

[Bldg. roof collapsed while undergoing renovation due to weight of ice buildup from storm.]

11/11	Bldg. Collapse	177 Sullivan St.	Manhattan	4	1

[Bldg. under partial renovation undermined due to excavation around foundation causing collapse.]

11/18	Hazardous Materials Spill	74-15 175th St.	Queens	0	0

[Ruptured Con. Ed. transformer spilled possibly containing PCB oil. Holy Family grammar school closed for day. PCB level determined in safe range (4 PPM).]

12/28	Snow	City wide	All	0	0

[Dept. of Sanitation activated 2100 hrs. for 5" accumulation. At 0445 OEM ECS convened 12/29 for rush-hour periods. ECS disbanded 1900 hrs.]

*Internal Office Records of NYPD Office of Emergency Management, compiled March 8, 1988. Acronyms are,

Con. Ed.=	Consolidated Edison, New York area electric utility company
DEP=	NYC Department of Environmental Protection
ECS=	Emergency Coordinating Section
EPA=	U.S. Environmental Protection Agency
NJ EPA=	New Jersey Environmental Protection Agency
OEM=	NYC Police Office of Emergency Management
PCB=	polychlorinated biphenyls

New York is a major industrial center that produces and uses innumerable materials that are hazardous to the public or to the natural environment. The city sits in the middle of a transportation corridor through which vast quantities of hazardous materials are carried each day. Still, it seems remarkable that New York averages two hazardous materials incidents every day. One benefit from the frequency of hazmat incidents is that the city has developed well prepared and highly experienced hazardous materials emergency response teams.

Table X-1 discloses that of the total 34 major incidents of 1987, at least 15 were hazardous materials accidents or hazmat public safety threats.

These emergencies resulted from improper storage of chemicals, ruptured tanks or pipelines, uncontrolled airborne releases of dangerous chemicals, chemical transportation accidents, transformer fires involving polychlorinated biphenyls (PCBs), human exposures to asbestos indoors, hazmat spills inside multistory buildings, and, in one incident, the discovery of potentially explosive chemicals in an illegal PCP drug lab. The ECB's hazardous materials accident plan details the duties of the police and fire departments, as well as the tasks assigned to the departments of environmental protection and sanitation.

Labor Strikes

Many public servants do work that is essential to public health, safety, and welfare. There also are many workers in utilities, municipal corporations, and the private sector whose jobs significantly affect the public. When major segments of this work force engage in a job action that impedes or suspends the service performed, the public may be imperiled. What happens to trauma victims when prehospital emergency care providers go out on strike? Who guards the prisoners when city corrections workers go out on picket line? Who plows snow or picks up refuse when sanitation workers strike? Who patrols the city's streets when "blue-flu" absenteeism decimates police manpower?

Municipal labor strikes do not easily fit standard conceptions of natural or technological disaster. Nevertheless, strikes can precipitate city emergencies having disastrous consequences. To a degree, job actions by those who supply essential public services are intended to prove to management and taxpayers the true social value of the work performed. The more harm or disruption caused by the job action, the more leverage union negotiators believe they have with city management. Not many years ago New York's bridge operators went on strike over a pay dispute. When operators of moveable bridges walked off their jobs they raised or turned all the bridges so vehicular traffic could not cross and they took all bridge machinery keys home. Colossal traffic jams ensued forcing a speedy resolution of the labor dispute, but at considerable cost to the city. Strikes by workers in vital public services can create conditions under which the health and welfare of the general public is put at serious risk and in many instances emergency managers are expected to help alleviate this risk.

The NYPD OEM has a closely-guarded emergency plan for labor

strikes. Much of this planning seeks to identify people in nonstriking departments who have the qualifications and who could be reassigned temporarily to departments or agencies seriously understaffed because of a job action. Not surprisingly, this type of planning is politically controversial. Striking workers and their unions often vehemently oppose city management efforts to put substitute workers into positions held by those out on strike. They argue that this is a management effort to weaken the union's bargaining position or to break the strike altogether. Moreover, reassigning nonstriking city workers to duties that fall outside their formal job classification and contract obligations may meet with resistance by reassigned workers and their labor unions.

Emergency planning for job actions has to be handled diplomatically and discreetly. In the winter of 1988, after prehospital care providers went out on strike, OEM helped identify and temporarily reassign police officers who held emergency medical technician or nursing credentials. After four days, the striking emergency medical workers returned to the job and the police officers who had temporarily replaced them went back to their original posts. In this and in other cases strikes by municipal workers, and sometimes by workers in key private sector occupations, expose the city to unacceptable risks and vulnerabilities that trigger an emergency management response.

Crowd Control And Civil Order

As a leading cultural, entertainment, and population center, New York hosts a great many events each year that attract large crowds. The St. Patrick's Day and Macy's Thanksgiving Day parades, the New York Marathon, and New Year's Eve in Times Square are just a few of the better known events requiring considerable crowd control and emergency medical service efforts. Add to this large conventions, major rock concerts, entertainment extravaganzas, other major sporting events, with some events occurring at the same time or near other events, and clearly mass participation events impose demands on city services, most especially city emergency services. Mass participation events that go awry can become mass casualty events. Mass political protests are a special category of this phenomenon for which extensive police training has been conducted.

Major city parades or celebrations are perceived by New York emergency managers as having disaster potential. St. Patrick's Day, an official city holiday, is celebrated each year with a huge parade down Fifth Avenue. Emergency planning for this event is extensive and the parade itself usually requires a full mobilization of the city police force, as well as special preparations by other city agencies. Crowd control usually involves handling drunk and disorderly individuals. A mishandling of these duties or some spontaneous provocation could trigger a major disturbance. The Macy's Thanksgiving Day parade is a family-oriented event that makes it owns special demands on emergency officials to protect spectators and control crowds. Many months of extremely elaborate planning and emergency preparedness exercises went into the city's July 4, 1986 Liberty Weekend Celebration, an event that saw several million people massed in the areas of lower Manhattan, Brooklyn, Staten Island, and New York Harbor. Police officials are justifiably proud of their preparations for the Liberty Day Celebration and greatly pleased with the success of the event itself. There were no serious accidents, injuries, or disturbances and only minor crime control problems during the event.[19]

New York has earned a good reputation for its success and professionalism in handling mass crowd events and political protests. Despite its extensive experience and training, however, the Police Department occasionally fails to meet its responsibilities to maintain order while protecting civil liberties. In the summer of 1988 police officers and neighborhood residents clashed in Manhattan's Tomkins Square. It illustrates how mishandling a crowd control problem can escalate into a serious public relations problem for the Police Department. In the incident, individual officers responded to taunts and rock throwing by beating whomever they could catch, whether protesters, onlookers, or passersby. More than forty injuries were reported and over one hundred police brutality charges have been filed. The incident was triggered by community residents' protests against a police precinct commander's decision to enforce a 1 a.m. park curfew, the curfew imposed earlier by Mayor Koch. The confrontation could have been better controlled if the police commanders had managed their personnel in accord with standard police crowd control procedure.

Building Collapse

New York is a city under constant demolition, reconstruction, renovation, and new construction. Moreover, the city has an enormous number of old and deteriorating residential, commercial, and industrial buildings, many of which have been condemned because of poor structural integrity. Building collapse, owing to the effects of age, weather, poor quality construction, and renovation or excavation accidents, is an ongoing concern for the city.

Table X-1 shows that in 1987 alone, building collapses resulted in seven deaths and 44 injuries. In other words, for all major emergency incidents recorded in 1987, building collapse caused a third of the deaths and a quarter of the injuries.[20] Collapsed multistory structures require sophisticated search and rescue operations, crowd control, fire suppression, emergency medical services, and temporary sheltering or housing of displaced occupants.

Major Fires

The Police Department assumes lead agency responsibility in virtually all nonfire emergencies. The "in-the-box" fire, meaning the active fire area itself, is the exclusive responsibility of the Fire Department. However, management of the area around the fire scene is the job of the Police Department. This may entail crowd control, evacuation and sheltering of those who have escaped from the fire, and other duties. Fire personnel not only extinguish the fire, but evacuate trapped or incapacitated occupants, investigate the post-fire scene for hidden secondary fires or other dangers, and investigate the cause of the fire.

Fire Department emergency notification can come directly to fire dispatch telephone operations or through a 911 emergency operator alerting fire dispatchers. In addition to having fire fighting capability, the force has trained emergency medical technicians. The department's Bureau of Fire Prevention also sends out firefighters to inspect buildings for adequate alarms, water sprinklers, and fire extinguishers.

The distinction between a "routine" fire call and a "major fire emergency" sometimes is tenuous. The OEM operationally defines a major fire emergency condition as one that requires the help of other city departments besides Fire. For example, Table X-1 discloses that a major fire at an electric switching station in Brooklyn required the response of eight fire houses and two police precincts.

Overlap of police and fire functions is inescapable in city emergency management. Consequently, there sometimes appears to be a duplication of effort between the departments. For example, waterway emergencies often involve public safety and fire hazard concerns. Consequently, both the Police Department and the Fire Department use boats and scuba diver units. Marine police and police scuba units handle waterborne emergencies while fireboat crews and firefighter scuba divers also assist in this type of emergency.

Fire fighting in New York is often "on the vertical." The city has more than 100 buildings that exceed 500 feet in height. The twin towers of the World Trade Center, the second and third tallest buildings in the U.S., each are 110 stories, standing 1,350 feet high. The Major Incident List for 1987 shows that two of the three major fire events of 1987 occurred in high-rise buildings, including the tragic March 22 fire inside the Schaumburg Plaza apartments mentioned previously. The fire originated in a basement trash compactor and migrated up a chute and emerged unexpectedly on floors 23 to 35 stories above the street. The deaths included several children who jumped from upper floors to escape the flames and smoke. This tragedy proved to be the most deadly and controversial city fire of 1987. Investigations showed that firefighters were slow to recognize that the fire had spread to upper floors and that the apartment complex had a criminally negligent sprinkler and alarm system.

Only 55 buildings in the city are now capable of handling helicopter rooftop landings without special preparation. The Police Department has specially-trained helicopter-borne teams capable of descending by rope to the rooftops of high-rise buildings. They are trained to remove from the rooftop anything that impedes helicopter landings. When their work is completed firefighter teams and equipment are flown to the roof and if necessary, building occupants are then evacuated by copter. This capability furnishes firefighters with another means of search, rescue, and fire suppression in high-rise environments.

Utility Failures And Transportation Disruption

New York's high population density is a decisive factor in emergency preparedness. With more than 23,000 people per square mile, the city's population density far exceeds second place Chicago's 13,000 per square mile. New York's resident population is more than 7 million, with commuters adding as many as two million more each weekday.[21]

Mass transit is an essential component of urban life, most particularly for New Yorkers. The New York metropolitan area is home to 17 million. Demographic studies of the metropolitan area show that 45 percent of those who are employed and older than 15 use mass transit to get to and from work each day. Indeed, New York's public transit ridership accounts for a third of all the nation's public transit passengers.[22] This passenger volume imposes immense strains on the mass transit system both within and around New York.

Even the city's subterranean environment poses challenges to emergency managers. The city sits atop an elaborate, intricate, and vulnerable underground infrastructure of subway stations and tunnels, underground building structures and vaults, some extending 100 feet below the surface. There also are telecommunications cables, relay stations, electrical conduits, water and sewer pipes, pump stations, steam and pneumatic lines, and ventilation shafts, which make what would be a routine underground equipment malfunction in a smaller city, a potential emergency in New York.[23]

Utility failures underground often require extraordinary responses on the surface. For example, in most cities a water main break seldom has serious consequences, but water main breaks in New York have been known to halt N.Y. Stock Exchange trading operations for hours and to have disrupted international telex communications essential to the world financial community. Similarly, in June 1986 more than a quarter million rush-hour passengers were seriously delayed by a water main break that stopped service on the Lexington Avenue subway line. The 82-year-old main flooded the 51st Street IRT station with four feet of water, caused a water shut-off for buildings between 51st and 58th Street, and created major traffic delays in the closed portion of Lexington Avenue.[24] An unrelated fire in a below-track service corridor at Grand Central Terminal, occurring within a few hours of the early morning water main break, knocked out signals and switching mechanisms from the station at 42nd Street north to 59th Street. This forced all incoming trains to discharge passengers in the Bronx or in upper Manhattan. About 63,000 commuters on the Metro-north lines were delayed and 60 buses were dispatched to assist them.

Given the city's frequent disruptions of transit service, emergency managers may have come to regard it as an almost routine event. Still, the secondary consequences of these disruptions continue to challenge emergency managers.[25] The New York Transit Authority and metro area commuter railways have grown accustomed to water damage, electrical fires, equipment breakdowns, etc. and are adept at responding to, and recovering from, the transit service disruptions they often produce. However, other city systems are affected by mass transit disruption. Increased ground-level police security at subway passenger choke-points, availability of emergency medical services for people whose health is taxed by the effects of transit failure, rerouting of vehicular traffic, and site management that expedites repair and restoration of services, are but a few ways that city emergency officials work to mitigate the problems created by transit service disruptions.

Decay from age, weather exposure, or overuse represents a city infrastructure problem with disaster potential. As Cigler points out, "Many infrastructure disasters occur . . . because no one notices maintenance of sewer or water lines, or bridges."[26] The city's Department of Environmental Protection is responsible for maintenance of New York's water and sewer systems. The Metropolitan Transit Authority, the Port Authority of New York and New Jersey, the Triborough Bridge and Tunnel Authority, and a succession of city departments such as transportation, ports and terminals, buildings, parks, general services, and others hold various bridge or building maintenance responsibilities.[27] Pressed by apparently more immediate priorities and constrained by inadequate funding, the city administration periodically has been accused of acting irresponsibly by continually deferring maintenance of essential city structures, most particularly, bridges.

Electric power outage represents another potential disaster agent. As stated earlier, any blackout that affects 3500 people or more and that lasts at least two hours is treated as an emergency. City-wide power failures, as those of 1965 and 1977, can have immeasurable secondary consequences.[28] The major objectives of the ECB's *Power Failure Contingency Plan* are: to monitor levels of load shedding and/or power reductions; to provide protection, safety, and security by controlling looting and other criminal activities; to provide emergency service to those who are stranded or who require medical or welfare assistance; to regulate surface traffic to ensure smooth flow and to reduce hazards; to ensure both adequate supply and transport of emergency generators and fuel as needed; and to furnish relevant information to the public in ways that promote understanding, cooperation, and the alleviation of anxiety.[29]

LESS COMMON DISASTER THREATS

Emergency officials also have developed contingency plans for disaster threats that are less common, but nonetheless of serious concern. These include airplane crashes, hurricanes and floods, radiation incidents, city water shortages, and credible terroristic threats with potential disaster consequences.

Aviation Disaster

While aviation accidents may be considered low-probability events, they can be disasters for a city. New York's high population density raises dramatically the probability that a crash will result in a great many fatalities and injuries to people on the ground.

New York has experienced major aviation accidents, some with disastrous consequences. For example, in 1945 a B-25 bomber flew into the side of the Empire State building. In the 1950s two commercial airliners collided in mid-air and plummeted to the ground in the borough of Queens. Nearly all passengers on each plane were killed and there were numerous injuries to people on the ground. Most aviation disasters occur on or near airport grounds. Crashes into Flushing Bay near LaGuardia Airport and runway over-runs at Kennedy and LaGuardia are more likely to occur than are crashes over populous city areas. Both airports are located in the borough of Queens. New York has an operational plan for aviation accidents applicable to any location in the city. The Port Authority of New York and New Jersey owns and operates the three major metropolitan airports and maintains an elaborate and fully operational crash plan for incidents that occur at the Kennedy, LaGuardia, or Newark (New Jersey) airports.

The three airports handle as many as 7000 commercial flights a day. Crash dangers also exist from private aviation into, out of, and over the city, and from commercial or military traffic that flies over city air space.[30] Were a major crash to occur within the city, the Office of Emergency Management would set up a temporary Emergency Coordinating Section near the crash site to expedite search, rescue, and recovery, calling in and coordinating the work of other public agencies.

Hurricanes And Floods

Hurricane and flood contingency planning is a serious concern for New York's emergency managers. The city has experienced three major hurricanes since 1975 but, fortunately, suffered minimal life and property loss as a result of each storm. Nevertheless, according to the National Oceanic and Atmospheric Administration, New York City can expect a major hurricane every five to seven years.[31] The city's maze of underground structures, most particularly its subway facilities, make it vulnerable to flood damage. However, windswept high tides and heavy rain are more probable damage agents than flash flooding or overflow from New York area rivers. Coastal damage to shore areas of Brooklyn, Queens, and Staten Island has been common in previous hurricanes.

The city's *Hurricane and Flood Emergency Plan* calls for timely warning and response; for coordination of all agency mitigation, preparedness, response and recovery operations; for alerting the public about storm conditions, including appropriate safety precautions to be taken; and for prompt and accurate reporting of storm damage and dollar losses, needed to secure federal disaster aid. The plan relies heavily on the National Weather Service for storm advisories. It also outlines specific tasks for virtually every city department. Detailed elements of the plan include special bus routes, collection points, and shelter locations to be used during limited evacuation of seriously threatened sections of the city. Police preparedness in flood vulnerable precincts is to be maintained through regular drills, exercises, and field simulations. Planning for hurricanes and floods is so well developed that the plan even contains a seating chart for the Emergency Coordinating Section headquarters room where representatives of some 32 organizations or offices assemble in an emergency mobilization.[32]

Radiation Incidents

The city's planning for nonwarfare radiological accidents can be classified into three general categories. The first is concerned with an uncontrolled accidental release of radioactive substances to the air by a nuclear power plant. Consolidated Edison's Indian Point complex, located about forty miles north of the city, contains two reactor units with one in regular operation. Current Nuclear Regulatory Commission (NRC) emergency planning requirements for civilian nuclear reactors apply to localities within a ten-mile radius of a nuclear power plant. New York is outside Indian Point's civil evacuation zone but is within the plant's 50-mile radius ingestion pathway zone.[33]

A major nuclear accident at Indian Point would disrupt New York measurably. First, some degree of spontaneous evacuation from the city would occur even if authorities announced that evacuation was not necessary. Second, the city's food supply over a period of days and weeks would be diminished if extensive farming areas inside the ingestion pathway zone of Indian Point could not ship produce. The so-called "milkshed" which supplies New York's dairy products would be disrupted.

A second major category of concern about radiation emergencies involves transport of high-level and low-level nuclear waste. The U.S. Department of Energy's (DOE) contractor-operated Brookhaven National Laboratory (BNL) at Upton, Long Island, conducts extensive radiological research. BNL generates quantities of both high- and low-level nuclear waste.[34] For years, shipment of BNL's nuclear waste through New York was a source of conflict between the city and the federal government. City officials maintained that they could block shipment of the radioactive waste through the city in the interest of public health and safety. BNL and the DOE countered by claiming that this represented a violation of interstate commerce laws. Eventually, the city and the DOE reached an agreement that permits BNL to truck its nuclear waste through New York, but at city scheduled times, along city-approved routes, and with police escort.

New York's 100 hospitals generate tremendous quantities of low-level radiological waste as a function of x-rays and other areas of nuclear medicine.[35] Radioactive waste is generated from clinics, doctors' and dentists' offices, as well as from medical, university, pharmaceutical and industrial labs. This waste requires shipment to disposal or storage sites. Consequently, city emergency managers have had considerable experience responding to low-level radiation incidents, particularly transportation accidents. Radiological waste is treated as a category of hazardous materials and so is addressed in the city's *Hazardous Material Response Plan.*

In spite of the high frequency of radioactive materials incidents, there have been few cases in which the public has been exposed to harmful levels of radiation. A recent exception may be the case of the Queens-based Radium Chemical Company, a firm that so mismanaged radioactive materials that New York State has ordered it to vacate and decontaminate its plant site because it poses "a major potential threat to public safety."[36] Significant highly radioactive amounts of radium were discovered to be contaminating the firm's buildings, grounds, and sewers.[37] There was evidence that radioactive substances were carried airborne across a nearby expressway.

The third category, a new area of concern for the city, has arisen over the "home port" docking of the battleship U.S.S. Iowa in Staten Island. The ship itself is not nuclear powered, however, it does carry nuclear weapons. Antinuclear groups in the New York area have demanded that the city develop an emergency response plan that prepares for an accidental radioactive material release in the port area. The groups fear that a fire or industrial accident might emit into the air, plutonium or other radioactive substances contained in nuclear weapons stored at the facility. The city's "home port" emergency plan was filed with the Board of Estimate by OEM on July 7, 1988.[38]

Water Shortages

New York City has had a succession of water shortage emergencies usually attributable to drought in areas around its upstate reservoir and aqueduct system. About half of the city's water is supplied from impoundments at the headwaters of the Delaware River and the other half from impoundments in the Catskill region and in nearby northern counties. New York is vulnerable to water shortages during droughts not only because of low reservoirs but because the city does not, for the most part, meter water consumption by homes and businesses. Only recently has the city begun an effort to install and monitor water meters. It may take ten years or more to meter all water consumption in the city. Consequently, water conservation efforts in drought emergencies are largely voluntary and violation of many water conservation measures are virtually unenforceable in the absence of metering.

The NYC Department of Environmental Protection prepares and maintains a drought plan. The plan focuses heavily on water conservation measures, but it also provides for trucking water into particularly hard-hit sections of the city if necessary. The bulk of New York's water is conveyed by two major upstate aqueducts, both of which cross under the Hudson River miles north of the city. One was built shortly after the turn of the century and another about twenty years later. Should either aqueduct experience structural failure, New York would confront a water shortage disaster, as alternate water sources and pipelines would be inadequate to supply the city and repair or replacement of sections of an aqueduct, particularly sections running under the Hudson, could take years. Therefore, this type of utility failure could cause an emergency water shortage.

Terrorism

New York has considerable experience dealing with the threat of political terrorism. Typically, terrorists use or threaten to use explosive devices or arson to manifest a grievance against a foreign government, the U.S. government, or the city government.

For example, recently radical groups have bombed military recruiting centers in the city to protest U.S. support of the Contras in Nicaragua. Two military reserve centers in Queens were firebombed by six conspirators in May 1983.[39] In March 1986 a distraught Nigerian national attempted to burn down the Nigerian Consulate in Manhattan.

Bomb defusing and disposal traditionally has been the responsibility of the Police Bomb Squad but, as reported earlier, the Fire Department also is placed on standby alert. The city does not make public its antiterrorism plans, tactics, resources, and procedures for the justifiable reason that such information would compromise its ability to deal with terrorism and terroristic threats.

LOWEST PROBABILITY DISASTER AGENTS

Several disaster agents are regarded as so remote to New York's emergency managers that they are not given high priority. Nuclear war, earthquakes, tornados, and food shortages fall far down the list of perceived major threats to the city.

Nuclear War

There has been a longstanding, but muted, disagreement between New York City's political officials and federal emergency management authorities over civil defense against nuclear attack. The city has no formal antinuclear attack plan and standing policy is to refuse to prepare one. In 1982 the City Council voted against preparing a crisis relocation plan and the current city administration does not accept the premise that New York can ever be fully evacuated.[40]

Nevertheless, the city's emergency management authorities understand that they must comply with federal and state laws or regulations that require them to have and maintain such a plan. To approach conformity with these requirements, OEM has provided state and federal authorities with evacuation profiles for each of the city's five boroughs. These profiles contain data that could, in theory, be used to coordinate a city-wide evacuation before a nuclear attack. However, this information has been gathered chiefly for all-hazards planning, not specifically for nuclear attack preparedness.

New York emergency officials' resistance to nuclear attack planning is rooted in their acceptance of the practical impossibility of evacuating the entire city. One official of the Office of Emergency Management remarked that an evacuation of New York would take at least three weeks! The city's response to FEMA's nuclear attack Crisis Relocation Planning (CRP) exemplifies what Peter May calls "degenerative collaboration." This occurs "when some subnational partners in a collaborative effort opt not to participate," therefore undermining the partnership.[41] The conflict has been somewhat defused by federal termination of the CRP program in fiscal year 1984, but nuclear attack evacuation planning now comes under FEMA's population protection program that today encompasses evacuation planning for all war and nonwar-related hazards.[42]

Earthquakes, Tornados, And Food Shortages

In a similar sense, city emergency managers incorporate earthquake emergency preparedness into generic all-hazards planning. While there are moderately active fault zones as nearby as Westchester county, the city has no modern experience with major seismic activity.[43] Consequently, the threat of an earthquake is given low priority in city emergency management.

From a meteorological perspective, the city rarely experiences tornados or tornado-like winds. Much more probable is the danger of snowstorms and hurricanes. In recent history, New York has not suffered major threats to its food supply. This category of threat becomes most credible as a secondary consequence of a prolonged snowstorm, during which food supply interruptions and hording behavior could create serious problems for the city.

RELATIONSHIPS WITH EXTERNAL EM ORGANIZATIONS

The Office of Emergency Management regularly and routinely inter-acts with numerous federal, state, and local agencies. For example, New York State Emergency Management Office administrators often work with OEM personnel, usually as liaison between the U.S. Federal Emergency Management Agency and the city. The state "backstops" the city in major emergencies, sometimes with the state Emergency Response Team. New York City emergency managers also interact occasionally with their metropolitan counterparts in New Jersey, Nassau County, and Westchester County, typically in joint emergency exercises or through joint training activities. There are mutual aid agreements between the New York Fire Department and those of adjacent municipalities.

OEM devotes about half of its labor to necessary clerical work to maintain city compliance with FEMA and state regulations. The remaining staff time is devoted to city-specific requirements of daily emergency preparedness, much of it in the field. New York is one of ten federal government regional centers, so the NYPD OEM is near many federal agency offices. For example, the FBI and other federal agencies engaged in antiterrorism activities have briefed or worked with the NYPD emergency managers in investigations of politically-motivated threats against persons and property in the city. With the United Nations in Manhattan, along with a host of foreign missions, legations, and overseas offices, city authorities are constantly concerned about the threats to public health and safety posed by political protests, demonstrations, and terroristic acts.

CONCLUSION

Several findings stand out in this study. New York City conducts all-hazards planning to meet requirements imposed by federal and state government, but emergency officials also sensibly set emergency planning priorities based on the city's experience with different disaster threats. Because the police have the lead role in management of most emergencies, there is a para-military character to emergency operations in New York. For example, clear lines of authority, chains of command, and deference to rank permeate published emergency plans. At the same time, the city's emergency planning effort seeks to achieve what Haas and Drabek refer to as "domain consensus," i.e., mutual agreement among the heads of agencies involved in emergency management on the goals and priorities that they should have for their organizations."[44]

There is a high degree of formalization in city emergency preparedness planning, evidenced in the numerous interdepartmental memoranda fashioned through meetings between OEM and other city agencies. The Office of Emergency Management is a small unit, but it exhibits high EM professionalism and is able to amplify its role in emergency circumstances by drawing on other offices of the Police Department and on the staff and resources of other city departments. The OEM also appears to have the support of the Mayor and his staff, a critical factor for success in emergency management.[45] Moreover, police responses during the dispute with the Fire Department over aspects of emergency management, suggest that police leaders and rank-and-file officers believe maintaining and improving emergency management jurisdiction is an important way to sustain the Police Department's administrative integrity.

Overlapping federal, state, and special district government organizations, complicated further by the number and variety of emergency-related organizations in New York, make the problem of "unit diversity" a serious one for city emergency managers. Problems of unit diversity are posed, for example, when an on-scene police commander must direct and coordinate the actions of emergency responders who are not from the police department, who are trained to handle problems and tasks that are not police-related, and who may be from a profession very different from that of a police officer.[46] When a host of these organizations converge on a disaster scene, say in a major aviation accident, a clear assignment of previously-agreed on tasks and a para-military approach to managing the site may serve to speed and simplify emergency response. Nevertheless, unit diversity of city departments and interorganizational conflict will be a persistent challenge for NYPD officers managing and coordinating response and recovery at any disaster scene.

As Cigler has observed, "The intergovernmental paradox for emergency management is that the governments least likely to perceive emergency management as a key priority—local governments—are at center stage in terms of responsibility for emergency management."[47] While this may be valid for most local governments, New York does not appear to keep emergency management "in the wings." To the contrary, predisaster preparedness, disaster response, and postdisaster recovery receive serious political and administrative attention in "the Big Apple."

Recent conflict between the city's police and fire departments over matters of emergency management do not easily lend themselves to judgments of right or wrong. What is indisputable is that the resources and expertise of both departments are needed in many emergencies. Cooperation in emergency response is critical in protecting the health, safety, welfare, and property of New Yorkers. Since interdepartmental coordination is at the heart of city emergency management, anything that triggers or inflames departmental conflict to the extent that it affects police or firefighter behavior in the field, should be considered in and of itself a vulnerability for the city.

Notes

[1] As stated in the city's official basic emergency management plan, "New York City's vast resources provide the opportunity for effective management of most emergencies." See New York City Mayor's Emergency Control Board, *Emergency Management Plan*, ECB publication BM 327 [8-85], 1985, I-3. Hereafter referred to as "ECB Main Plan."

[2] Multi-agency mitigation efforts are common as well as site-specific mitigation planning. By definition, pre-disaster mitigation involves both hazard assessment and actions to reduce the probability of disaster. See Beverly A. Cigler, "Emergency Management and Public Administration," in *Crisis Management: A Casebook*, Michael T. Charles and John Choon K. Kims, eds. (Springfield, Ill.: Charles C Thomas Publisher, 1988), p. 7.

[3] Wallace B. Sayre and Herbert Kaufman, *Governing New York City* (New York: W. W. Norton, 1965), pp. 710 and 716.

[4] ECB Main Plan, 1985, p. I-3.

[5] Ibid., pp. I-8, I-9.

[6] Telephone interview with Lt. Eugene Guerin, NYC Office of Emergency Management, 13 July 1988.

[7] ECB Main Plan, 1985, p. I-20.

[8] Ibid., p. I-21.

[9] The public enquiry unit also relieves pressure on the 911 system by absorbing calls about the specific emergency event, enabling 911 to better handle other emergencies. Interview of Lt. Eugene Guerin, NYPD Office of Emergency Management, 2 March 1988. Hereafter referred to as "Guerin office interview."

[10] Hostage incidents are so commonplace that the Mayor's Office will be notified only if the incident lasts for more than an hour or involves the threat of harm to many people. Source: Guerin office interview.

[11] "Firefighters Hurt in Incident with Police," *New York Times* (November 3, 1987), p. II-20.

[12] Bruce Lambert, "Clash of Police and Fire Dept. Brings Warning," *New York Times* (November 4, 1987), p. II-3.

[13]Bruce Lambert, "Police-Fire Feud Reflects Concern on Pay and Jobs," *New York Times* (September 22, 1987), pp. B1, B2.

[14]Bruce Lambert, "Koch Rules Against Wider Role for Firefighters," *New York Times* (November 13, 1987), p. II-3.

[15]Chris Bastian, "A Hazards Analysis of the New York City Area," unpublished paper for the New York City Office of Civil Preparedness (September 9, 1983), p. 5.

[16]Ibid., p. 5.

[17]Since the Streets and Sanitation Department will be fully committed to snow removal operations, garbage pick-up in the city will be curtailed until the snow emergency ends.

[18]Release of some types of chemicals can cause asphyxiation, respiratory ailments, cancer, mutagenic damage, eye or skin damage including burns, or other harmful effects.

[19]See *A Report: The New York City Police Department's Report on the Policing of the Statue of Liberty Centennial Celebration.* July 3rd–6th, 1986.

[20]Note that the explosion of July 21 is not classified as a building collapse even though the explosion flattened three buildings when, as they fell, killed four people and injured 32 more.

[21]Eastbound crossings of the Hudson River into New York were estimated to be 1.54 million a day during the 1987 Thanksgiving period. In the same five-day period 957,000 commercial airline passengers were expected to use New York's three major airports. See Michael Frietag, "In Manhattan, It'll Be No Holiday for Drivers, Traffic Officials Say," *New York Times* (November 25, 1987), p. B24.

[22]Wilfred Owen, *Transportation for Cities* (Washington, D.C.: Brookings Institution, 1976), pp. 5–6, 10.

[23]Moreover, the city has four underwater vehicular tunnels, with the Brooklyn-Battery, Holland, and Lincoln tunnels being the second, third, and fourth longest in the United States. These, too, are vulnerable to over-use, deterioration, congestion, and major accidents.

[24]Todd S. Purdum, "Main Break and Fire Create Havoc in Rush-Hour Service," *New York Times* (June 25, 1986), p. II-3.

[25]The New York City Transit Authority reported 3,090 subway car fires in 1985 alone. *New York Times* (April 20, 1986), p. I-33.

[26]Cigler, 1988, p. 14.

[27]It is noteworthy that the Mayor is represented on the boards of some of the area's transportation authorities through appointments he makes.

[28]Problems can range from computer failures, loss of refrigeration, and food spoilage, to trapped victims, health emergencies for those who rely on a constant flow of electricity for essential life-support, massive traffic tie-ups, and looting to name a few. In the 1977 city-wide power outage some 3500 people were arrested for looting, compared to only 100 or so during the 1965 blackout. See Nicholas Henry, *Governing at the Grassroots: State and Local Politics.* 3rd ed. (Englewood Cliffs, N.J.: Prentice-Hall Inc., 1987), pp. 32–33.

[29]See *Power Failure Contingency Plan.* New York City Mayor's Emergency Control Board BM 181 (3-85), 1985, pp. III-1 and III-4. Load shedding refers to controlled

power reductions or outages to areas of the power grid made by utility operators either in circumstances in which power demand exceeds on-line generating capacity or when generating facilities or transmission systems fail to feed the full grid with enough electric current.

[30]Helicopter and seaplane traffic, both heavy in the metropolitan area, also pose an aviation disaster threat.

[31]Guerin office interview.

[32]*Hurricane/Flood Contingency Plan.* New York City Mayor's Emergency Control Board, BM 181-G (Rev. 6-87), 1987, p. 30.

[33]The term "ingestion zone" applies to areas of land suspected to be contaminated by radioactive matter. Agricultural produce and, most particularly, produce from grazing animals such as dairy cows, may be subject to quarantine or destruction to prevent human ingestion of radiation-tainted foodstuffs.

[34]It operates a small radiomedical reactor and other research devices which periodically yield radioactive waste products that must be shipped elsewhere for long-term storage and disposal.

[35]There are 13 municipal hospitals in the city. The remaining 87 include all other public, private, and university hospitals.

[36]David E. Pitt, "Safety Accusations Surround Radium Plant," *New York Times* (October 4, 1987), pp. I-1 and I-42.

[37]Radium has a half-life of 1,607 years and it emits alpha, beta, and gamma rays during decomposition, therein posing a potential health hazard to those exposed.

[38]The plan does not address what to do if a nuclear weapon at the port is accidentally detonated. See *Staten Island Naval Homeport Plan.* New York City Mayor's Emergency Control Board, BM 181-I (6-88)-92, 1988.

[39]Leonard Buder, "Mistrial Motion Denied in Terrorist Bombing Case," *New York Times* (March 6, 1986), p. II-4.

[40]Guerin office interview.

[41]Peter J. May, "FEMA's Role in Emergency Management: Examining Recent Experience," *Public Administration Review* 45: Special Issue (January 1985), pp. 41 and 43.

[42]Ibid., p. 48.

[43]New York's last experience with quakes strong enough to topple chimneys occurred in 1737, 1783, and 1884. However, nearby Westchester County experienced a magnitude 4 Richter Scale earthquake in October 1985. Most of the city's high-rise buildings are not considered vulnerable to major damage in moderately severe seismic events. However, water tanks atop many older buildings are vulnerable to serious damage in moderate quake conditions. See Walter Sullivan, "New Seismic Studies in City Increase Concern," *New York Times* (April 5, 1986), p. 32.

[44]J. Eugene Haas and Thomas E. Drabek, *Complex Organizations: A Sociological Perspective* (New York: The MacMillan Company, 1973), cited in Thomas E. Drabek, *The Professional Emergency Manager.* Program on Environment and Behavior, Monograph #44 (Boulder, Col.: Institute of Behavioral Science, University of Colorado, 1987), pp. 132, 141 and 161.

[45]The support of the mayor has been found to be an essential ingredient of effective local emergency management. See Drabek, 1987, p. 50.

[46]For a review of "unit diversity," see Drabek, 1987, p. 48.

[47]Cigler, 1988, p. 10.

Chapter XI

EMERGENCY MANAGEMENT AND STATE AND LOCAL GOVERNMENT CAPACITY

WILLIAM L. WAUGH, JR.

INTRODUCTION

The current literature on emergency management describes a field of study and a governmental function undergoing fundamental change. For centuries, governments responded to threats of major and frequent catastrophes, such as floods and fires, by mandating or banning certain building materials or limiting development in some areas—or simply accepting the loss of life and property. But, for the most part, serious attention to the need to plan, organize, and prepare for and to allocate resources in anticipation of major natural and technological disasters is a relatively new phenomenon. Until very recently, national, regional, and local emergency responses tended to be *ad hoc* reactions to disaster events rather than considered and proactive programs designed to prevent disasters when possible or at minimum lessen their effects, plan for and develop the capacities of communities to respond effectively to potential disasters, and create mechanisms for restoring essential services in the wake of catastrophe.

Comprehensive emergency management programs now pose great challenge for national, regional, and local authorities and demand considerable government capacity to implement, maintain, and operate. But, it is uncertain whether governments at any level have the resources and political wherewithal to respond effectively and very questionable whether local governments have the capacity to design, administer, and finance such programs without considerable technical and financial assistance. The first task here will be to examine what is meant by government capacity and what is necessary to design, implement, and operate an effective emergency management program. Questions will be raised about the abilities of state and local governments to support effective programs. The questions are ones common to the literature and ones that perhaps should be studied in greater depth to ascertain their validity. The second task will be to examine the emergency management function itself to develop some expectations concerning the economic and political costs of such programs and the administrative demands that they may place on a state or local government.

The third task in the analysis will be to identify the major obstacles to effective emergency management at the state and local levels. Those obstacles represent many of the assumptions on which emergency management policymaking is based. The last task will be to examine state and local government capacities to design, implement, operate, and maintain effective programs given limits in resources and authority and the special problems encountered with emergency management programs.

What the literature suggests is that the dilemma of emergency management has been the problem of developing strong, effective programs when public attention and government resources are scarce. That dilemma is particularly acute at the state and local levels where administrative, fiscal, and political capacities may be the weakest. In most cases, these jurisdictions are the first responders to major disasters, responsible for setting the emergency response in motion, and restoring essential life support systems quickly to reduce the likelihood of secondary damage. The problem of capacity is further complicated by the fact that the success of effective state and regional emergency management programs may hinge on the abilities of the first agencies on the scene of a disaster.

STATE AND LOCAL GOVERNMENT CAPACITY

In 1967 Terry Sanford's *Storm Over the States* painted a grim picture of state governments as being indecisive, antiquated, ineffective, unwilling to face problems, and unresponsive to the needs of constituents. Other critics added charges that state legislatures and, to a lesser extent, governors and other officials were not responsive to the needs of local, particularly large urban, governments because of the overrepresentation of rural interests. Federal support for local and state programs was more often than not predicated on those perceptions.[1]

In 1972, Ira Sharkansky challenged those views in his book *The Maligned States*[2] and other scholars and political writers joined battle over the issue of state and local capacity and responsiveness. In 1974, for example, Daniel Elazar examined and challenged the negative views or "myths" of state and local governments that:[3]

1. States are not responsive to local interests;
2. Cities are distrustful of states;
3. States and communities are administratively weak;
4. Corruption and influential interests prevent states and communities from acting effectively;
5. States and communities do not live up to their fiscal obligations to support programs; and,
6. States and communities need federal guidance to target funds where they are most needed.

Those issues are by no means dead. The debate over the "New Federalism" proposals during the first years of the Reagan Administration revived the controversy some and scholars are now examining the impact of federal transfers of program responsibility. The recent studies suggest that there are significant differences among state and local governments in terms of their capacities to respond to their own needs[4] and, perhaps, that state and local governments are generally becoming more professional and capable.[5] Also, increased state targeting of federal funds in recent years and fewer "pass throughs" from federal to local governments has had a negative impact on the distribution of resources, with lesser amounts actually apportioned to less affluent communities. That suggests that the resource gap is widening between poor and affluent communities and, as a result, many communities are not as able to respond to hazards and disasters as they might be. The demise of general revenue sharing, too, has had a negative impact on the monies available for local programs, both because of the reduction in funding and because of the loss of funds that permitted a fair amount of local discretion in spending.

Government "capacity" can be defined in a number of ways. The most common measures of capacity are in terms of fiscal resources, discretionary authority, and administrative sophistication, or some combination thereof. Initially, studies focused on GNPs (or some other measure of economic activity) or tax bases. More recently, the focus has been on some combination of tax base and tax effort or tax capacity.[6] Measures of the ability *and* willingness of states and communities to tax themselves intrinsically involve issues of politics as well as economics, to be sure.

Discretionary authority is a measure of policymaking or political capacity. Because of the constraints imposed on local policymakers by state constitutions and statutes, the abilities of communities to respond to their own needs may be very limited. Even relatively minor local concerns may require state intervention. State law may also dictate every-thing from limits on the taxing and borrowing authority of communities to the number and salaries of local officials. Maximum capacity to respond to local needs, by those terms, infers that communities enjoy local home rule powers, high tax effort, and broad borrowing authority. But, there is tremendous variation in how much local discretion is permitted by states.

Administrative capacity generally focuses on the use of modern, sophisticated management techniques and/or the diffusion of innovative techniques and technologies, such as program budgeting, target-based budgeting, financial trend monitoring, strategic planning, performance monitoring systems, productivity bargaining, quality circles, and auto-mated information processing systems. The assumption is that govern-ments using such techniques are better able to address the complex issues that communities face today.

The simplest approach is to view capacity as the ability to do what one wants.[7] Sufficient capacity exists when a state or community has the administrative, fiscal, and policymaking or discretionary wherewithal to do what it wishes. By that logic, if a community wants only to support basic services and few amenities, little policymaking and fiscal authority is necessary and, perhaps, less sophistication is needed in the manage-ment techniques used.

Certainly emergency management programs are "basic services" but they are more often viewed as amenities by state and local authorities and, for that reason, support is dependent upon the extra resources that can be brought to bear. In short, fiscal capacity is a determinant of how well or poorly communities prepare for disasters and manage risk. Because of the heavy reliance on land use regulation and structural programs in local disaster mitigation efforts, political authority or discre-tion may also be a determinant of how well a community can respond to threats to public safety. Moreover, the relatively high levels of sophistica-tion required for effective disaster planning, risk assessment, and other program functions strongly suggests that expertise and technique are necessary, as well as financial resources and policymaking authority.

Comprehensive Emergency Management

In 1979 the National Governors' Association developed a four-phase model for a comprehensive emergency management program.[8] In brief, the model suggests that emergency management programs should have four functions or phases:[9]

Mitigation — Deciding what to do where a risk to the health, safety, and welfare of society has been determined to exist; and implementing a risk reduction program;

Preparedness — Developing a response plan and training first responders to save lives and reduce disaster damage, including the identification of critical resources and the development of necessary agreements among responding agencies, both within the jurisdiction and with other jurisdictions;

Response — Providing emergency aid and assistance, reducing the probability of secondary damage, and minimizing problems for recovery operations; and,

Recovery — Providing immediate support during the early recovery period necessary to return vital life support systems to minimum operation levels, and continuing to provide support until the community returns to normal.

There are ample discussions of the four-phase model and its components in the emergency management literature.[10] What is important here is the interrelatedness among the functions and the need to coordinate the activities of the variety of agencies responsible for those functions. The level of sophistication required by such a complex of programs is also important. Indeed, the administrative and political sophistication required to coordinate such programs is even more evident in the Integrated Emergency Management System (IEMS) being promoted by the Federal Emergency Management Agency.

IEMS represents a means of tying together emergency management programs designed or intended to address particular hazards. The premise behind the IEMS model is that there are common responses to many hazards and actual disasters. If those common elements can be identified and developed, programs can be more flexible and resources can be better utilized. A comprehensive program is, or can be made, applicable to any number of situations that may arise. The political utility of such an all-hazard program is in its appeal to federal officials primarily concerned with, and most willing to spend money on, civil defense but which allows state and local officials to apply it against the more commonplace natural and technological hazards their jurisdictions increasingly confront.

In brief, the IEMS model suggests that an effective emergency management program will include:

1. Hazard analyses, including hazard identification; disaster probability, likely intensity, and likely location; potential impact; community exposure; and, priorities for the emergency management program.

2. Capability assessment, including organizational and plan assessments; capability shortfalls; and, long- and short-range plans for improving capabilities.

3. Emergency planning, including coordination of emergency and other officials; anticipating the unexpected; setting capability standards; and, planning for the improvement of capabilities.

4. Capability maintenance, including testing and updating plans; testing and maintaining equipment; and, training and educating emergency personnel and the public.

5. Emergency response, including putting the plans into operation; making necessary adjustments; evaluating the response; and, using that information to improve the hazard analyses and capability assessments.

6. Recovery efforts, including the restoration of life support systems; and, the evaluation of the disaster experience so that mitigation, preparedness, and response programs can be improved.[11]

In essence, the IEMS model ties the emergency management function together by focusing on the use of information, the need to learn from disasters and emergency responses, and the development of capabilities. More importantly here, the model raises questions concerning the administrative system required to coordinate and support such a program. It would necessarily have to be a relatively sophisticated and well-financed program and it is uncertain whether states and communities are up to the task. Quite apart from the issue of capacity, emergency management programs characteristically face significant political, economic, and administrative/technical obstacles.

Obstacles To Effective Emergency Management

Diversity of Hazards

The wide range of potential hazards that may put a community at risk strongly suggests that it is difficult to design effective programs to address each. The problems of identifying and assessing hazards is exacerbated by the sheer number of possibilities as new technologies create new hazards, old technologies are found to have left behind hidden hazards, and transportation networks bring in unanticipated hazards. Waste storage sites, landfills, transit systems, and high-rise buildings, to mention but a few possibilities, may pose significant risks. As the proponents of integrated emergency management systems suggest, however, there are generic functions that may be adapted to the kinds of unique circumstances that a disaster may present. Much of the effectiveness of the disaster response to the Mount St. Helens eruption in May of 1980, for example, can be credited to the U.S. Forest Service's adaptation of their incident command model of fire fighting to the emergency management response demanded by the eruption. Few agencies in North America had experience with explosive volcanic eruptions.[12] Flexibility, then, is a fundamental requirement for effective emergency management.

Flexibility does not appear to be a common attribute of local emergency management programs, however. Most local governments do have formal planning for disasters and, according to the ICMA, approximately 80 percent do have disaster plans, but few address the range of possibilities that a community may face.[13] Managers and political leaders are surprised when their detailed response plans do not fit the circumstances.

Low Issue Salience

By and large, emergency management programs do not compete well for public attention or public resources until a disaster occurs.[14] In the U.S., for example, approximately two-thirds of the twenty-five principal disaster relief laws passed since 1950 have been direct results of specific disasters and often have limited applicability to future disasters.[15] Low-probability events do not encourage the development of emergency programs, nor do high-probability but low-damage events. For example, there is increasing concern in Florida about public perceptions of hurricane dangers. The long period of time since the last major hurricane on and along Florida's highly developed and exposed coastlines has led to problems in implementing effective preparedness and mitigation programs. The problem is exacerabated because the state's population has increased considerably in the past several decades so more people are at risk; most of the new residents have little experience with hurricanes and little appreciation for their destructiveness, and many of the residents, particularly the elderly and infirm, may be hard to evacuate if a storm threatens. In many communities development has been permitted in locations that will be at very high risk during a major hurricane. Current technologies do not yet provide the accuracy necessary to pinpoint the likely landfalls of hurricanes in time to identify the populations most threatened and in need of evacuation.[16]

By contrast, volcanoes are very visible hazards, but their destructive periods are infrequent, often centuries between major eruptions, and there is a tendency to increase development nearby. The threat loses its potency over time. Hazards presented by acid rain, pesticide contamination of groundwater, subsidence, depletion of the ozone layer, long-term climatic changes, and other less familiar dangers are difficult to sell to the public because of the complexity of the phenomena and the problem of articulating the risk.

Resistance to Regulatory Efforts

In general terms, opposition to government regulatory efforts is accepted as a given in the U.S. Certainly many regulatory efforts find opposition from strong political and economic interests. Mitigation programs most often include the design and enforcement of building codes and land use regulations.[17] It is difficult to design, implement, and enforce building codes and land use regulations at any level of government, especially so at the local level. Land use regulation is one of the most intensely political issues in local government[18] and, thus, is a difficult issue for local administrators and politicians to handle in the face of strong opposition.

However, there is also ample evidence that the public strongly supports regulatory efforts when hazards are understood and the risk is credible. The recent experience of the Reagan Administration in attempting to reduce environmental regulation supports that conclusion. Polls show strong public support for environmental programs. Similarly, there is strong evidence that the American public is aware and supportive of regulatory programs to reduce the risk from nuclear power, handguns, industrial chemicals, and other technological hazards.[19] The resistance to regulatory programs may be largely due to public officials and strong interest groups, in other words. But, its impact on emergency management efforts is still significant.

Resistance to Planning Efforts

Similarly, there has generally been strong resistance to planning efforts, particularly more centralized planning efforts, because such plans may interfere with the prerogatives of officials and influential interests.

As noted earlier in discussion of the diversity of hazards that a community may face, communities typically do not plan for the full range of possibilities, and plans frequently fail to anticipate or include all the tasks demanded by an emergency. Indeed, the social demands, rather than the physical demands caused by the disaster itself, are most often neglected in the planning process.[20] Disaster plans tend to be static, detailed documents that are difficult to put into operation, rather than the dynamic and frequently evaluated programs suggested by the IEMS model.

Lack of a Strong Political Constituency

While politicians and interest groups do not want to be blamed following a major disaster for either obstructing or failing to provide adequate support for emergency management programs, there are many reasons why such efforts do not find strong appeal in the political process.[21] Land use regulation, strict building codes, and restrictions on access to potentially dangerous areas near a major hazard, for example, may be very unpopular actions among some of the most influential interests in an affected community. Elected officials, moreover, generally have short time perspectives and many political interests to serve, and so prefer to allocate scarce resources to projects that will bear fruit quickly.

To the extent that emergency management in the U.S. is closely associated with civil defense programs, there has been considerable resistance to develop programs that may have military applications. Dozens of communities have refused to prepare mass evacuation plans because a sizable segment of local leaders and citizens believe that such plans might indirectly provoke a Soviet nuclear first-strike if Soviet leaders suspect U.S. civil evacuations are taking place in preparation for a U.S. first-strike.[22] The contamination effect" of civil defense is less apparent in state and local civil defense activities, but the involvement of FEMA and other federal defense-related agencies in emergency management may always raise suspicion that nuclear war strategies are a hidden agenda. Communities are likely to look more kindly toward the U.S. Geological Survey and the U.S. Army Corps of Engineers, agencies perceived more benignly by the public and agencies respected for their technical competence.

Lack of a Strong Administrative Constituency

Notwithstanding recent efforts to stimulate support for emergency management as an academic field of study and as an area of professional expertise, the professionalization of the field has been slow. There is no single professional orientation toward emergency management, although many managers are former military. Due to the lack of professionalism, emergency managers typically encounter credibility problems within their own governments and with the residents of their communities. The trend, however, is toward greater attention to emergency management by elected officials and general administrators because of increased risk of civil liability for failures to exercise discretion effectively. In short, public officials may be liable for failures in disaster response.

There are some small state and national organizations of emergency managers, as well as larger organizations of public works managers, architects, applied geographers, public health officials, and other related professionals, that do provide some standard-setting and professional development. But, those organizations are not yet very influential. However, in the early 1980s, the Federal Emergency Management Agency and the National Association of Schools of Public Affairs and Administration began to stimulate academic interest in the field of emergency management as an area for research and as an appropriate area for academic programs and professional training. Many of the references cited here are products of that effort. The American Society for Public Administration and the American Public Works Association are also promoting greater professionalism in emergency management and attempting to bring together practitioners and academics. Nonetheless, the stereotype of the World War II air raid warden, a civil defense functionary, still is the common perception of emergency managers.[23]

Problem of Measuring Effectiveness of Programs

Unless disasters are frequent and of relatively predictable intensity, it is difficult to measure the effectiveness of emergency management efforts. Program success or effectiveness is demonstrated when it prevents a disaster altogether, lessens its effects, assures a timely and adequate response, or leads to a quick recovery. Those results are difficult to establish, however. The critical question is how much is enough. Too little preparation for disaster can leave a community vulnerable and too much preparation is at the expense of other necessary programs. Even the best laid plans may prove inadequate when a major catastrophe strikes.

The effectiveness of responses, too, are a matter of interpretation. Premature evacuation of population centers threatened by hurricanes, for example, can be very expensive in terms of the costs of providing transportation, food, and shelter for those evacuated, the losses experienced by businesses in and around the affected area, the medical risks caused by moving large numbers of people, and the financial and manpower burdens placed on local public safety agencies, to mention but a few of the effects of evacuation. If the evacuation proves unnecessary, a common difficulty with hurricanes because of the long lead times required to effect an evacuation and the short lead times afforded by current technologies for predicting landfall, authorities are left open to criticism.

Success or effectiveness may also be measured quite differently among the major actors. Emergency managers in Salt Lake City during the major floods of the mid-1980s found that their sandbagging of city streets to channel water out of the downtown area was effective in reducing damage to businesses, but they were severely criticized for reducing damages to levels that would not justify low interest federal business loans for recovery. That is an extreme case and it can be argued that the disaster response was effective in that it reduced property damage to relatively low levels.

The costs of emergency management programs, however, are very visible.

Technical Complexity of Many Emergency Management Efforts

Many technological and even natural hazards present very uncertain risks to the public. For example, the very limited experience that North Americans have had with volcanoes in modern times provides little instruction in how to respond to very real threat of explosive volcanic activity in the Cascade Range in the Pacific Northwest and in other parts of the "rim of fire" around the Pacific. The Mount St. Helens eruption in 1980 represents the limited experience that Americans have with explosive volcanism and current programs are largely based on that meager knowledge.[24]

Many emergency management programs are not highly technical at all, but the coordination of many such programs does represent a difficult task. For example, disaster preparedness is generally thought of as disaster planning, but it is much more than that. Preparedness programs may involve the development of an emergency organization, emergency plans, identification of real and potential resources, communication networks for the organization itself and with other jurisdictions and agencies, warning systems, public information systems, shelter programs, evacuation plans, training programs for emergency services personnel, education programs for public officials and the general public, and so on.[25] Administrative capacity is required even if technical sophistication is not.

Vertical Fragmentation of Federal Systems

Federal systems characteristically have ambiguous and overlapping responsibilities between the central and regional authorities, as well as among the geographic units. Local and regional authorities are generally the first responders to disasters and, thus, may have principal responsibility for the success of the overall response. In fact, the national authorities may have little or no jurisdiction unless aid is requested. Unfortunately, state and local governments may have much less experience with the management of hazards and disasters simply because they have had so few to address. A few states, on the other hand, may have much more experience with certain types of disasters and may well have greater technical expertise and willingness to invest in mitigation and preparedness programs than the national government. A case in point is California and its earthquake hazard reduction programs. In general terms, however, federal agencies have more resources, if not expertise, to invest in emergency management programs. The development of state preparedness programs for earthquake and hurricane hazard reduction has hinged on federal financing and guidance and, in recent years, funding has dwindled and direction has been lacking or inconsistent.[26] In focusing resources where and when they are most needed, May and Williams[27] suggest decentralizing authority to allocate resources and developing response options to assure that local authorities on-site, the first responders, have the flexibility necessary to adapt plans and procedures to emergency situations. The inability to pinpoint hurricane landfalls, earthquake epicenters, tornado touchdowns, and other disaster locales mitigates against centralized decisionmaking.

Horizontal Fragmentation of Governments and Communities

States and urban areas are by their very nature complexes of jurisdictions with overlapping and conflicting responsibilities, some containing functional areas in which no government has clear responsibility. Coordination of emergency management efforts is critical and difficult given local prerogatives, differences in fiscal and administrative capacity, and the fragility of communications networks. Conflict and jealousy are common sentiments expressed by agency officials within a single jurisdiction, so it should come as no surprise to see them also exhibited in interjurisdiction relations. Developing effective programs is complicated further when disasters or hazards extend beyond the borders of a community and principal responsibility, i.e., the lead agency, is difficult to identify.

Current Political and Economic Milieu

The "New Federalism" theme of the Reagan Administration has emphasized the need for a realignment of governmental functions with a greatly reduced federal role in most policy areas and, presumably, a corresponding increase in state and local roles. The exception to that theme has been the emphasis placed on defense programs. While few of the "New Federalism" initiatives of the early 1980s were implemented as proposed, there has been a very significant decrease in federal support for nondefense programs. For American civilian emergency management programs, the 1980s has been a decade of budget reduction. Some FEMA military-related programs, as in civil defense against enemy attack, benefited from the nation's huge across-the-board increases in defense spending. But unfortunately, this only encouraged FEMA to burrow back into its legendary mission of civil defense,[28] at the expense of other types of disaster and emergency management programs.

Reductions in federal support for many if not most nondefense emergency management programs has also to be viewed in the context of other changes in the fiscal milieu, including fiscal crises in many states in the early 1980s (continuing through the decade for some) and corresponding cuts in spending, the termination of general revenue sharing, and a series of tax revolts and antitax administrations. Despite increases in state aid to local governments from $82.8 billion in 1980 to $129.9 billion in 1986, much of which has been earmarked for education,[29] the amount of noncategorical aid that might be spent on emergency management programs is still relatively small.

State and Local Capacity

State and local capacity in itself has also to be viewed as an obstacle to effective emergency management. While it is dangerous to generalize about the administrative capacities of state and local governments, some observations can be made in addition to those already mentioned. Certainly the picture of state and, by extension, local government painted by Terry Sanford[30] in 1967 has improved in the past two decades. Indeed, it is clear that many states and localities have the political, economic, and administrative wherewithal to design, implement, maintain, and operate effective emergency management programs. Having said that, it must also be mentioned that many states and localities may not be easily able to do so. Fiscal stress caused by general economic conditions, reduced federal and state transfers of discretionary funds, and resistance to increased taxes have had an effect on local capacity. The reticence of state officials to expand the policymaking, taxing, and borrowing authority of local governments also has had an impact in many states. Increased responsibility for many administrative tasks, too, places demands on local resources.

CONCLUSION

This review of obstacles to effective emergency management suggests that more fiscal resources, more political authority, and improved administrative skills will help surmount the obstacles described. Funds must be sufficient to support comprehensive programs. Emergency managers, as well as local officials, need the authority to design and implement hazard reduction and emergency response programs, including discretion to target resources where they are most needed. And, emergency managers and local officials need to develop relatively sophisticated administrative tools to address complex problems.

The reality for emergency managers in the 1980s, however, has been shrinking federal funding for programs that do not have defense applications, "decentralization" of national programs with either corresponding recentralization at the state level or no support at any level, local self-reliance most often conveyed as more administrative responsibility with little or no policy making authority, and few states acting to increase the fiscal resources available to local governments.[31] In short, local policy making, administrative, and fiscal capacities have not been expanded in most states to accommodate local needs. Those shortfalls have to have an inhibiting effect on emergency management programs.

There are more optimistic signs, however. Greater professionalization of emergency managers will increase administrative and political capacity. Increased official attention to emergency management, even if only to reduce the potential for lawsuits, will enhance political capacity. Increased state involvement in many policy and program areas also should lead to greater state political and administrative capacity as state bureaucracies and legislatures gain experience. Nonetheless, the development of capacity has been very uneven and progress may be slow.

The objective here has been to outline the questions that are still unanswered about state and local capacity. It is uncertain how capable states and communities are to respond to hazards and disasters, but it should not be assumed that they are always less capable than the federal government. The range of capacities among local governments and the need for capacity-building are issues that should be addressed if emergency management programs are to be effective.

Notes

[1]Ann R. Markusen, Annalee Saxenian, and Marc A. Weiss (1981) "Who Benefits from Intergovernmental Transfers?," *Publius* 11 (Winter), pp. 5–35.

[2]Ira Sharkansky, *The Maligned States* (New York: McGraw-Hill, 1972).

[3]"The New Federalism: Can the States Be Trusted?," *The Public Interest* (Spring 1974), pp. 89–102.

[4]Advisory Commission on Intergovernmental Relations, *Tax Capacity of the Fifty States: Methodology and Estimates,* Washington, D.C.: ACIR, M-134, March 1982; Beth Walter Honadle, "A Capacity-Building Framework: A Search for Concept and Purpose," *Public Administration Review* 41 (September/October 1981), pp. 575–580; Joseph F. Zimmerman, *Measuring Local Discretionary Authority,* Washington, D.C.: Advisory Commission on Intergovernmental Relations, M-131, November 1981.

[5]For example, see: Mavis Mann Reeves, "Look Again at State Capacity: The Old Gray Mare Ain't What She Used to Be," *American Review of Public Administration* 16 (Spring 1982), pp. 74–89; and, David H. McKay, "Fiscal Federalism, Professionalism and the Transformation of American State Government, *Public Administration* 60 (Spring 1982), pp. 10–22.

[6]Advisory Commission on Intergovernmental Relations, *Tax Capacity of the Fifty States: Methodology and Estimates.*

[7]John J Gargan, "Consideration of Local Government Capacity," *Public Administration Review* 41 (November/December 1981), pp. 649–658; William L. Waugh, Jr.,

"States, Counties, and the Questions of Trust and Capacity," *Publius* 18 (Winter 1988), pp. 189–198; William L. Waugh, Jr., and Ronald John Hy, "The Administrative, Fiscal, and Policymaking Capacities of County Governments," *State and Local Government Review* 20 (Winter):

[8]National Governors' Association, *Comprehensive Emergency Management: A Governor's Guide* (Washington, D.C.: U.S. Government Printing Office, 1979).

[9]William J. Petak, "Emergency Management: A Challenge for Public Administration," *Public Administration Review* 45 (January 1985): 3–7.

[10]Louise K. Comfort, "Designing Policy for Action: The Emergency Management System," in *Managing Disaster: Strategies and Policy Perspectives* (Durham, N.C.: Duke University Press, 1988), pp. 3–21.

[11]Federal Emergency Management Agency (1983) *Process Overview: Integrated Emergency Management System* (Washington, D.C.: FEMA, CPG 1–100, September 1983); and, David McLoughlin, "A Framework for Integrated Emergency Management," *Public Administration Review* 45 (January 1985): 165–172.

[12]William L. Waugh, Jr., "Volcanic Hazard Reduction and Management," in *Handbook of Emergency Management Policies and Programs*, edited by William L. Waugh, Jr., and Ronald John Hy (Westport, Conn.: Greenwood Press, forthcoming 1988).

[13]G. Hoetmer, G., "Interorganizational Relationships in Emergency Management," paper prepared for the NASPAA/FEMA Public Administration Faculty Workshop on Emergency Management, National Emergency Training Center, Emmitsburg, Maryland, May 20–June 2, 1984.

[14]William L. Waugh, Jr., "Policy and Implementation Issues in Disaster Preparedness," in *Managing Disaster*, pp. 111–125.

[15]Peter J. May, "Disaster Recovery and Reconstruction," in *Managing Disaster*, pp. 236–251.

[16]Waugh, "Hurricane Hazard Mitigation and Preparedness," in *Handbook of Emergency Management Policies and Programs*.

[17]Beverly A. Cigler, "Current Policy Issues in Mitigation," in *Managing Disaster*, pp. 39–52.

[18]Waugh, "Policy and Implementation Issues in Disaster Preparedness," in *Managing Disaster*.

[19]Leroy C. Gould, et al., *Perceptions of Technological Risks and Benefits* (New York: Russell Sage Foundation, 1988).

[20]Jack D. Kartez and William J. Kelley, "Research-Based Disaster Planning: Conditions for Implementation," in *Managing Disaster*, pp. 126–146.

[21]Bruce B. Clary, "The Evolution and Structure of Natural Hazards Policies," *Public Administration Review* 45 (January 1985): 20–28.

[22]Peter J. May, "FEMA's Role in Emergency Management: Recent Experience," *Public Administration Review* 45 (January 1985): 40–48.

[23]Ronald John Hy and William L. Waugh, Jr., "The Emergency Management Function," in *Handbook of Emergency Management Policies and Programs*.

[24]Waugh, "Volcanic Hazard Reduction and Management."

[25]McLoughlin, "A Framework for Integrated Emergency Management."

[26]U.S. General Accounting Office, *States Can Be Better Prepared to Respond to Disasters,* Washington, D.C.: US GAO, CED-80-60, March 31, 1980; U.S. General Accounting Office, *Review of the Federal Emergency Management Agency's Role in Assisting State and Local Governments to Develop Hurricane Preparedness Planning,* Washington, D.C.: US GAO, GAO/RCED-83-182, July 7, 1983; U.S. General Accounting Office, *Consolidation of Federal Assistance Resources Will Enhance the Federal-State Emergency Management Effort,* Washington, D.C.: US GAO, GAO/GGD-83-92, August 30, 1983; Waugh, "Policy and Implementation Issues in Disaster Preparedness." Also see: Alvin H. Mushkatel and Louis F. Weschler (1985) "Emergency Management and the Intergovernmental System," *Public Administration Review* 45 (January): 49–56.

[27]Peter J. May and Walter Williams, *Disaster Policy Implementation: Managing Programs Under Shared Governance* (New York and London: Plenum Press, 1986).

[28]May, "FEMA's Role in Emergency Management: Recent Experience."

[29]"More State Dollars for the Localities," *Governing* (May 1988), pp. 60–61.

[30]*Storm Over the States* (1967).

[31]Waugh, "States, Counties, and the Questions of Trust and Capacity;" and, Waugh and Hy, "The Administrative, Fiscal, and Policymaking Capacities of County Governments."

SELECTED BIBLIOGRAPHY

Ackerman, C., *Flood Hazard Mitigation* (Washington, DC: Engineering and Applied Sciences Division, National Science Foundation, 1980).

Aldrich, Howard, *Organizations and Environments* (New York: Prentice Hall, 1979).

Algermissen, S.T., *A Study of Earthquake Losses in the San Francisco Bay Area* (Washington, DC: U.S. Department of Commerce, NOAA, 1972).

_____, *A Study of Earthquake Losses in the Los Angeles, California Area* (Washington, DC: U.S. Department of Commerce, NOAA, 1973).

American Friends Service Committee, *In the Wake of Hurricane Camille: An Analysis of the Federal Response* (Philadelphia: The Committee, 1969).

American Red Cross, *Disaster Relief Program* (Washington, DC: ARC, 1975).

_____, *Hurricane Action* (Washington, DC: ARC, 1975).

Anderson, William A., *Local Civil Defense in Natural Disaster: From Office to Organization* (Washington, DC: Office of Civil Defense, Disaster Research Center Report No. 7, 1969).

_____, *Some Observations on a Disaster Subculture* (Columbus, Ohio: Ohio State University Disaster Research Center, 1965).

_____, "Disaster Warning and Communication in Two Communities," *Journal of Communication* 19 (1969): 92–104.

Andrews, Richard R., "Seismic Safety Planning in California: An Overview of Recent Initiatives," *Proceedings of the Third International Conference on Microzonation* 3 (1982), pp. 1503–1512.

Applied Technology Council, *Tentative Provisions for the Development of Seismic Regulations for Buildings* (Washington, DC: U.S. GPO, ATC Publication ATC-3-06, NBS Special Publication 510, NSF Publication 78-8, 1978).

Association of Bay Area Governments, *Will Local Government Be Liable for Earthquake Losses?* (Berkeley, Calif.: ABAG, 1979).

Association of Flood Plain Managers, *FEMA and the States: A Cooperative Effort in Flood Hazard Mitigation* (Madison, Wisconsin, 1982) (Unpublished).

Ayre, Robert S., *Earthquake and Tsunami Hazards in the U.S.* (Boulder, Colorado: Institute of Behavioral Sciences, University of Colorado, Monograph, 1975).

Baker, Earl T., and Tae Gordon McPhie, *Land Use Management and Regulation in Hazardous Areas* (Boulder, Colorado: University of Colorado, IBS#6, 1975).

Baker, George W., and Dwight W. Chapman, eds., *Man and Society in Disaster* (New York: Basic Books, 1962).

Banks, Herman J., and Anne T. Romano, *Human Relations for Emergency Response Personnel* (Springfield, Ill.: Charles C Thomas, 1982).

el Barakei, Mohammed, *Model Rules for Disaster Relief Operations* (New York: UN Institute for Training and Research Policy and Efficacy Studies No. 8, 1982).

Baram, Michael, *Alternatives to Regulation: Managing Risks to Health, Safety and the Environment* (Lexington, Mass.: Lexington Books, 1981).

Barberi, R., and P. Gasparini, "Volcanic Hazards," *Bulletin of the International Association of Engineering and Geology* 14 (1976): 217–232.

239

Barton, A., *Communities in Disaster* (New York: Doubleday, 1970).

Bates, F.L. et al., *The Social and Psychological Consequences of a Natural Disaster: A Longitudinal Study of Hurricane Audrey* (1957) (Washington, DC: National Academy of Sciences, National Research Council, 1963).

Bloomgren, Patricia A., *Strengthening State Floodplain Management* (Boulder, Colorado: Natural Hazards Research and Applications Information Center Special Publication 3, Institute of Behavioral Science, University of Colorado, 1982).

Bristow, Allen P., *Police Disaster Operations* (Springfield, Ill: Charles C Thomas, 1972).

Brown, Barbara J., *Disaster Preparedness and the U.N.: Advance Planning for Disaster Relief* (Elmsford, NY: Pergamon Press, 1979).

Burby, Raymond J., and Steven P. French, *Flood Plain Land Use Management: A National Assessment* (Boulder, Colo.: Westview Press, 1985).

Burton, Ian; Robert W. Kates; and, Gilbert F. White, *The Environment as Hazard* (New York: Oxford University Press, 1978).

Carson, William D., *Estimating Costs and Benefits for Nonstructural Flood Control Measures* (Davis, Calif.: Hydrolic Engineering Center, Corps of Engineers, October 1975).

Charles, Michael T., and John Kim, eds., *Emergency Management: A Casebook* (Springfield, Ill.: Charles C Thomas, 1988).

Chayet, Neil L., *Legal Implications of Emergency Care* (New York: Appleton-Century-Crofts, 1969).

Comfort, Louise, ed., *Managing Disasters: Strategies and Policy Perspectives* (Durham, N.C.: Duke University Press, 1988).

Cohen, Raquel E., and Frederick L. Ahearn, Jr., *Handbook for Mental Health Care of Disaster Victims* (Baltimore: Johns Hopkins University Press, 1980).

Cornell, James, *The Great International Disaster Book* (New York: Scribner, 1976).

Council of State Governments, *Comprehensive Emergency Preparedness Planning in State Government* (Lexington, Ky: CSG, 1976).

_____, *The States and Natural Hazards* (Lexington, Ky: CSG, 1979).

Cuny, Frederick C. (ed. Susan Abrams for Oxfam America), *Disasters and Development* (New York: Oxford University Press, 1983).

Dacy, Douglas, and Howard Kunreuther, *Economics of Natural Disasters: Implications for Federal Policy* (New York: Free Press, 1979).

Douty, Christopher M., *The Economics of Localized Disasters: The 1906 San Francisco Catastrophe* (New York: Arno Press, 1977).

Drabek, Thomas; Harrett Tansminga; Thomas Kilijanik; and, Christopher Adams, *Managing Multiorganizational Emergency Responses* (Boulder, Colorado: Institute of Behavioral Sciences, Publication No. 6, University of Colorado, 1981).

_____; Alvin H. Mushkatel; and, Thomas S. Kilijanik, *Earthquake Mitigation Policy: The Experience of Two States* (Boulder, Colorado: Institute of Behavioral Sciences, Publication No. 37, University of Colorado, 1983).

_____, *Disaster in Aisle 13: A Case Study of the Coliseum Explosion at the Indiana State Fairgrounds, October 31, 1963* (Columbus, Ohio: OSU College of Administrative Science, Monograph D-1, 1968).

Dynes, Russell R., *Organized Behavior in Disaster* (Lexington, Mass.: Lexington Books, 1970).

Executive Office of the President, *The National Earthquake Hazards Reduction Program* (Washington, DC: EOP, 1978).

Faster, Harold D., *Disaster Planning: Preservation of Life and Property* (New York: Springer-Verlag, 1980).

Federal Emergency Management Agency, *Civil Defense and the Public: An Overview of Public Attitudes Studies* (Washington, DC: FEMA, MP-62, September 1979).

——————, *An Assessment of the Consequences and Preparations for a Catastrophic California Earthquake: Findings and Actions Taken* (Washington, DC: FEMA, M&R-2, November 1980).

——————, *Questions and Answers on Crisis Relocation* (Washington, DC: FEMA, P&P-4, October 1980).

——————, *Early Progress to Implement Federal Guidelines for Dam Safety* (Washington, DC: FEMA, M&R-1, 1980).

——————, *Flood Hazard Mitigation: Handbook of Common Procedures* (Washington, DC: FEMA, FEMA-14, 1981).

——————, *Dam Safety Research: Current, Planned, Future* (Washington, DC: FEMA, FEMA-21, 1982).

Feigenbaum, Edward D., and Mark L. Ford, *Emergency Management in the States* (Lexington, Ky: Council of State Governments, 1984).

Foster, Harold D., *Disaster Planning: The Preservation of Life and Property* (New York: Springer-Verlag, 1980).

Friesema, H. Paul, ed., *Aftermath: Communities After Natural Disasters* (Beverly Hills, Calif.: Sage Publications, 1979).

Geipel, Robert (translated by Philip Wagner), *Disaster and Reconstruction: The Friuli, Italy, Earthquakes of 1976* (Boston: Allen and Unwin, 1982).

George, James E., *Law and Emergency Care* (St. Louis, Mo.: C.V. Mosby, 1980).

Glantz, Michael H., ed., *The Politics of Natural Disaster: The Case of the Sahel Drought* (New York: Praeger, 1976).

Gleser, Goldine C.; Bonnie L. Green; and Caroline Winget, eds., *Prolonged Psychosocial Effects of Disaster: A Study of Buffalo Creek* (New York: Academic, Press, 1981).

Goldstein, Arnold S., *EMS and the Law: A Legal Handbook for EMS Personnel* (Bowie, Md.: R.J. Brady, 1983).

Green, Stephen, *International Disaster Relief: Toward a Responsive System* (New York: McGraw-Hill, 1977).

Griggs, Gary, and John A. Gilchrist, *Geological Hazards, Resources and Environmental Planning,* 2nd Edition (Wadsworth, 1983).

Grigsby, Gordon, *Tornado Watch* (Columbus, Ohio: Ohio State University Press, 1977).

Grosser, George H.; Henry Wechsler; and Milton Greenblatt, eds., *The Threat of Impending Disaster: Contributions to the Psychology of Stress* (Cambridge, Mass.: The MIT Press, 1964).

Haas, J. Eugene; Robert W. Kates; and, Martyn J. Bowden, eds. *Reconstruction Following Disaster* (Cambridge, Mass.: The MIT Press, 1977).

Hayes, Walter W., *Facing Geological and Hydrological Hazards: Earth-Science Considerations,* Professional Paper No. 1240B (Alexandria, Va.: USGS Distribution Branch, 1981).

_____, Editor, *Preparing for and Responding to a Damaging Earthquake in the Eastern U.S.: Proceedings of Conference XIV, September 16-18, 1981, Knoxville, Tennessee* (Reston, Va.: USGS, Open File Report 82-220, 1982).

Healy, Richard J., *Emergency and Disaster Planning* (New York: Wiley, 1969).

Hoyt, William G., and Walter B. Langbein, *Floods* (Princeton, NJ: Princeton University Press, 1955).

Hutchinson, Sally A., *Survival Practices of Rescue Workers: Hidden Dimensions of Watchful Readiness* (Washington, DC: University Press of America, 1983).

ICMA and FEMA, "How Prepared is Your Community for Its Next Emergency: A Manager's Checklist," *Local Government Emergency Management: A Practitioners' Workbook* (Handbook Series No. 3), International City Management Association and Federal Emergency Management Agency, 1980.

Jelenko, Carl III, and Charles F. Frey, eds., *EMS: An Overview* (Bowie, Md.: R.J. Brady, 1976).

Kennedy, Will C., *The Police Department in Natural Disaster Operations* (Washington, DC: Office of Civil Defense, Office of the Secretary of the Army, 1969).

Kreps, Gary A., "Sociological Inquiry and Disaster Relief," *Annual Review of Sociology* 10 (1984): 309–330.

Kunreuther, Howard, *Disaster Insurance Protection: Public Policy Lessons* (New York: Wiley, 1978).

_____, *Recovery from Natural Disasters: Insurance or Federal Aid?* (Washington, DC: American Enterprise Institute, Evaluative Studies #12, 1973).

Leaning, Jennifer, and Langley Keyes, eds., *The Counterfeit Ark: Crisis Relocation for Nuclear War* (Cambridge, Mass.: Ballinger, 1984).

Leonard, Vivian A., *Police Pre-Disaster Preparation* (Springfield, Ill: Charles C Thomas, 1973).

Lucas, Rex A., *Men in Crisis: A Study of Mine Disaster* (New York: Basic Books, 1969).

Maass, Arthur, *Muddy Waters: The Army Engineers and the Nation's Waters* (Cambridge, Mass.: Harvard University Press, 1951).

MacAlister-Smith, Peter, *International Humanitarian Assistance: Disaster Relief Actions in International Law and Organization* (Boston: M. Nijhoff, 1985).

May, Peter J., *Recovering from Catastrophes: Federal Disaster Relief Policy and Politics* (Westport, Conn.: Greenwood Press, 1985).

May, Peter J., and Walter Williams, *Disaster Policy Implementation: Managing Programs Under Shared Governance* (New York: Plenum Press, 1986).

Medvedev, Zhores A., (translated by George Saunders), *Nuclear Disaster in the Urals* (New York: Norton, 1979).

Meehan, Richard L., *The Atom and the Fault: Experts, Earthquakes, and Nuclear Power* (Cambridge, Mass.: The MIT Press, 1984).

Meltsner, Arnold J., "Public Support for Seismic Safety: Where Is It in California," *Mass Emergencies* 3 (1978): 167–184.

Mileti, Dennis; Thomas E. Drabek; and J. Eugene Haas, *Human Systems in Extreme*

Environments: A Sociological Perspective (Boulder, Colorado: Institute of Behavioral Science Monograph, University of Colorado, 1975).

National Governors' Association, *Emergency Mitigation: Strategies for Disaster Prevention and Reduction* (Washington, DC: NGA, 1980).

_____, "Lessons Learned—The FEMA/States Cooperative Agreement," *Emergency Management Bulletin* (Washington, DC: NGA, May 1982).

_____, *Comprehensive Emergency Management Bulletin* (Washington, DC: NGA, April 1982).

_____, *Domestic Terrorism* (Washington, DC: NGA, Emergency Preparedness Project, Center for Policy Research, State Emergency Management Series, 1978).

National Research Council, Committee on the Safety of Nonfederal Dams, *Safety of Nonfederal Dams: A Review of the Federal Role* (Washington, DC: FEMA, FEMA-31, November 1982).

_____, Commission of Engineering and Technical Systems, Advisory Board of the Built Environment, *Multiple Hazard Mitigation* (Washington, DC: National Academy Press, 1983).

_____, Committee on the Safety of Existing Dams, *Safety of Existing Dams: Evaluation and Improvement* (Washington, DC: National Academy Press, 1983).

_____, *Earthquake Prediction and Public Policy* (Washington, DC: National Academy Press, 1975).

National Science Foundation, *A Report on Flood Hazard Mitigation* (Washington, DC: NSF, 1980).

OECD, *Nuclear Third Party Liability and Insurance: Status and Prospects* (Paris: OECD, 1985).

Pan American Health Organization, *A Guide to Emergency Health Management After Natural Disasters* (Washington, DC: PAHO, 1981).

_____, *Environmental Health Management After Natural Disasters* (Washington, DC:P PAHO, 1982).

_____, *Medical Supply Management After Natural Disaster* (Washington, DC: PAHO, No. 438, 1983).

Parad, Howard J.; H.L.P. Resnik; and, Libbie G. Parad, eds., *Emergency and Disaster Management: A Mental Health Sourcebook* (Bowie, Md.: Charles Press, 1976).

Penick, James, Jr., *The New Madrid Earthquakes of 1811-1812* (Columbia, Mo.: University of Missouri Press, 1976, 1981).

Perry, Ronald W., *The Social Psychology of Civil Defense* (Lexington, Mass.: Lexington Books, 1982).

_____, and Alvin H. Mushkatel, *Disaster Management: Warning, Response and Community Relocation* (Westport, Conn.: Quorum Books, Greenwood Press, 1984).

Petak, William J., and Arthur A. Atkisson, *Natural Hazard Risk Assessment and Public Policy: Anticipating the Unexpected* (New York: Springer-Verlag, 1982).

Platt, Rutherford H., "The National Flood Insurance Program: Some Midstream Perspectives," *Journal of the American Institute of Planners* 42 (1976): 303–313.

_____, *Options to Improve the Federal Nonstructural Response to Floods,* Report

Prepared for the President's Committee on Water Policy (Washington, DC: U.S. Water Resources Council, 1979).

_____; M. Mullen; and J.A. Kusler, *Intergovernmental Management of Floodplains* (Boulder, Colorado: Institute of Behavioral Sciences, University of Colorado, Program on Technology, Environment and Man, Monograph No. 30, 1980).

Quarantelli, E.L., and Russell R. Dynes, "Response to Social Crisis and Disaster," *Annual Review of Sociology* 3 (1977): 23–49.

_____, *Disasters: Theory and Research* (Beverly Hills, California: Sage Publications, 1978).

_____, *Organizational Behavior in Disasters and Implications for Disaster Planning* (Emmitsburg, Md.: FEMA, National Emergency Training Center, Monograph Series, 1984).

Rossi, Peter; James D. Wright; and, Eleanor Weber-Burdin, *Natural Hazards and Public Choice: The State and Local Politics of Hazard Mitigation* (New York: Academic Press, 1982).

_____ et al., *Victims of the Environment: Loss from Natural Hazards in the U.S., 1970-1980* (New York: Plenum Books, 1983).

Rosenthal, Uriel; Michael T. Charles and Paul 'T Hart; eds., *Coping with Crises: The Management of Disasters, Riots and Terrorism* (Springfield, Ill.: Charles C Thomas, 1989).

Russell, Clifford S., "Losses from Natural Hazards," *Land Economics* 46 (1970): 383–393.

Savage, P.E.A., *Disasters: Hospital Planning* (New York: Pergamon Press, 1979).

Simpson, Robert H., and Herbert Riehl, *The Hurricane and Its Impact* (Baton Rouge: Louisiana State University Press, 1981).

Skeet, Muriel, *Manual for Disaster Relief Work* (New York: Churchill Livingstone, 1977).

Slovic, Paul; Howard Kunreuther; and Gilbert F. White, "Decision Processes, Rationality, and Adjustment to Natural Hazards," in *Natural Hazards: Local, National Global,* edited by Gilbert F. White (New York: Oxford University Press, 1974), pp. 187–205.

Smithsonian Institute, *Directory of Disaster-Related Technology* (Washington, DC: GPO, 1975).

Stephens, Lynn H., and Stephen J. Green, eds, *Disaster Assistance, Appraisal, Reform, and New Approaches* (New York: NYU Press, 1979).

Stern, Gerald H., *The Buffalo Creek Disaster* (New York: Random House, 1976).

Svenson, Arthur G., *Earthquakes, Earth Scientists, and Seismic Safety Planning in California* (Lanham, Md.: University Press of America, 1984).

Taylor, James B.; Louis A. Zurcher; and William H. Key, *Tornado: A Community Responds to Disaster* (Seattle, Wash.: University of Washington Press, 1970).

Tierney, Kathleen J., *A Primer for Preparedness for Acute Chemical Emergencies* (Columbus, Ohio: Disaster Research Center, Ohio State University, 1980).

Turner, Barry A., *Man-Made Disaster* (New York: Crane Russak, 1978).

UNESCO, *The Assessment and Mitigation of Earthquake Risk* (Intergovernmental Conference on the Assessment and Mitigation of Earthquake Risk, Paris, 1976) (Paris: UNESCO, 1978).

U.S. Comptroller General, General Accounting Office, *States Can Be Better Prepared to Respond to Disasters* (Washington, DC: GAO, CED-80-60, March 31, 1980).

_____. *National Flood Insurance: Marginal Impact on Flood Plain Development, Administrative Improvements Needed* (Washington, DC: GAO, CED-82-105, August 16, 1982).

_____, *Management of the Federal Emergency Management Agency: A System Being Developed* (Washington, DC: GAO, GGD-83-9, January 6, 1983).

_____, *Stronger Direction Needed for the National Earthquake Program* (Washington, DC: GAO, RCED-83-103, July 26, 1983).

_____, *Consolidation of Federal Assistance Resources Will Enhance the Federal-State Emergency Management Effort* (Washington, DC: GAO, GGD-83-92, August 30, 1983).

_____, *The Federal Emergency Management Agency's Plan for Revitalizing U.S. Civil Defense: A Review of Three Major Plan Components* (Washington, DC: GAO, NSIAD-84-11, April 16, 1984).

U.S. Congress, House of Representatives, *A Unified National Program for Managing Flood Losses*, Report of the Task Force on Federal Flood Control Policy, 89th Congress, 2nd Session, 1966, H.Doc. 465.

_____, Committee on Government Operations, *Reorganization Plan No. 3 of 1978*, Message from the President of the United States, 95th Congress, 2nd Session, 1978, H.Doc. 95-356.

_____, Committee on Public Works and Transportation, *Federal Disaster Relief Program*, Report by the Subcommittee on Investigations and Review, 1978.

_____, Committee on Government Operations, *FEMA Oversight: Will U.S. Nuclear Attack Evacuation Plans Work?* Hearing before the Subcommittee on Environment, Energy, and Natural Resources, 97th Congress, 2nd Session, 1982.

_____, Committee on Science and Technology, *Information Technology for Emergency Management*, Report prepared by the Congressional Research Service for the Subcommittee on Investigations and Oversight, 98th Congress, 2nd Session, October 9, 1984.

U.S. Congress, Joint Committee on Defense Production, *Civil Preparedness and Industrial Mobilization*, Report by the Committee, 95th Congress, 1st Session, 1977.

U.S. Congress, Office of Technology Assessment, *Issues and Options in Flood Hazard Management* (Washington, DC: OTA, OTA–BP–X-3, February 1980).

U.S. Congress, Senate, Committee on Commerce, Science, and Transportation, *Reauthorization of National Earthquake Hazards Reduction Act*, Hearings held by the Subcommittee on Science, Technology, and Space, 96th Congress, 2nd Session, 1980.

_____, Committee on Foreign Relations, *U.S. and Soviet Civil Defense Program*, Hearings held by the Subcommittee on Arms Control, Oceans, International Operations and Environment, 97th Congress, 2nd Session, 1982.

_____, Committee on Commerce, Science, and Transportation, *Earthquake Hazards Reduction Act Reauthorization*, 98th Congress, 1st Session, 1983.

_____, *Committee on Environment and Public Works, Omnibus Water Resources Legislation,* hearings held by the Subcommittee on Water Resources, 98th Congress, 1st Session, 1983.

U.S. Department of Housing and Urban Development, *Evaluation of the Economic, Social, and Environmental Effects of Floodplain Regulations* (Washington, DC: FEMA, FIA-8, March 1981).

U.S. Geological Survey, *A Study of Earthquake Losses in the Puget Sound, Washington Area* (Reston, Va.: USGS, 1975).

_____, *A Study of Earthquake Losses in the Salt Lake City, Utah Area* (Reston, Va.: USGS, 1976).

_____, *National Earthquake Hazards Reduction Program: Overview* (Alexandria, Va.: USGS, Circular 918, 1984).

_____, *National Earthquake Hazards Reduction Program: Fiscal Year 1983* (Alexandria, Va.: USGS, Circular 919, 1984).

Volcano: The Eruption of Mount St. Helens (Longview, Washington: Longview, 1980).

Waugh, William L., Jr., *Terrorism and Emergency Management: Administrative and Policy Perspectives* (New York and Basel: Marcel Dekker, 1989).

_____, and Ronald J. Hy, eds., *Emergency Management Handbook: Policies and Programs* (Westport, Conn.: Greenwood Press, 1990).

_____, "Integrating the Policy Models of Terrorism and Emergency Management," *Policy Studies Review* 6 (Fall 1986): 287–300.

Western, Karl A., *Epidemiological Surveillance After Natural Disaster* (Washington, DC: Pan American Health Organization, 1982).

White, Gilbert F., ed., *Natural Hazards: Local, National, Global* (New York: Oxford University Press, 1974).

Wood, William C., *Insuring Nuclear Power: Liability, Safety and Economic Efficiency* (Greenwich, Conn.: JAI Press, 1982).

Wright, James D., and Peter H. Rossi, "The Politics of Natural Disaster: State and Local Elites," pp. 45–67 in *Social Science and Natural Hazards,* edited by James D. Wright and Peter H. Rossi (Cambridge, Mass.: Abt Books, 1981).

_____, ed., *After the Clean-Up: Long Range Effects of Natural Disasters* (Beverly Hills, Calif.: Sage Publications, 1979).

Zucherman, Edward, *The Day After World War III: The U.S. Government's Plans for Surviving a Nuclear War* (New York: Viking Press, 1984).

INDEX

A

Acid rain, xvi–xvii, 91–104, 228
  abatement programs, 94, 98–102
  Congressional action on, 96–97
  (*see also* specific locales)
Acid Rain Office (Canada), 94
Adirondack Mountains, New York, acid rain in, 93
Agreement on Acid Rain Precipitation (1982), 101
Alberta, Canada, 166, 177 (*see also* Edmonton and Medicine Hat)
American Society for Public Administration (ASPA), 230
American Public Works Association (APWA), 230
Appalachian region, U.S., acid rain in, 99
Aviation disasters, xiii, xvii, 10, 109–128, 166, 172, 208

B

Bombings, 194
Britain, acid rain in, 93
British Columbia, Canada, 168, 177 (*see also* Courtney, Pemberton, Port Alice, Princeton, Terrace, and Vancouver Island)
Brezenoff, Stanley (First Deputy Mayor of NYC), 193
Brock, Robert, 103
Burby, Raymond J., 68
Bush, George, 97

C

California, city managers, 133–152
  Department of Fish and Game, 159, 161
disaster assistance, 139–140, 145, 150–151
earthquake hazard reduction, 232
Office of Emergency Services, 34, 36–37, 148
Office of State Fire Marshal, 157, 159–161
Regional Water Quality Board, 157
(*see also* Coalinga, Irvine, Orange County, Portugese Bend, San Diego, Santa Cruz County, and Tustin)
Canadian Aviation Safety Board (CASB), 121–122, 126
Canadian Emergency Preparedness College (CEPC), 177
Center for Governmental Studies (California State University, Fullerton), 133
Center for Urban and Regional Studies (University of North Carolina at Chapel Hill), 60
Centralized authority, need for, 7, 8, 83–84, 86, 101, 118, 168, 175, 179, 188, 214, 233
(*see also* Command center)
City attorneys, roles in emergency management, 28 (*see also* Legal aspects of emergency management)
City finance departments, roles in emergency management, 28, 34–35, 40, 174 (*see also* Financing emergency management programs)
City managers, roles in emergency management, xvi, xvii–xviii, xix, 66, 75, 78–79, 83–86, 133, 137–152, 166
City planners, roles in emergency management, 66
Civil defense, 225, 229, 233 (*see also* Nuclear war)
Civil disorders, 194, 202–203
Clearinghouse on Acid Rain, 101
Coalinga, California, earthquake, 40
Command centers, 113–115, 118, 119–121,

Command centers (*Continued*)
    127, 166, 168, 173–175, 177–179,
    190–193, 227
Connecticut (*see* Grasso, Windsor and
    Windsor Locks)
Convergence behavior, 6, 10, 21, 111–112, 116,
    123–126, 170 (*see also* Volunteers)
Coordinator of emergency management (*see*
    Emergency manager)
Corner Brook, Newfoundland, hazardous
    materials spill (1984), 171–176, 178
Courtney, British Columbia, hazardous
    materials spill (1983), 171, 173–176
Crawford, K. Grant, 166
Crisis relocation (*see* Evacuation)
Curling, Newfoundland (*see* Corner Brook)

D

Damage assessment, 34–39, 51, 53, 92
Dioxin contamination, 34
Disaster declaration (*see* Presidential
    isaster declaration)
Disaster plans (*see* Emergency plans)
Disaster Preparedness Improvement Grants,
    46, 54
Disaster Relief Act of 1974 (Public Law
    3-288), 36, 40, 41–42
Disaster Research Center, 7
Disaster Unemployment Assistance, 45
Drabek, Thomas, 7

E

Earthquakes, 40, 212–213, 232
Eastern Canadian Premiers, 101–102
Economic Injury Disaster Loan Program
    SBA), 41
Edmonton, Alberta, tornado (1987), 166, 168,
    169–170, 172–175, 177–178
Emergency communications, xx, 6, 16–17,
    8–19, 20–21, 25, 27, 111–121, 124–127,
    155, 157, 159–167, 169, 172–175, 177, 179,
    188–193, 208, 232, 233
Emergency Communications Research Unit
    (Carleton University), xix, 165–166, 179
Emergency exercises, 8, 12–13, 16–17, 20–21,
    26, 124–125, 176, 189, 203
Emergency managers, xviii–xix, 8, 113,

155–164, 179, 186–188, 202–203, 206–207,
    213–214, 230–231, 234 (*see also* City
    managers, Mayors, Fire departments,
    Local officials, Police, and Public works
    departments)
Emergency medical services, 28, 111–112,
    116–118, 119, 123, 125, 127, 128, 169, 170,
    174, 185, 191, 195, 201–202, 204
Emergency plans and planning, xi, xiv, xx,
    6–7, 39, 65, 66, 110, 113, 116, 123,
    124–125, 127, 140–141, 151–152, 165, 167,
    168, 172–180, 185, 194, 201–203, 208–210,
    212–215, 221, 224, 226–227, 229, 232
adaptive planning, 5–31
need for planning skills, 150
    (*see also* City planners and Preparedness)
Emergency Preparedness Canada, xix, 166
Environment Ontario, 95
Essential Emergency Assistance Program, 54
Europe, acid rain in, 93
Evacuation, 12, 17, 19–21, 149, 171, 174, 178,
    196–197, 204, 212–213, 227–228,
    231–232
Evaluation of emergency management
    programs, 20, 26–27, 29, 226, 230–231

F

Farmer's Home Administration, 41
Federal Aviation Administration (FAA), 121
Federal Emergency Management Agency
    (FEMA), xii, xiv–xv, xviii, xix, xxiii, 27,
    29, 34–55, 59–60, 76, 139, 145, 148, 150,
    151, 188, 213–214, 225, 229, 233
Federal Bureau of Investigation (FBI), 121,
    214
Federal Disaster Protection Act, 44
Federal Highway Administration, 40
Federal Temporary Housing program, 45, 47
    (*see also* Housing)
Financing emergency management programs,
    xx, 25–26, 27–29, 34–35, 40–42, 47–50,
    52, 174, 185, 188–189, 196, 209, 223–224,
    231, 233–234 (*see also* City finance
    departments and Presidential disaster
    declarations)
Fires, 138, 166, 170–172, 185, 190–192, 194,
    197–199, 204–207, 221, 227 (*see also* Fire
    departments)

Fire departments, roles in disaster response, 6, 28, 79, 83, 109, 110–113, 116–120, 123, 124, 125–126, 127, 156–157, 169, 170, 174, 177, 185–186, 189, 191–199, 204–205, 212, 215–216

Floods, 34, 46–47, 138, 151, 162, 166, 170–171, 173, 176–178, 190, 194, 208–209, 221
  hazard management, xv, 35, 40, 59–73
  (*see also* National Flood Insurance Program)

Flood Control Act of 1936, 61

Flood Disaster Protection Act of 1973, 61–62

Florida, hurricanes, 227–228

G

Gander, Newfoundland, aviation disaster (1985), xiii, xvii, 109–110, 116–128, 166, 172–175, 178

Gorham, Eville, 93

Gotlieb, Allan (Canadian Ambassador to U.S.), 97

Goulds, Newfoundland, fire (1976), 170, 173–177

Governors, roles in emergency management, xvi, 36–37, 42, 63, 76, 79–80, 82, 84–88, 222

Gramm-Rudman-Hollings Act of 1985, 34, 47

Grasso, Ella (Governor of Connecticut), 84, 88

Great Lakes region, acid rain in, 91, 99, 102–103

Great Lakes Charter agreement (1985), 102

Great Lakes Toxic Substances Control Agreement (1986), 102

H

Halifax, Nova Scotia, 128

Hazard assessment or analysis, 12, 20, 26, 226

Hazardous materials accidents, 34, 166, 171, 185, 194, 196–201, 210

Herrington, John S. (U.S. Secretary of Energy), 96–97

Hodel, Donald (U.S. Secretary of Interior), 97

Hostage-taking, 166, 170, 176, 192

Housing, 43, 45, 47, 79, 197–198, 204, 231, 232

Hurricanes, 190, 208–209, 213, 227–228, 231, 232

I

Illinois, acid rain in, 96

Incident command centers (*see* Command centers)

Indiana, acid rain in, 102

Individual and Family grants, FEMA, 43, 47, 54

Intergovernmental relations, xv, xvii, 16–17, 18–19, 59–60, 64, 72, 100–102, 148, 150, 151, 162–163, 186, 214–215, 232–233

International City Management Association, 5, 15, 134, 227

International Journal of Mass Emergencies and Disasters, xvi

Irvine, California, xviii–xix, 155, 158–163

J

Jefferson, Jim, 167

K

Kaiser, Edward J., 68

Kentville, Nova Scotia, 93

Koch, Edward (Mayor of NYC), 193, 194, 203

L

Labor strikes, 190, 194, 196, 201–202

La Cloche Mountains, Ontario, acid rain in, 93

Land use regulation, 35, 61, 62, 66

Law enforcement agencies (*see* Police)

Legal aspects of emergency management, xiv–xv, 17, 19, 20–21, 26, 28, 159–163, 174, 179, 189, 213, 227, 230, 235 (*see also* City attorneys)

Lindsay, Leon, 102

Local officials, roles in emergency management, 8, 13, 16, 20–21, 26, 27, 34–39, 42, 50, 52, 59, 63, 64–66, 75, 82–84, 86–88, 93, 104, 115, 148, 151, 156–157, 159–160, 166–168, 179, 186–187, 189–190, 207, 210, 214–215, 221, 228, 229, 233–235

Local officials (*Continued*)
    (*see also* Mayors, City attorneys, City
    managers, and City planners; Finance,
    Fire, Parks, Personnel, Police, and Pub-
    lic works departments)
Louisiana, aircrash in 1982, 6
Love Canal, Niagra Falls, New York, 33

M

Manitoba (*see also* Oak Lake), acid rain in, 94
Master of Public Administration degree,
    141–142
Mayors (including Canadian reeves, wardens,
    and council chairpersons), roles in
    emergency management, xvi, xvii–xviii,
    xix, 79–80, 83–84, 86, 115, 127, 156, 166,
    167–168, 172–180, 186–190, 215
Media, roles in disasters, xvii, 10, 16–17,
    18–21, 26, 113–115, 118, 120, 122–123,
    124, 126–127, 162, 190–191
Medical services (*see* Emergency medical
    services)
Medicine Hat, Alberta, hazardous materials
    accident (1984), 166, 171–177
Michigan, acid rain in, 102
Midwest U.S., acid rain in, 98–99
Minnesota, acid rain in, 96, 102
Mississauga, Ontario, hazardous materials
    spill (1979), 169, 171, 173–176, 178
Mitigation, xv–xvi, xx, 39, 40, 42, 44, 45, 55,
    59–60, 62, 70, 156, 185, 225, 227–228, 232
Montreal, 128
Mount St. Helens eruption (1980), 227, 231
Mudslides, 138, 166, 170, 176, 178
Mulroney, Prime Minister Brian, 94, 97–98
Mutual aid agreements or plans, 7, 20–21,
    25–26, 79

N

National Association of Schools of Public
    Affairs and Administration (NASPAA),
    230
National Emergency Training Center
    (FEMA), 29
National Flood Insurance Program, xv, 44, 47,
    61, 66–68, 70, 72–73 (*see also* Floods)
National Governors' Association, 224

National Guard, 75, 79
National Research Council, 8
National Transportation Safety Board, 121
National Weather Service, National Oceanic
    and Atmospheric Administration, 209
Neighborhood organizations (*see* Volunteers)
New England, acid rain in, 93, 98, 101
New England/Eastern Canada Sulfur
    Dioxide Emission Reduction Plan
    (1985), 101–102
New England Governors Conference, 102
Newfoundland, 168 (*see also* Corner Brook,
    Gander, Goulds, North Bay, and St.
    John's)
New Hampshire, acid rain in, 95
New York, State, acid rain in, 95, 101, 102
    Emergency response team, 214
    State Emergency Management Office, 188,
        214
    (*see also* Adirondack Mountains and Love
        Canal)
New York City, xiii, xx, 185–216
    Department of Environmental Protection,
        195, 207, 211
    Department of General Services, 189
    Department of Inspections, 186, 200
    Department of Streets and Sanitation,
        195–196
    Emergency Control Board (ECB), 187,
        189–190, 201
    Emergency Coordinating Section (ECS),
        190–191, 196–197, 200, 208–209
    Emergency Management Center, 190–191
    Human Resource Administration, 191, 195
    Office of Civil Defense, 188
    Office of Emergency Management (OEM),
        xx, 188–191, 196, 201–202, 208, 211,
        213–215
    (*see also* Koch, Police and Fire
        departments)
Nickabeau, Quebec, tornado (1984), 169, 173,
    175, 176–178
911 emergency number, xx, 174, 191–193, 204
North Bay, Newfoundland, building explo-
    sion (1975), 169, 170, 173, 175
North Carolina, acid rain in, 103
Nova Scotia, 168, 177 (*also see* Halifax and
    Sydney)
Nuclear emergencies, 148, 208–211, 228

Nuclear Regulatory Agency, 209–210
Nuclear war, 212–213, 229

O

Oak Lake, Manitoba, hostage-taking (1978), 170, 173–177
Oden, Svante, 93
Ohio, acid rain in, 96, 102
O'Neill, Tip, xiii
Ontario, 93, 99, 102, 177 (*see also* Mississauga, Ottawa, Petawawa, Prince Edward County, Sudbury, and Woodstock)
Ontario Hydro, 99
Orange County, California, Environmental Management Agency, 156, 159–162
    Fire Department, 156, 159, 160
    Health Department, 158–159, 162
Ottawa, Ontario, 165
Ouellette, Adrien (Canadian Minister of Environment), 101

P

Parks departments, roles in emergency management, 28–29
Parliamentary Committee on Acid Rain, 94–95
Pemberton, British Columbia, floods (1984), 171–178
Pennsylvania (*see also* Wilkes-Barre), acid rain in, 102
Personnel departments, roles in emergency management, 28
Petak, William J., 166
Petawawa, Ontario, hazardous materials accident (1985), 166, 171, 173–175, 178
Physical Disaster Loan Program, SBA, 47
Police, roles in disaster response, 7, 10, 13, 28, 78–79, 83, 109, 110–128, 156–158, 169, 170, 174, 176, 177, 185, 187–194, 201–205, 207, 212, 214–216 (*see also* Royal Canadian Mounted Police, Federal Bureau of Investigation, and U.S. Border Patrol)
Port Alice, British Columbia, mudslide (1975), 166, 169, 170, 173–179
Portugese Bend, California, 33–34
Preparedness, xiv, xv, xx, 5, 10, 11, 13, 14–15, 24, 25, 27, 29–30, 40, 109, 125, 127,
133–140, 167, 177–180, 186, 203, 205, 213–215, 225, 227, 232
Presidential disaster declarations, xiv–xv, 33–56
Prince Edward County, Ontario, snowstorm (1977), 169, 173–176
Princeton, British Columbia, floods (1984), xiii, 171, 173–176, 178
Private sector, roles in emergency management, 12, 17, 21, 27, 69–70, 75, 83, 93, 98–99, 156, 157, 158–159, 162, 186, 189–190, 201–202
Professionalization of emergency management, xi, xvii, xx, 7–9, 141–142, 188, 215, 230
Province roles in emergency management, xvi–xvii, xix, 92, 100–104, 170, 177–179
Public Assistance grants, 44
Public information, 21, 62, 65 (*also see* Media and Communications)
Public health agencies, roles in emergency management, 28, 230
Public works departments, roles in emergency management, 28–29, 66, 78, 159, 160, 230
Puerto Rico, disaster assistance, 138

Q

Quarantelli, Henry, xiii, 7
Quebec, 93, 99, 101–102, 169 (*see also* Nickabeau)
    acid rain in, 93, 99, 101–102

R

Reagan Administration, xvi, xx, 62, 91–92, 94, 96–98, 100, 228, 233
Reagan, President Ronald (*see* Reagan Administration)
Recovery, xvi, xx, 33, 41–42, 49, 52, 55, 110, 113, 127, 158–159, 160, 185, 215, 225–226, 230 (*see also* Presidential Disaster Declarations and specific disaster aid programs and agencies)
Red Cross, 75, 189–190
Response, xv, xvi, xvii, xix, xx, 5–7, 10–12, 16, 110–128, 156, 158–160, 168, 172–175, 186, 192, 193, 196–200, 202, 209, 211, 215, 222, 225–226, 230–231, 232, 234 (*see also* specific response agencies)

Rossi, Peter, 65
Royal Canadian Mounted Police (RCMP),
    109, 117–123, 126–127, 170, 172, 177

S

St. John's, Newfoundland, snowstorm (1974),
    169, 173–175, 178
Salt Lake City, Utah, floods, 231
Salvation Army, 122, 190
San Diego, California, xvii, 109–116, 122, 123
San Diego Pipeline Company, 156–159, 160,
    162–163
Santa Cruz County, California, floods (1982),
    27
Saskatchewan, acid rain in, 94
Scanlon, Joseph, 167
Search and rescue, 204, 205, 208
Shelter (*see* Housing and Federal Temporary
    Housing Program)
Small Business Administration (SBA), 41, 47
Snow emergencies, 166, 169, 173–174, 176, 190,
    194–197, 200, 201, 213
Soil Conservation Service, 40
Sproat, Debbie, 167
Stafford Act (Robert T. Stafford Relief and
    Emergency Assistance Act) of 1988, xv,
    44–46, 54–55
State roles in emergency management,
    xvi–xvii, 36–39, 50, 62–66, 79–88, 92,
    103–104, 125, 148, 160, 161–162, 189,
    213–214, 222, 232, 233
Sudbury, Ontario, 93
Sweden, acid rain in, 93
Sydney, Nova Scotia, windstorm (1974), 166,
    169, 172–175, 177, 178

T

Tennessee Emergency Management Agency,
    29
Terrace, British Columbia, floods (1978),
    170–171, 173–175
Terrorism, 185, 212, 214
Times Beach, Missouri, dioxin contamination,
    34
Tornadoes and windstorms, xvi, 75–90, 166,
    169, 173–174, 178, 212, 232
Training programs, 10, 12, 16, 26–27, 178,

188–189, 202, 203, 215, 226 (*see also*
    Preparedness)
Tustin, California, pipeline disaster (1986),
    155, 158, 162

U

U.S. Army Corps of Engineers, 40, 229–230
U.S. Border Patrol, 111
U.S. Coast Guard, 121, 161–162
U.S. Department of Defense, 45
U.S. Department of Education, 40
U.S. Department of Energy, 97–98
U.S. Department of Housing and Urban
    Development, 41
U.S. Department of the Interior, 97
U.S. Department of Labor, 43
U.S. Department of Transportation, 41
U.S. Environmental Protection Agency, 161
U.S. Forest Service, 227
U.S. General Accounting Office, 34, 46–47
U.S. Geological Survey, 229–230

V

Vancouver Island, British Columbia, 169
Virginia, floods (1985), 46–47
Volcanoes, 227, 231
Volunteers, roles in disaster responses, 6,
    16–17, 18–19, 20–21, 79, 83, 122, 190 (*see
    also* Convergence behavior)

W

Warning systems, 12, 21, 62, 65, 149, 189, 209
Weller, Jack, 7
West Virginia, disaster assistance, 138
    floods (1985), 47
Wilkes-Barre, Pennsylvania, floods, 151
Windsor, Connecticut, tornado, xvi, 77–88
Windsor Locks, Connecticut, tornado, xvi,
    77–88
Wisconsin, acid rain in, 95–96, 102
Woodstock, Ontario, tornado (1979), 169,
    173–175, 178

Z

Zoning (*see* Land use regulation)